T0271141

ANARCHY UNBOUND

Why Self-Governance Works
Better Than You Think

In *Anarchy Unbound*, Peter T. Leeson uses rational choice theory to explore the benefits of self-governance. Relying on experience from the past and present, Professor Leeson provides evidence of anarchy "working" where it is least expected to do so and explains how this is possible. Provocatively, Leeson argues that in some cases anarchy may even outperform government as a system of social organization, and demonstrates where this may occur. *Anarchy Unbound* challenges the conventional self-governance wisdom. It showcases the incredible ingenuity of private individuals to secure social cooperation without government and how their surprising means of doing so can be superior to reliance on the state.

Peter T. Leeson is Professor of Economics and the BB&T Professor for the Study of Capitalism at George Mason University. He is also the North American editor of *Public Choice*. Previously, he was a Visiting Professor of Economics at the University of Chicago, the F.A. Hayek Fellow at the London School of Economics, and a Visiting Fellow in Political Economy and Government at Harvard University. Professor Leeson is the author of *The Invisible Hook: The Hidden Economics of Pirates* (2009) and a recipient of the Fund for the Study of Spontaneous Order's Hayek Prize, which he received for his research on self-governance.

Cambridge Studies in Economics, Choice, and Society

Founding Editors

Timur Kuran, *Duke University*
Peter J. Boettke, *George Mason University*

This interdisciplinary series promotes original theoretical and empirical research as well as integrative syntheses involving links between individual choice, institutions, and social outcomes. Contributions are welcome from across the social sciences, particularly in the areas where economic analysis is joined with other disciplines, such as comparative political economy, new institutional economics, and behavioral economics.

Books in the Series:

Terry L. Anderson and Gary D. Libecap, *Environmental Markets: A Property Rights Approach* 2014
Morris B. Hoffman, *The Punisher's Brain: The Evolution of Judge and Jury* 2014
Peter T. Leeson, *Anarchy Unbound: Why Self-Governance Works Better Than You Think* 2014
Benjamin Powell, *Out of Poverty: Sweatshops in the Global Economy* 2014

Anarchy Unbound

*Why Self-Governance Works
Better Than You Think*

PETER T. LEESON

George Mason University

CAMBRIDGE
UNIVERSITY PRESS

CAMBRIDGE
UNIVERSITY PRESS

32 Avenue of the Americas, New York NY 10013-2473, USA

Cambridge University Press is part of the University of Cambridge.

It furthers the University's mission by disseminating knowledge in the pursuit of education, learning and research at the highest international levels of excellence.

www.cambridge.org
Information on this title: www.cambridge.org/9781107025806

First published 2014

A catalogue record for this publication is available from the British Library

Library of Congress Cataloguing in Publication data
Leeson, Peter T., 1979–
Anarchy unbound : why self-governance works better than you think / Peter T. Leeson, George Mason University, VA.
pages cm. – (Cambridge studies in economics, choice, and society)
Includes bibliographical references and index.
ISBN 978-1-107-02580-6 (hardback) – ISBN 978-1-107-62970-7 (paperback)
1. Anarchism.   2. Autonomy.   I. Title.
HX833.L4135   2014
321'.07–dc23   2013024739

ISBN 978-1-107-02580-6 Hardback
ISBN 978-1-107-62970-7 Paperback

In loving memory of Douglas Bruce Rogers:
student, collaborator, and friend

Contents

Acknowledgments

The ideas presented in Chapters 5, 7, and 10 of this book were developed with coauthors to whom I'm greatly indebted: Alex Nowrasteh, David Skarbek, and Claudia Williamson. I also thank Scott Parris, my editor at Cambridge University Press, and Peter Boettke and Timur Kuran, the editors of Cambridge Studies in Economics, Choice, and Society, the series in which this book appears, for their encouragement and for providing me the opportunity to share my thinking about self-governance with others. As usual, Chris Coyne provided excellent thoughts and suggestions, which improved my discussion considerably. My discussion also benefited from the comments of three anonymous reviewers. Finally, I thank the Earhart Foundation for generously supporting this book.

Anarchy Unbound

This book consists of several essays. Their central argument is simple: *anarchy works better than you think.*

My thesis sets a low argumentative bar. If you're like most people, you don't think anarchy works at all. Such readers are in good company. One of the most important figures in the history of social thought, Thomas Hobbes, shared that thinking.

In 1651 Hobbes famously described life in anarchy as "solitary, poor, nasty, brutish, and short." His reasoning is familiar. In anarchy, property is unprotected: there's nothing to prevent the strong from plundering the weak, the unscrupulous from bamboozling the unwitting, and the dishonest from defrauding the honest. There's no social cooperation, only social conflict, no civilization, only chaos.

Hobbes's path out of this anarchic jungle was government. By making and enforcing rules that protect individuals' property, he argued, government will create social harmony. Indeed, government will create society.

Hobbes was wrong – on both counts. Individuals have secured property protection and social cooperation without government and still do. Moreover, in much of the world, government has proved to be the greatest depredator of property rights, creator of conflict, and instigator of chaos, rather than an innocuous antidote to anarchic afflictions.

Govern*ance* – social rules that protect individuals' property and institutions of their enforcement – doesn't require govern*ment*, which is but one means of supplying governance. Hobbes overlooked the possibility of *self*-governance: privately created social rules and institutions of their enforcement. He also underestimated the possibility of truly horrible governments. It's therefore unsurprising that he saw anarchy as anathema to society and government as its savior.

Some readers may not be quite so optimistic about government, or quite so pessimistic about anarchy, as Hobbes was. Today it's widely acknowledged that many governments fail to live up to what their advocates hope for. Indeed, some governments do far worse than that. Instead of promoting cooperation, governments in the Soviet Union, Nazi Germany, and North Korea, to name but a few, severely undermined cooperation in their societies (and in the case of North Korea still do), with devastating consequences. Because of this, you may be (or at least should be) less sanguine about the possibility of government as society's savior than Hobbes's rhetoric suggests.

Today it's also acknowledged that at least some social interactions can be, and are, carried off cooperatively without government's assistance. Hobbes's characterization of anarchy expresses basic "prisoners' dilemma" logic. A well-known result of that logic is that mutual noncooperation is the unique Nash equilibrium when such games are played but once. An equally well-known result is the possibility of cooperative equilibria when they're played infinitely or terminate with some constant known probability.

This "folk theorem" result of iterated noncooperative games supplies a ready mechanism of self-governance: the discipline of continuous dealings. Individuals may adopt strategies in their interactions with others whereby they refuse to interact with uncooperative persons in the future, cutting them off from the gains of additional interactions. By penalizing uncooperative behavior, such strategies can induce cooperation. If we consider more than two persons, reputations become possible, further strengthening the penalty for uncooperative behavior. Now, by having developed a negative reputation, uncooperative persons may lose the gains from interacting even with persons toward whom they haven't behaved uncooperatively.

Hobbes's reasoning sets the bar required to make the argument that anarchy works better than you think on the floor. Reasoning about anarchy and government that incorporates the foregoing considerations sets that bar higher, but only a few inches so. Even persons who recognize self-governance's existence quickly follow their recognition with the caveat that self-governance's scope of effective application is severely limited. And even persons who acknowledge that some governments are truly horrendous are still sure that any government is better than none at all.

This book challenges the conventional wisdom that sees successful self-governance's range as severely limited. It finds private social order where conventional wisdom says we shouldn't. Roughly speaking, that's where the discipline of continuous dealings has difficulty securing cooperation by itself, such as when populations are large or diverse, when interactions aren't repeated or persons are impatient, and when violence is possible or individuals are devoted to plunder as a way of life.

Persons who find themselves in anarchy are considerably more creative in finding solutions to their problems than the academics who study them. Unlike academics, these persons reap large rewards if they solve those problems and suffer large penalties if they don't. They must live (or die) with the consequences of either floundering in the face of, or overcoming, the obstacles that stand in the way of their ability to realize the gains of social cooperation without government. Given such powerful incentives, it would be surprising if persons in anarchy did *not* develop effective mechanisms of self-governance in a wide variety of difficult circumstances, including those where the discipline of continuous dealings alone is insufficient. And, as this book evidences, they do.

Those mechanisms take several forms. Some, such as those that leverage the discipline of continuous dealings, enforce social rules internally – through punishments that persons who are themselves parties to the relevant interactions threaten. Others, such as private professional judges, enforce social rules externally – through punishments that third parties to the relevant interactions threaten instead. Some mechanisms of self-governance enforce social rules with threats of peaceful punishments, such as shaming. Others enforce social rules with threats of violent ones, such as blood feuding. The essays in this book consider mechanisms of self-governance that rely on both internal and external enforcement, as well as those that rely on both peaceful and violent punishments.

This book also challenges the conventional wisdom according to which self-governance always performs worse than government. There are some conditions under which even an ideal government – the imaginary sort that has never existed, but most people imagine anyway – turns out to be less sensible than no government at all. More important, by understating the degree of social cooperation that self-governance can secure, and overstating the degree of social cooperation that many actual governments do secure, conventional wisdom ignores the possibility that citizens living under ultra-predatory and dysfunctional governments might fare better under anarchy. As this book also evidences, in one case at least, this possibility is almost certainly a reality.

A mechanism of self-governance can be said to "work" if it tolerably solves the problem that persons in anarchy rely on it to address. None of the mechanisms I consider solve the problems they address perfectly. Then again, neither would any mechanism of governance, including government.

Anarchy can be said to "work better than you think" if the mechanisms of self-governance that undergird it work in circumstances where you thought self-governance couldn't. This book considers several such circumstances. Part I contains essays that address self-governance when populations are socially diverse. Part II contains essays that address self-governance when individuals face the specter of physical violence. Part III contains essays that address self-governance in societies composed exclusively of "bad apples" – persons whose way of living is devoted to theft and murder.

Each of these circumstances poses a different obstacle for the discipline of continuous dealings in securing self-governance. To work well, and some would argue to work at all, in addition to requiring repeated interaction, the discipline of continuous dealings requires small and socially homogeneous populations, populations whose members don't confront the prospect of violence, and populations whose members don't discount the future too heavily. The essays in Parts I–III analyze cases of successful self-governance despite deviations from these conditions, and thus mechanisms of self-governance that go beyond the discipline of continuous dealings alone.

Anarchy can also be said to work better than you think when (assuming you didn't believe as much already) a society whose governance is based on such mechanisms produces higher welfare than it could enjoy under its feasible government alternative. The essays in Part IV consider self-governance in this vein.

The key to finding such a self-governance "unicorn" is to compare a society with a recent experience under anarchy to the same society under the government *it actually had* before or after moving to anarchy – or, somewhat more difficultly, if that society hasn't had a recent experience under anarchy, to compare that society's likely experience under anarchy to its experience under the government *it's currently under*. This kind of comparison forces one to restrict his attention to relevant governance alternatives – to the kind of anarchy and government actually available to some society – and precludes the comparison of irrelevant governance alternatives, such as poorly functioning anarchy and exceptionally high-functioning government, which is the kind of comparison most people are prone to make. The self-governing society that outperforms the state-governed one is only impossible to find if one is simultaneously pessimistic about anarchy in some society and optimistic about government in that same society, which, ordinarily, he probably shouldn't be given that the same historical constraints that limit the potential effectiveness of one kind of governance arrangement are likely to limit the potential effectiveness of other kinds.

Anarchy working better than you think does *not* mean that the mechanisms of self-governance I discuss always, or even often, work better at solving the problems they address than some kind of government could – especially if that government is the rare, extremely well-functioning kind most people pretend is the rule instead of the exception. I will argue that in *some* cases those mechanisms can work better than government – especially if one compares their performance to the comparatively common, extremely poorly functioning kind most people pretend is the exception instead of the rule. But my argument doesn't imply that *any* anarchy is superior to *any* government one could conceive of. Nor does anarchy's superiority in a particular case necessarily generalize.

So much for what I mean (and don't mean) by anarchy working better than you think. What do I mean by "anarchy"? I mean government's absence, of course. And by "government" I mean . . . Well, here things become a bit more complicated.

It's tempting to define government following Max Weber's (1919) classic characterization: as a territorial monopoly on violence – on social rule creation and enforcement. As a rule, this is the conception of government this book's essays have in mind. But there are several problems with this conception that compel me in at least two essays to conceive of government, and thus anarchy, somewhat differently.

If we follow Weber, government's presence or absence depends on what one considers the relevant territory. If we define that territory narrowly enough, every authority, even private ones we wouldn't normally call by the name, is a government. For example, if we call my condominium building the relevant territory, my homeowner's association could be considered a government, for it alone has the authority to make and enforce social rules regulating activity in the condo. Under a sufficiently narrow territorial definition, government is everywhere. In contrast, if we define the relevant territory broadly enough – say, the world – the reverse is true. The absence of a global government means countries exist vis-à-vis one another as individuals would in Hobbes's state of nature. Now government is nowhere.

This feature of the Weberian conception of government poses a potential problem, but not an insurmountable one. One simply needs to be clear about scope of the territory he's considering and to make an argument about why that territory is the relevant one for the purpose at hand. For example, to examine the political economy of Arlington, Virginia, where my condominium building is located, I think everyone would agree the relevant territory is Arlington, Virginia, rather than my condominium building. In contrast, to examine the political economy of international relations, I think everyone would agree the world, or some other region encompassing multiple countries, is the relevant territory rather than one country in particular. Reasonable persons could disagree in specific cases about whether the appropriate territorial unit had been selected for some analysis. But, at least in principle, we could have a clear, common definition of where we have government and where we don't.

The more serious difficulty in trying to apply consistently a Weberian conception of government – and the one of much more importance for this book – is illustrated by the following example. Suppose that for some purpose under consideration everyone agrees that some small isolated community is the relevant territory of analysis. Suppose further that every person in this community has explicitly and voluntarily agreed that a single third party's decisions shall govern them, say the community elder's, enforced with threats of violence exclusively by his command. Is the elder this community has decided shall govern it a government? He has a monopoly on social rule creation and enforcement in the territory in question. A Weberian conception, then, would seem to suggest he is.

Yet I'm reluctant to call him a "government." And I suspect I'm not alone. The reason for my discomfort with the Weberian conclusion here is that the persons this third party governs have *unanimously consented* to it as their governance agency. It seems just as sensible to characterize this community's governance arrangement as a private club as it does to characterize it as a government. But our intuition suggests to us that there's an important difference between clubs and governments.

Because the possibility of explicit unanimous consent seems to be the source of uneasiness with the Weberian conception in such cases, it's natural to seek a modified conception of government, and thus anarchy, that considers not only whether a governance authority or arrangement has a territorial monopoly, but also whether the persons it governs have unanimously and voluntarily consented to be governed by it. Under this conception, coercion at the level of whether or not you will be bound by a governing authority's decisions, in addition to a territorial monopoly, is what makes for a government.

A monopoly governing agency that compels persons to abide by the social rules it creates, but which all those persons haven't explicitly consented to be governed by, is a government. In contrast, a governance agency, even if it's the sole agency in a territory that creates and enforces social rules, and even if it enforces those rules violently, is an example of self-governance provided that every person it governs has previously and explicitly consented to as much.

Oddly, in this conception of government, if Hobbes's "government" actually emerged in the way that he and other social contractarians hypothesize – through the unanimous consent of the people it governs – it would *not* be a government. It would be an example of self-governance.

Unfortunately, what seems like a natural way to modify the Weberian conception of government turns out to be just as problematic as the unmodified conception, but in a different way. Consider an isolated community in which the only social rules that exist are norms – unwritten property customs that evolved organically over centuries – and the only means of enforcing those rules is a norm of stoning, which community members resort to when there's consensus that an important rule has been broken. The persons who populate this community have never explicitly consented to be governed by the set of norms that are the only source of rules that regulate their behavior, and do so violently at that.

Are these persons living under a government? I think most everyone would answer no. Yet because the rule and enforcement norms that provide governance in this community haven't received explicit unanimous consent, the modified conception of government described in the preceding paragraph would seem to suggest they are.

If this norm-based governance, which is decentralized and unconsciously created, doesn't seem to capture what we mean by a "monopoly authority" (even though it's the only source of social rule creation and enforcement that exists and, moreover, that enforcement is violent), consider another example. Suppose an organized crime family uses threats of violence to run its neighborhood in some country where a state officially exists but pays scant attention to its duties, leaving the neighborhood's inhabitants to their own devices. Is the crime family a government?

While the modified conception of government described in the preceding paragraph suggests it is, I don't think most readers would be prepared to call it one. On the contrary, I suspect most readers would say the crime family is a result of government's *absence*. They would characterize the crime family as a consequence of anarchy. And I would agree.[1]

---

[1] A closely related way of trying to negotiate this difficulty of the Weberian conception involves modifying government's definition with the word "legitimate" such that government becomes a "legitimate monopoly on force in a given territory" (indeed, Weber himself at times used "legitimate" as part of government's definition). Unfortunately, this modification fails in much the way that, I have argued earlier, the coercion-inclusive conception of government fails. If "legitimate" is a normative statement about the moral right of a monopoly agency on force to govern a certain territory, there's the obvious problem that individuals' understandings about what's morally right are subjective, precluding an

Yet another possible approach to identifying government is to appeal to the notion of "exit costs." But this approach fails to deliver an unambiguous definition of government for similar reasons. Exit costs are, quite literally, the costs of exiting life under one governance arrangement to live life under another. The trouble with using exit costs to define government is that it's costly to exit any governance arrangement unless there are an infinite number of such arrangements in a territory, which there never are.

Because government monopolizes governance in some territory, exit costs under government will very likely be higher than under self-governance, which, at least in principle, doesn't preclude the possibility of multiple governance arrangements operating in the same territory. But this difference doesn't get us far. What is the "cutoff cost" – the exit cost above which we definitively have government and below which we definitively have anarchy – that unambiguously defines government? There isn't one. And unlike when one must make an argument for the relevant territory of analysis to define government, where there will ordinarily be a "natural" or "obvious" reason for selecting one territory over another that everyone can assent to, it's hard to see on what grounds one could make a persuasive argument that the cutoff cost they have chosen is anything other than arbitrary. Our intuition about the exit cost that makes for government is weak, as is the extent to which we share that intuition.

Equally important, one can imagine a self-governance arrangement that is more expensive to exit than government. A government that monopolizes governance in a territory that's much smaller than the territory governed exclusively by, say, a set of norms, or even a unanimously selected third party, is cheaper to exit than these alternative governance arrangements. Yet it would be strange if a system of norms or a unanimously selected third party metamorphosed into a government because it happened to govern a larger territory. And no reasonable person would claim that it did.

Hopefully it's clear now why defining government precisely is problematic. In light of this, unsatisfying though it may be, this book's essays sometimes conceive of government, and thus anarchy, with the Weberian

objective definition of government. If instead "legitimate" is a positive statement about the fraction of a population governed by a monopoly agency on force that approves of this agency – that is, sees it as legitimate, in which case calling government a "legit*imized* monopoly on force in a territory" would be more accurate – a different difficulty emerges. In the case where every person approves of the monopoly, it's sensible to call the monopoly legitimate. But in this case we have a self-governing club, as previously described. In the case where there's anything short of unanimous approval of the monopoly, we have ambiguity about whether the monopoly is legitimate and thus whether we have government.

conception in mind, and sometimes with the modified, coercion-inclusive conception in mind instead. I'm unwilling to call the governance system that prevailed on pirate ships – the subject of one of the essays in Part III – government, even though this system constituted a monopoly on violence on each pirate ship, because the pirates it governed explicitly and unanimously consented to that system. At the same time I'm unwilling to call the governance system that prevails in Somalia – the subject of one of the essays in Part IV – government, even though this system governs many persons who never consented to be governed by it and does so partly with threats of violence, because that system reflects the absence of what every reasonable person calls government rather than government's presence.

My approach to identifying government is therefore like Justice Potter Stewart's approach to identifying pornography: you know it when you see it. Unlike intuitions about exit costs, most people do seem to share strong intuitions about whether government governs some set of social relations or not. Thus our (or, at least, my) inability to define government in a fully satisfactory manner in theory needn't prevent us from identifying government's presence or absence in practice. I realize this approach creates scope for disagreement about whether we have government or anarchy in a particular instance. But I see no alternative approach that seems likely to produce less disagreement. Moreover, I hope – and indeed suspect – that you will agree in each case I examine that anarchy is in fact present in the sense I consider.

Note that under either conception of government described earlier, anarchy doesn't preclude multiple governments' presence, such as in international contexts. The international arena encompasses interactions between multiple sovereigns and thus presents formally ungoverned interstices. There's no supranational agency with monopoly power to create and enforce social rules that cover multiple sovereigns. There are supranational organizations, such as the United Nations, as well as a large variety of multinational treaties for governing various interstate relationships. These organizations sometimes perform adjudication services for member countries and threaten punishments for noncompliance. But members of such organizations and treaties are members voluntarily. Ultimately they abide by, or refuse to abide by, such organizations' or treaties' directives voluntarily as well. This doesn't mean supranational organizations' directives aren't often enforced. But, ironically, given that such organizations are often justified by the need to remove the world's governments from international anarchy, their enforcement power derives from self-governing mechanisms, such as those rooted in the discipline of continuous dealings, not from government.

This book's method of analysis is decidedly economic. It uses rational choice theory to understand the anarchic environments and mechanisms of self-governance that individuals develop to cope with those environments. This isn't the only method one could imagine using. But I'm an economist and, even for an economist, I believe strongly that the economic approach is by far the most productive.

One recommending feature of the economic approach is its ability to supply insight into the underlying *mechanisms* that do or don't enable anarchy to work in particular cases.[2] This emphasis on mechanisms permits me to move beyond mere descriptions of anarchy working in various circumstances toward a better understanding of the logic underlying *why* it succeeds in those circumstances and precisely *how* it manages to do so.

My essays are in the form of what are sometimes called analytic narratives. In them, economic logic shapes and illuminates the data of the historical or contemporary case under consideration. This approach necessarily involves abstracting from much descriptive detail to make an intelligible analysis possible. At the same time it retains and brings to the foreground other descriptive detail that frames, and is equally important for making intelligible, the case under consideration.

As in my other work, the economic logic deployed here is overwhelmingly verbal. I hope this makes this book accessible to a wider audience. This is also the manner in which I "think economically" and thus the manner in which I write. I point this out, first, with the aim of retaining non-economist readers, or others more comfortable with nontechnical analyses, who might otherwise set this book aside now in the mistaken belief that a flurry of equations are to follow. I point this out, second, so that readers committed to the view that formalism is the only, or the only legitimate, way to say anything useful can set me aside now and return to their mathematical exercises.

This book's analyses are positive, not normative. They describe how the world is (or was), not how it should be. One could use my discussions of how the world is to support arguments about how it should be. And in this book's penultimate chapter I consider one such argument. That discussion is partly normative, however, so I have separated it from the positive analyses in the essays that inform my normative claim.

It's inevitable that some persons will be unable (or unwilling) to accept the claim that the analyses in Chapters 2 through 9 are positive. They

---

[2] On the importance of focusing on mechanisms of self-governance in discussions of anarchy, see Boettke (2012a, 2012b) and Leeson (2012a).

will jump from the fact that I'm challenging conventional wisdom about self-governance to the mistaken belief that the essays I use to do so are normative. If you're one of these persons, go back and read the allegedly normative essay(s) again. You will see that the discussion is in fact positive. If you don't see this, consult a dictionary for the definitions of "positive" and "normative." If you still remain unconvinced, consider the possibility that it's not me who has difficulty escaping normative thinking.

A fundamental task of social science is to understand how individuals secure social cooperation under the division of labor. Where government exists and functions well, developing such an understanding is relatively easy. In contrast, as Hobbes's (mistaken) thinking about anarchy clearly attests, where government is absent or highly dysfunctional, doing so is much harder. The challenge this book puts to you is my attempt to contribute to our understanding of how individuals secure social cooperation in circumstances where the idea that they could do so seems illusory. The invitation this book extends to you is to join me in exploring the possibility that it's not.

PART I

SELF-GOVERNANCE AND THE PROBLEM
OF SOCIAL DIVERSITY

2

Social Distance and Self-Enforcing Exchange*

Mechanisms of self-governance grounded in the discipline of continuous dealings come in two basic forms: bilateral-punishment strategies and multilateral-punishment strategies. Bilateral-punishment strategies involve a single person refusing to interact in the future with persons who cheated them in the past. They constitute "one-man boycotts." Multilateral-punishment strategies involve multiple persons refusing to interact in the future with persons who cheated them *or others* in the past. They constitute multi-person boycotts. Because they punish uncooperative behavior more severely, multilateral-punishment strategies supply the stronger threat to uncooperative behavior. Thus, in principle, they're able to secure cooperation under a wider variety of circumstances.

Consider two societies: one populated by highly patient individuals, the other populated by highly impatient ones. Because highly patient individuals discount the earnings from interacting in the future with others minimally, the threat of losing the earnings from interacting in the future with even a single person if they cheat that person today may be enough to lead the former society's members to behave cooperatively. For these individuals, the discounted value of the revenue lost from being unable to interact in the future with just one other person exceeds the one-shot payoff of behaving uncooperatively toward him. Bilateral punishment is fully effective here.

This isn't so in the society of highly impatient individuals. Because these individuals discount the earnings from interacting in the future with others

* This chapter is based on and uses material from Leeson, Peter T. 2008. "Social Distance and Self-Enforcing Exchange." *Journal of Legal Studies* 37(1): 161–188 [© 2008 The University of Chicago], and Leeson, Peter T. 2006. "Cooperation and Conflict: Evidence on Self-Enforcing Arrangements and Heterogeneous Groups." *American Journal of Economics and Sociology* 65(4): 891–907 [© 2006 American Journal of Economics and Sociology, Inc.].

steeply, the threat of losing the earnings from interacting in the future with even, say, 50 percent of other persons in their population may not be enough to deter them from behaving uncooperatively. For them, the discounted value of the revenue lost from being unable to interact in the future with half the population is less than the one-shot payoff of behaving uncooperatively toward someone. Bilateral punishment, and even 50 percent-encompassing multilateral punishment, is ineffective here.

Imagine, however, that multilateral punishment was *more encompassing*. Suppose, for instance, that it was fully encompassing – that cheating one person involved foregoing the earnings of interacting in the future with *every* person in the population. Now the punishment for behaving uncooperatively would almost certainly be severe enough to induce even persons in the highly impatient society to behave cooperatively. More effective multilateral punishment is more encompassing multilateral punishment.

The same point applies to a society composed of persons of varying degrees of patience, some of whom discount the future relatively little and some of whom do so a lot. Bilateral or less encompassing multilateral punishment will prevent uncooperative behavior by the more patient members of such a society. But more encompassing multilateral punishment is needed to prevent uncooperative behavior by less patient members. The implication is the same: to be more effective, multilateral punishment must be more encompassing.

What, then, determines how encompassing multilateral punishment is? The first important factor is the ease with which information about the history of individuals' conduct – about whether individuals have behaved cooperatively or uncooperatively in the past – reaches their population's other members. Where such information flows with less difficulty, a higher proportion of the population knows who to punish. The second important factor is the extent to which members of the population share ideas about what kinds of behaviors are uncooperative – which kinds constitute "cheating" and which don't. Closely related is the extent to which members of the population share ideas about the appropriate way to respond to uncooperative behaviors, namely through the termination of future interaction. Where more of the population's members share these ideas, a higher proportion of them will respond to undesired behaviors with the punishment required to deter uncooperative behavior.

Large or socially diverse populations (demographic features that often move together), pose several problems for multilateral punishment's encompassing-ness and thus its ability to support cooperation under anarchy. The larger the population, the more people information about one individual's uncooperative behavior must reach to cut that person off from the same proportion of potential exchange partners. Social diversity compounds this problem. A population consisting of persons who, for instance, speak different languages will find it harder to communicate cheaply the history of individuals' conduct to others than if everyone spoke the same language. Socially diverse populations' members are also less likely to share ideas about what constitutes uncooperative behavior and how to respond to it. For example, persons from one cultural background may view contractual obligations differently than persons from another. Similarly, one group of persons within a population may see a single instance of another's cheating as sufficient grounds to boycott her perpetually, whereas another group of persons in that population may have, say, a "three-strike rule" before they're willing to initiate such a boycott. Because of the difficulties that large, socially diverse populations pose for multilateral punishment's encompassing-ness, conventional wisdom concludes that self-governance's effective scope is limited to small, socially homogeneous ones. Given that most of the gains from social cooperation lie outside one's small, homogeneous group, this seems to be a severe limitation on self-governance. And indeed it would be.

But there's an important problem for this conclusion: *reality*. History, it turns out, defies what conventional wisdom dictates. As Fearon and Laitin (1996: 718) point out, in "most places where ethnic groups intermingle, a well-functioning state and legal system does not exist." Still, interaction between socially distant persons in these places is common and overwhelmingly peaceful. How can this be?

This essay explores the answer to that question. Existing discussions of self-governance treat the extent of homogeneity between individuals as exogenously determined and social distance between actors as fixed. However, a literature addressing the economics of identity, led by Akerlof (1997) and Akerlof and Kranton (2000), points out that individuals can and do manipulate their social distance from others. Building on their insight, I treat social distance as a variable of choice, endogenously determined by individuals themselves. Doing so has important implications for self-governance's ability to secure cooperation in large, socially diverse populations. It points to a mechanism of self-governance that conventional wisdom overlooks.

In that mechanism socially distant individuals adopt "degrees of homogeneity" with outsiders they want to trade with. Doing so signals their credibility to one another. The use of social-distance-reducing signals separates cheaters from cooperators ex ante, ensuring that in equilibrium only cooperators exchange. By supplementing partially encompassing multilateral punishment, this mechanism of self-governance promotes cooperation between the members of large and diverse populations under anarchy. Evidence from precolonial Africa and medieval international trade illustrate how.

SIGNALING WITH SOCIAL DISTANCE IN THEORY

Social distance is the extent to which individuals share beliefs, customs, practices, appearances, and other characteristics that define their identity. Socially distant individuals share few or none of these categories. They're socially heterogeneous. Individuals who are socially close share many or all of these categories. They're socially homogeneous.

Homogeneity is multidimensional. There are innumerable potential dimensions across which individuals may have commonality. Two persons might share some of the same categories of belief, such as religion or political persuasion. They may share appearance, such as the way they dress, or practices, such as how they settle disputes. Individuals might also share customs, such as the way they greet strangers, the way they deal with colleagues, or other social rules that guide their behavior.

Some dimensions of homogeneity are more significant than others. For instance, social rules may often be a relatively significant dimension, whereas style of dress may often be insignificant.[1] Which dimensions matter more depends on the context in which persons find themselves. The sports team one supports is (usually) a more significant dimension of potential homogeneity between persons interacting at an athletic event than their religious affiliations. On the other hand, one's religious affiliations are (usually) a more significant dimension of potential homogeneity between persons interacting at church than the sports team one supports.

Homogeneity is also continuous. For each dimension of homogeneity, individuals may share various margins of commonality over that dimension. Consider the dimension of language.[2] If some individual has a complete understanding of English and some other individual has, say, a 5 percent understanding of English, the two share marginal homogeneity over the dimension of language. Individuals needn't completely share a dimension of homogeneity for there to be some homogeneity over it. To avoid

---

[1] However, Rafaeli and Pratt (1993) find that in at least some cases dress does constitute a significant dimension of homogeneity.
[2] Lazear (1999) examines minority populations' incentives to adopt majority populations' languages as a means of enabling cooperative interaction.

cumbersome talk of multiple "marginal dimensions of homogeneity" that two persons may share, I call the bundle of dimensions of homogeneity that persons may share, completely or only marginally, their degree of homogeneity.

Nature exogenously fixes some dimensions, and thus degrees, of homogeneity, such as ethnicity and (to a lesser extent) gender. But it doesn't fix many others, such as religion, language, and customs. These degrees of homogeneity are alterable and thus choice variables for individuals. By manipulating these variables, individuals can affect their position vis-à-vis others in social space. They can reduce the social distance between themselves and outsiders through the decisions they make.[3]

Consider two distinct social groups, each composed of n members. Each group's members are completely heterogeneous with respect to the other group's members but highly homogeneous with respect to their own. There's no government in either social group. Nor is there an overarching government that could oversee interactions between the groups' members.

The population containing both groups, $2n$, is too large and diverse to permit the effective flow of information about individuals' histories throughout it. So multilateral punishment alone can't sustain cooperation here. However, this doesn't mean multilateral punishment is useless. Large population and significant social heterogeneity don't impinge the flow of information about traders' past conduct *within* an in-group. In-group members, recall, are relatively few and socially close.

Information about cheaters can therefore spread inside a group, but not outside its bounds where increased population and social heterogeneity prevent this.[4] So, if any member of one social group cheats another member of *his* group, all members of *his* group learn this but no member of the other group does. More important, if any member of one social group cheats a member of the *other* group, all members of the *other* group learn this but no member of the cheater's group does. Multilateral punishment is present, but it's only partially encompassing. Punishment for cheating involves foregoing trade opportunities with the members of the social group one cheated, but not the members of the other.

---

[3] Clay's (1997) work alludes to this fact as well. She notes how in Mexican California, American traders gained access to Mexican communities' internal contract-enforcement institutions by investing in Mexican identities. For example, American traders married locally, spoke Spanish in the home, and accepted Catholicism.

[4] Iannaccone (1992) considers religious sacrifice as a mechanism of securing intragroup cooperation. As I discuss later in the chapter, religious sacrifice has also been used as a form of social-distance-reducing signaling to facilitate intergroup cooperation.

Partially encompassing multilateral punishment can't secure the same level of cooperation as totally encompassing multilateral punishment involving the entire population, $2n$, can. But it can secure some. Sufficiently patient persons – those who value the discounted stream of indefinite future trades with the group members their trading partner is a part of more than the one-shot payoff of cheating – will cooperate when threatened with partially encompassing multilateral punishment. They always trade honestly with persons who are outside their group.

In contrast, sufficiently impatient persons – those who don't value the discounted stream of indefinite future trades with the group members their trading partner is a part of more than the one-shot payoff of cheating – won't trade honestly with persons who are outside their group when threatened only with partially encompassing multilateral punishment. They will be unable to realize the benefits of trading with outsiders indefinitely if they cheat. But because they discount those benefits steeply, they find cheating outsiders profitable nonetheless. These persons always take advantage of persons who are outside group.

Suppose that all of one social group's members are highly patient – patient enough that even the partial multilateral punishment described earlier is sufficient to induce them to always cooperate in their interactions with the other social group's members. In contrast, the other social group contains some positive proportion of highly impatient members – persons for whom totally encompassing multilateral punishment would be sufficient to induce cooperation with the highly patient social group's members, but for whom the previously described partial multilateral punishment is insufficient.

Because they never cheat trading partners who are outside their group, let's call the highly patient type of persons, who compose the entire former social group but only part of the latter, cooperators. Because they always cheat trading partners who are outside their group, let's call the highly impatient type of persons, who compose no part of the former social group but part of the latter, cheaters.

Consider a member of the social group whose members include some cheaters, p, who approaches for exchange a member of the other group whose members are all cooperators, q. p privately observes his type. He alone knows whether he himself is highly patient – that is, a cooperator – or highly impatient – that is, a cheater.

q's problem is straightforward: he knows nothing about p except that p is a foreigner – a member of another social group whose beliefs, practices, and so on are very different from his – and that p may be a cheater. If p is one of the cooperative members of his group, q will benefit handsomely from trading with p. But if p turns out to be a cheater – something q can only learn after it's too late – q will lose substantially from having traded with p.

If multilateral punishment were fully encompassing, q would have no reason to fear trading with p. Even if p is a cheater, he cooperates when threatened with comprehensive multilateral punishment. But because of the large and socially diverse population that constitutes $2n$, multilateral punishment isn't comprehensive and thus can't be relied on to ensure cooperative exchange with p if p is a cheater. If the probability that p is a cheater is sufficiently high, q will decline to trade with p. Because p may have been a cooperator, gains from intergroup trade go unrealized.

The breakdown described here is not, as commonly believed, a breakdown of self-governance. It's a breakdown of multilateral punishment. Multilateral punishment aims to secure self-governance by "sorting" individuals according whether they're cooperators or cheaters ex post. Herein lays its problem.

Sorting individuals by whether they're cooperators, who should be interacted with again, or cheaters, who shouldn't be, *after the fact* is an ineffective way of trying to support cooperation when populations are large and heterogeneous, as the combined population that p and q inhabit is. Large, diverse populations impinge the information flow and coordination needed for fully effective ex post sorting. Such sorting requires everyone to learn about everyone else's histories and to share notions about what those histories mean and how to behave in light of them. These are precisely the requirements that large, socially heterogeneous populations can't fulfill.

But what about the possibility of sorting individuals by whether they're cooperators or cheaters ex ante – that is, *before* trade takes place? If that could be achieved, q could confidently interact with p and realize the gains from trade that lie outside his small, socially homogeneous group. He could be confident because he could be sure to interact with p only if p had already been sorted into the "cooperator class" despite the fact that he lacks information about p's history, that p is, moreover, an unknown foreigner, and the fact that the members of q's social group may have, for instance, different ideas about how to respond to uncooperative behavior.

Unfortunately for q, p's cheater or cooperator status isn't stamped on his forehead. Only p has that information. But if q could somehow incentivize q to reveal it, he could sort q by whether he's a cheater or a cooperator ex ante nonetheless.

Enter signaling. Unlike mechanisms of self-governance based purely on ex post sorting, such as the discipline of continuous dealings, those based on ex ante sorting, such as signaling, require neither small population size nor social homogeneity to work. If q requires p to make a costly up-front investment before he's willing to trade with p – an investment the value of which p can only recoup over time in the course of many cooperative interactions with q – q can incentivize p to reveal his status as a cheater or cooperator and then sort p on that basis before they trade.

Such an investment on p's part acts as a signal to q: an action that accurately communicates to q the type of person p is and in doing so reveals p's otherwise private information about his status. If the investment q requires p to make is expensive enough, p's willingness to make that investment will be perfectly correlated with his status as a cooperator or a cheater.

The reason for this is simple: it costs p more to make such an investment if he's a cheater than if he's a cooperator. The value of the investment q requires p to make to trade with him can only be recovered through repeated interactions over time. And, because of partially encompassing multilateral punishment, q only has the opportunity for such interactions as long as he doesn't cheat p, in which case q and the other members of q's social group cut p off. Cheaters, however, are more impatient than cooperators. They discount the gains from future interactions more than cooperators do. That, recall, is why cheaters cheat in the first place. Because of this, cheaters find it more expensive than cooperators to make long-term investments of the kind q requires to enable exchange.

This difference between cheaters' and cooperators' expected payoff of making some costly up-front investment means that, at some level of investment q can require of p to enable exchange, q will find it unprofitable to make that investment if he's a cheater but profitable to make if he's a cooperator. Conditional on observing this level of investment by p, q can confidently trade with p. If q doesn't observe that p has made this investment, he declines to trade with p. Because gains from trade between p and q are only available if p is a cooperator, signaling ensures that, while the potential dangers of trading outside one's social group are averted, the potential gains available from doing from doing so are captured.

The investment, or signal, that q requires to be willing to trade must have certain attributes to be effective. It must be publicly observable. If it's not, q won't know whether p has made it, so p's status as a cheater or cooperator will remain p's private information. The investment must be sufficiently specific. It must have value predominately in its ability to enable trade with q or other members of his social group rather than in other purposes too. If the investment isn't specific, p won't lose much if he decides to cheat q because, even though q and q's fellow group members will boycott p thereafter, p will be able to redeploy his investment for other useful purposes without significant loss. The investment q requires of p must also satisfy the single-crossing property: it must be more expensive for p to make if he's a cheater than if he's a cooperator. A sufficiently large investment, the value of which can only be recovered down the road, ensures this because cheaters and cooperators have different degrees of patience.

What kind of investment, or signal, that q could require of p satisfies these conditions? One rooted in social distance.

p and q are socially heterogeneous. That's what created the problem for anarchy we're concerned with in the first place. So, if in order to enable exchange with p, q requires p to invest in adopting various social attributes that q and his fellow group members share – some degree of social homogeneity with them – but p, as an outsider, doesn't share, q can use his social distance from p, which would otherwise make him distrustful of p, to facilitate intergroup exchange instead of precluding it.

Examples of degrees of homogeneity that q may require p to adopt for this purpose include q's language, his group's customs, their religious rituals, dress, and so on. Investments in such social-distance-reducing signals are costly, so their value can only be recovered through repeated, cooperative interactions with p or other members of his social group over time. Some, such as learning an outsider's language, are quite costly by themselves. Others, such as adopting an outsider's dress, aren't, but when combined with others, can become so in aggregate. Investments in degrees of homogeneity are also publicly observable. It's easy to tell if an outsider has adopted one's customs, for example, or not. Further, as "cultural" attributes, these investments tend to be social-group-specific. Because p's potential investments have these features, by requiring a social-distance-reducing signal from him, q can turn the central bug of intergroup trade under anarchy into a feature.[5]

---

[5] In some cases decreasing one's social distance with an outsider will increase his social distance with the members of his in-group. Although this could reduce the scope for intragroup exchange in certain cases (e.g., converting to an outsider's religion, which could sever some ties with in-group members who practice an opposing religion), in general it shouldn't. In-group members have very good information about the credibility of one another. Unless the practice a person adopts from an outsider reduces his patience (and thus credibility), members of his in-group should be equally willing to trade with him after he adopts this practice as before he has done so. In fact, adopting costly behaviors of outsiders may indicate a person's greater patience (and thus greater credibility), making him a more attractive trading partner among his in-group members. However, this relies on persons placing greater weight on monetary payoffs, which are unchanged or increase

Social-distance-reducing investments aren't the only kind of signals individuals might use to facilitate exchange where multilateral punishment alone is ineffective for this purpose. But in the context of socially diverse populations in particular, these sorts of investments may be privileged over others. Where individuals are socially homogeneous, there's little room for social-distance-reducing signals to play a role in conveying credibility. Adopting the behaviors and practices of someone like you isn't costly. Adopting the behaviors and practices of someone unlike you is. This makes adopting degrees of homogeneity with an outsider a useful signal of the sender's credibility. In this sense social-distance-reducing signals are specially suited to *inter*group interactions.

Social-distance-reducing investments also exhibit what Bliege Bird (1999), Smith and Bliege Bird (2000), and Smith et al. (2001) call "broadcast efficiency." Because in-group members are socially close, degrees of homogeneity that an individual from one group adopts to enable trade with an individual from another group also create degrees of homogeneity with the other members of that group. The social-distance-reducing investments that one member of this group interprets as a signal of credibility are interpreted this way by other members of his group as well. The adopting individual therefore benefits through such investments not only by the trade he enables with the particular individual he initially approaches for exchange, but also by the trade he consequently enables with every other member of that individual's social group. Because of this, persons may often gain more by making social-distance-reducing investments, which have a wider "audience," to enable exchange with outsiders than by using other costly investments for that purpose.

The signaling mechanism just described illustrates why the conventional wisdom that sees self-governance's effective scope as limited to small, homogeneous groups is mistaken. That wisdom stems from approaching social distance as though it were exogenous and fixed when in fact it's endogenous and variable. It also stems from a preoccupation with mechanisms of self-governance that sort persons ex post, which ignores mechanisms of self-governance that sort persons ex ante. Most important, this signaling mechanism helps explain the observation with which this essay began: in the world we actually live in, cooperation is common between socially

with respect to an in-group member who reduces his social distance with outsiders, over psychic payoffs, which may fall if in-group members believe it's important to maintain one's own customs.

distant persons, even where effective government is absent. In the sections that follow I turn to some historical examples of such cooperation and the role that social-distance-reducing signaling played in promoting it.

SOCIAL-DISTANCE-REDUCING SIGNALING IN PRACTICE

Precolonial Africa

In precolonial Africa, relations between different social groups' members occurred frequently without government (see, for instance, Curtin et al. 1995; Bohannan 1968). Despite this, "[l]ong before the Europeans appeared on the scene," precolonial Africans had established domestic and "international trade, with developed systems of credit, insurance ... [and] arbitration. Law and order were normally maintained and strangers honored their business obligations" (Cohen 1969: 6). There was "intensive social interaction between various ethnic groupings" that involved "extensive credit arrangements, often between total strangers from different tribes" (Cohen 1969: 6).

To make this intergroup cooperation under anarchy possible, members of different social groups invested in the customs and practices of outsiders with whom they wanted to exchange, signaling their credibility by reducing their social distance. Three potential dimensions of homogeneity that precolonial Africans used for this purpose proved particularly important: relationships to authority, land practices, and religious practice/association.

Relationship to Authority

In the absence of formal governments, informal community leaders, or headmen, governed many precolonial Africans. These leaders were typically village elders or others of high social standing in their communities, who established social rules for community members and resolved disputes that might emerge between them (see, for instance, Middleton 1971). Some informal leaders also acted as community "gatekeepers," requesting gifts from individuals as a sign of good faith to access their communities.

In some cases refusing to abide by social rules could lead to formal punishment, such as imprisonment. But more often it led to informal punishment, such as ostracism. For example, if an individual "chose to ignore a ruling given by the chief, he could do so with impunity; but if public opinion was behind the chief's decision, he might lose the privileges" of membership in that community (Howell 1968: 192). The informal nature of many precolonial communities thus made submission to a leader's authority largely a matter of choice.

Internally, precolonial communities tended to be highly homogenous. Individuals shared the same customs, practices, appearances, religion, language, methods of handling disputes, property arrangements, and many other significant potential dimensions of commonality, making them socially close. In contrast, between groups there could be considerable social distance. Different headmen led different communities, and headmen established important social rules in their communities, so many of these potential dimensions of homogeneity differed from one community to the next. The informal leader one chose to follow was therefore an important part of one's social identity.

Both gift giving and submitting oneself to the authority of a community's rulers and dispute resolution procedures reduced social distance between outsiders and in-group members over important potential dimensions of homogeneity: usage of the same social rules, including the custom of gift giving, methods of settling disputes, and more generally recognizing the same informal leader's authority.

These social-distance-reducing investments were costly. Adopting the practice of gift giving involved investing tangible resources – the gift – to reduce social distance with the community an outsider desired to interact with. Submitting to the headman's social rules and authority involved investing intangible resources – placing one in a vulnerable position vis-à-vis an unknown community leader – to achieve the same purpose. A newcomer might be uncertain whether he would receive less favorable decisions in disputes with existing community members, imposing on him a cost of submitting to the leader's rulings.

An outsider who behaved uncooperatively after adopting such degrees of homogeneity lost his investment because, as previously noted, bad behavior led the community to reject him. Because of this, as long as the one-time payoff of cheating was smaller than the value of the gift the outsider was required to give in the gift-giving case, or the cost of potentially unfavorable decisions in the submitting-to-authority case, requiring outsiders to adopt these practices as a precondition of "entry" permitted communities to identify outsiders with whom they could profitably interact. Partly as a result of signaling with social distance, "far from there being a single 'tribal' identity, most Africans moved in and out of multiple identities, defining themselves at one moment as subject to this chief, at another moment as a member of that cult, at another moment as part of this clan, and at another moment as an initiate in that professional guild. These overlapping networks of association and exchange extended over wide areas" (Ranger 1985: 248).

Property Practices

Precolonial Africans also adopted the property practices of outsiders with whom they wanted to interact to facilitate intergroup trade. Precolonial communities didn't own the land they used in the sense that they could sell it to others. However, they did exercise some control over who may use the land they currently occupied and how it could be used. Informal community leaders often directed community members in this regard. Elsewhere, Earth Priests – community leaders representing a link to the historical first user of the land – performed this function.

Land was often seen as having mystical properties, which entailed the performance of ritual customs and taboos that Earth Priests established. To assimilate to the community, outsiders who desired to engage it agreed to participate in these customs and respect the taboos that Earth Priests identified. Further, similar to the gift-giving practice described earlier, outsiders seeking to interact with a particular land-using community often made gifts to the Earth Priests "as an expression of goodwill" (Colson 1969: 54).

Submitting to the Earth Priest's ritual taboos was costly. For example, one of the Earth Priest's taboos might be a prohibition on cultivating the more fertile land in the area because of its sacred status. Alternatively, if he wanted to join a land-using community, an outsider might have to accept the Earth Priest's decision that directed him to work a less productive plot of land on the grounds that he was a newcomer, or because the more productive land was already in use.

Only by remaining in good standing in the community could an outsider recoup his gift's cost, or the cost of cultivating less fertile ground, through continual interaction with its members. Consequently, only outsiders who intended to behave cooperatively agreed to adopt a community's ritual land customs and taboos, making this an effective social-distance-reducing signal of credibility.

Religious Practices and Associations

Precolonial Africans also used religious practice and association as social-distance-reducing signals to enable intergroup cooperation. One way to reduce social distance along these lines was to participate in an outsider's religious practices and beliefs. Alternatively, one might join an outsider's religious association or convert completely to her religion.[6]

Cults and fraternal societies, such as the Ekpe, Okonko, and Ogboni, often performed quasi-religious and judiciary functions in precolonial African communities. As one European observer noted, in the absence of "any thing like our establishment of Judges, Police, Prisons, and Penal Servitude," such quasi-religious societies "are simply [the] methods by which law and order is secured" in many African communities (Stopford 1901: 95). These societies often created religious customs and practices, as well as dispute resolution procedures, which outsiders could adopt to reduce their social distance with in-group members. In some cases societies such as the Ekpe charged a "membership fee" to join. In others, "cult membership was open to any who wished to join" and agreed to adopt the customs and practices of the society (Colson 1969: 59).

In both cases religious adoption was costly to outsiders, and more so for impatient outsiders than for patient ones. If a membership fee was required to join the society, this cost was partly financial. Even when it wasn't, outsiders who participated in or converted to these quasi-religious associations had to adopt costly customs that could include surrendering their goods to spirits, submission to potentially costly procedures for conflict resolution, restrictions on behavior such as diet, and the recurrent investment of their time in society-related activities.

Impatient outsiders didn't find making these costly investments worthwhile. Because they intended to cheat, and cheating was frequently punished with rejection from the community, cheaters couldn't profit from investing in the costly religious activities of in-group members. For patient outsiders things were different. Because their honest conduct ensured they would remain in the community long enough to recover the investment cost of engaging in the community's religious practices, they willingly did so. By sorting outsiders according to their willingness to make costly religious investments ex ante, precolonial Africans selected outsiders they could cooperate with, facilitating intergroup trade.

The point of this brief discussion of precolonial Africa isn't that every intergroup interaction was peaceful and cooperative. It most certainly wasn't. The point is that there was significant cooperation between large numbers of socially diverse people without government. That cooperation was supported by mechanisms of self-governance based partly on

---

[6] For instance, some precolonial Africans converted to Christianity to facilitate interaction with European visitors.

social-distance-reducing signaling where the discipline of continuous dealings alone was insufficient.

Medieval International Trade

Medieval international traders also used social-distance-reducing signals
to facilitate exchange in their large, socially diverse population without
government.[7] The evidence of how they did so is based on documents
from the thirteenth through fifteenth centuries left by merchants engaged
in international trade under what is known as the *lex mercatoria*, or law
merchant. Lopez and Raymond (1990) have collected and translated many
of these documents, which I draw on in the discussion that follows.

The law merchant is a polycentric system of customary law. It arose from
the desire of socially distant traders in the late eleventh century to engage
in cross-cultural exchange. In the absence of a supranational agency of
formal enforcement in particular, and often of national state-based means
of such enforcement more generally, this custom-based system relied heavily
on private arbitration via merchant courts for resolving disputes. Between
the early twelfth and late sixteenth centuries, virtually all European trade
between socially distant persons operated on this basis, with great success.

Reputation played an important role in supporting this trade. But because
of international traders' large and socially diverse population, multilateral
punishment was only partially encompassing and thus often inadequate to
protect traders' property without government. Traders supplemented the
discipline of continuous dealings with social-distance-reducing signals.

Merchants engaged in medieval international commerce had the opportunity to exchange with outsiders from many different social groups. Thus
they had to adapt themselves to their circumstances to enable intergroup
trade. Frequently this involved adopting the manners and disposition of the
outsiders with whom one desired to trade.

For instance, according to a Neapolitan merchant writing in 1458, in order
to "enjoy as much reputation or credit" as needed to facilitate exchange,

---

[7] The brief discussion that follows is intended to illustrate how social-distance-reducing
signaling facilitated intergroup trade in the medieval period, not to suggest that this
was the only informal mechanism operating to enable exchange under the medieval law
merchant. It certainly wasn't. For example, as Greif, Milgrom, and Weingast (1994) have
pointed out, merchant guilds were also among those private institutions used to facilitate
medieval trade. Milgrom, North, and Weingast (1990) point to the presence of yet another
private institutional arrangement that may have contributed to the growth of medieval
exchange.

"merchants must not have the fierce manners of husky men-at-arms, nor must they have the soft manners of jesters and comedians, but they must be serious in speaking, walking, and in all actions" (Lopez and Raymond 1990: 418). Marginal homogeneity over the dimension of "manners" contributed to a signal of trustworthiness that enabled intergroup trade. So did marginal homogeneity over the dimension of "appearance." Thus a merchant writing from Florence sometime in the early fourteenth century advises traders traveling to England to "[w]ear modest colors, be humble, [and] be dull in appearance " (Lopez and Raymond 1990: 423).

Other dimensions of homogeneity also served as the basis for signaling credibility among heterogeneous medieval merchants. Writing in Florence at the beginning of the fourteenth century, for instance, Dino Compagni, in his poetry, points to the importance of homogeneity over two particular dimensions in enabling intergroup trade. The successful merchant, he writes, will be "Genial in greeting without complaints," and "He will be worthier if he goes to church" (Lopez and Raymond 1990: 426). Shared manners and religious practice signaled credibility to outsiders, making exchange possible. Traders adopted the language of outsiders toward this end too. For instance, a trader writing between 846 and 886 writes: "The merchants speak Arabic, Persian, Roman, Frankish, Spanish, and Slavonic" to enable exchange with foreign traders (Lopez and Raymond 1990: 31).

A merchant practice guide written in Florence between 1310 and 1340 provides particularly clear evidence of reliance on social-distance-reducing investments as a means of enabling intergroup trade. This guide is explicit about how traders created degrees of homogeneity with the outsiders they desired to exchange with. In a telling passage it imparts advice to Western traders who desire to exchange with the Chinese. Advising the Western trader, the passage reads: "First, it is advisable for him to let his beard grow long and not shave. And at Tana he should furnish himself with dragomans.... And besides dragomans he ought to take along at least two good manservants who know the Cumanic tongue well. And if the merchant wishes to take along from Tana any woman with him . . . he will be regarded as a man of higher condition than if he does not take one" (Lopez and Raymond 1990: 356–357).[8]

Perhaps most significantly, traders' voluntary submission to the business and arbitration practices embodied in the *lex mercatoria* created an important degree of homogeneity between them. For example, traders voluntarily adopted, among others, certain media of exchange, standardized weights

---

[8] "Dragomans" is a medieval term for guides in Eastern regions.

and measures (Lopez and Raymond 1990: 147–150), notaries (Lopez 1976: 108), witnesses to contract (North 1990: 121, 129), and membership in transnational trading associations and guilds (Berman 1983: 342). Dimensions of homogeneity besides those under the rubric of the law merchant were used to enable intergroup trade too. For instance, traders used intermarriage, citizenship in multiple countries (Lopez 1976: 67, 63), and religious affiliation (Berman 1983: 346) for this purpose.

Medieval international trade was essential to the economic growth of Europe. Self-governance under the law merchant was its foundation. As Benson (1990: 31) puts it, "the commercial revolution of the eleventh through fifteenth centuries that ultimately led to the Renaissance and industrial revolution could not have occurred without . . . this system." In establishing this system of self-governance, the medieval law merchant also laid the foundation for modern international trade, which I consider in a later essay. Because of this system, medieval trade flourished, often without the benefit of government.

Conventional wisdom has it partly right: if the only mechanisms of self-governance persons could rely on to promote cooperation without government were based on the discipline of continuous dealings alone, successful self-governance would indeed often be limited to small, socially homogenous groups. What that wisdom has wrong is the implicit suggestion that these are the only mechanisms of self-governance available to persons in anarchy. The fact that they're not helps explain why we observe successful self-governance even in large populations of socially diverse persons.

Social-distance-reducing signaling is itself but one, supplementary mechanism of self-governance that facilitates intergroup cooperation without government. Like all such mechanisms, this one too will only sometimes be effective, and thus be used by persons in anarchy, while many other times it will not. Social-distance-reducing signaling shouldn't be seen as a panacea for overcoming the problems of intergroup cooperation without government. But it should open our minds to the possibility of a variety of mechanisms that serve this purpose. As the next chapter illustrates, that variety is as rich as the variety of context-specific problems that persons in anarchy confront.

3

The Laws of Lawlessness*

Cooperation under anarchy when persons are from different social groups is one thing. When those groups are avowed enemies, it's quite another. The idea that self-governance could promote cooperation between socially distant *hostiles* seems absurd.

Yet it can, and it has. In the words of John Stuart Mill (1848: 882), "Insecurity paralyzes only when it is such in nature and in degree that no energy of which mankind in general are capable affords any tolerable means of self-protection." That energy, you will see, is substantial.

This essay examines a significant and long-lasting era of intergroup anarchy among English and Scottish citizens on the Anglo-Scottish border in the sixteenth century.[1] The border people pillaged, plundered, and raided one another as a way of life they called "reiving." To regulate this system of intergroup banditry and prevent it from degenerating into chaos, border inhabitants developed a self-governing system of cross-border criminal law called the *Leges Marchiarum*. These "laws of lawlessness" governed all aspects of cross-border interaction and spawned novel institutions of their enforcement, including "days of truce," bonds, "bawling," and "trod."

In contrast to the previous essay, where the central problem that socially distant persons confronted under anarchy was enabling exchange, in the context this essay considers, where such persons under anarchy are bitter hostiles, the central problem they confront shifts from supporting intergroup trade to regulating intergroup violence. The issues considered here

---

* This chapter is based on and uses material from Leeson, Peter T. 2009. "The Laws of Lawlessness." *Journal of Legal Studies* 38(2): 471–502 [© 2009 The University of Chicago].
[1] While historians have explored the Anglo-Scottish border (see, for instance, the excellent work by Fraser 1995; Neville 1998; Lapsley 1900), economists have neglected this episode.

therefore overlap and foreshadow the ones that are the direct focus of the essays in Part II of this book.

The sixteenth-century Anglo-Scottish borderlands aren't unique in giving rise to a self-governing system of rules regulating violent conflict between socially distant enemy groups. Trench warfare between German and British soldiers during World War I, for instance, also gave rise to related, private, violence-reducing rules. Interactions between opposing soldiers established norms governing permissible times and locations for sniper fire. Unwritten, spontaneously emerged rules also created unofficial (and, from their governments' perspectives, undesirable) truces and permitted opposing soldiers to receive rations (see, for example, Axelrod 1984; Ashworth 1980). Similarly, during the wars between Britain, France, and Spain throughout the eighteenth and early nineteenth centuries, private men-of-war operated under a self-governing system of rules that regulated violence and prize taking at sea. This system, which I examine closely in Part II, facilitated prisoner exchanges, the ransom rather than seizure of captured vessels, and agreements to abstain from destructive conflict. Like these self-governing systems for controlling intergroup violence between enemies, the *Leges Marchiarum* didn't eliminate such conflict. But it did regulate it, reduce it, and provide social order to an otherwise bloody and chaotic environment.

My discussion draws on primary source documents left behind by border inhabitants and observers between 1249 and 1603. Foremost among these is the *Leges Marchiarum* itself – a series of documents pertaining to the rules of the border from the mid-thirteenth century to 1597. William Nicolson, Lord Bishop of Carlisle, collected and complied these documents about a century after the Anglo-Scottish union brought the era this essay describes to a close. I also use a series of sixteenth-century manuscripts called *The Border Papers*. The British crown compiled these records, which contain correspondence between various border inhabitants and the monarchs of England. Together with the *Leges Marchiarum*, these papers form the most important and detailed firsthand accounts of life on the Anglo-Scottish border.[2]

INTERGROUP ANARCHY

The Anglo-Scottish borderlands extended on the Scottish side from the River Cree to the North Sea coast and on the British side from the coast

---

[2] Additionally, this essay relies on, and is greatly indebted to the work of, contemporary historians who have discussed the border people and their unique international legal system. See, especially, Fraser (1995), Tough (1928), Neville (1998), and Armstrong (1883).

of Cumberland to the coast of Northumberland. This territory was divided into six "Marches," three on each side: the English and Scottish East, Middle, and West Marches. The Marches covered the areas that today roughly encompass the Southern Uplands and Lowland of Scotland on the Scottish side and counties of Cumbria and Northumberland on the English side (Fraser 1995). The Anglo-Scottish marches were thus home to two distinct social groups: the English and Scottish borderers, separated by cultural, geographic, political, and national boundaries.

For much of the 250-year period between the first War of Scottish Independence in 1296 and the Treaty of Norham in 1551, England and Scotland were in open conflict with one another. Because the borderlands separated the warring nations, the border people were ensconced in this conflict, facing one another in battles during official Anglo-Scottish war and often existing in a state of undeclared conflict with one another when official war wasn't raging. March inhabitants thus grew to be bitter enemies of their counterparts on the opposite side of the frontier. Inter-borderer acrimony wasn't exclusively divided along national lines. Inhabitants on the same side of the Anglo-Scottish border could and did clash with one another as well. But in light of the continued state of open conflict between the two countries, which side of the border the March people found themselves on was a crucial and powerful factor in shaping their friends and their enemies.

The second half of the sixteenth century saw a period without official Anglo-Scottish war. Still, more than 250 years of protracted and bloody battle between England and Scotland, and consequently the English and Scottish border people, left the frontier citizens in a state of severe distrust and acrimony toward the citizens on the opposite side of the border. Despite this period of tenuous peace, the "tradition of enmity" between English and Scottish borderers continued, each group's members viewing the others as targets who they might murder, kidnap, and despoil without compunction.

Officially, each March was governed by a "warden" appointed by their respective monarch. Wardens in turn appointed various underlings to help administer their areas. In theory, wardens administered their countries' domestic laws in peacetime between the two nations and mustered military forces in their areas during times of military conflict. In practice, however, things were very different.

"[L]ack of a strong settled government" characterized the Marches (Tough 1928: 28). Several reasons account for this. Some wardens were engaged in the very violent behaviors they were supposed to control. In other cases they were weaker than the powerful clans they were supposed to oversee. England and Scotland's frequent indifference to controlling their borderlands, which forced wardens to administer their Marches "on myne owne purse," as one warden complained, meant that in some cases wardens didn't bother with trying to enforce domestic laws. And some Marches experienced periods without any warden at all (see, for instance, Fraser 1995: 34; *The Border Papers* 1583: vol. 1, no. 197; Tough 1928: 35; *The Border Papers* 1594: vol. 1, no. 948, see also, vol. 1, nos. 916, 930; *The Border Papers* 1585: vol. 1, no. 341).[3]

Despite the weakness of March governments, the most important sense in which the borderlands were anarchic wasn't internal to each March, or even between Marches on the same side of the border. They were most importantly anarchic in the sense that each kingdom, its March wardens, and the rest of its March citizens existed in a state of nature vis-à-vis the kingdom, March wardens, and March citizens on the other side of the border. Until the first decade of the seventeenth century, England and Scotland remained sovereign kingdoms. Each country's domestic system of law and order extended only to the Marches in its territory.[4] As border historian Cynthia Neville (1998: 192) points out, "Scottish miscreants," for instance, "whether they crossed the border in large numbers in organised raids or individually as free-booting felons, were outside the king's allegiance and, in turn, beyond the reach of the king's common-law judges."

No supranational sovereign existed to eliminate intergroup anarchy. There was no government with authority to promulgate rules over both groups of frontier citizens. Common formal laws and courts, and rules for dealing with cross-border interactions, such as a murder in one realm by an inhabitant of the other, didn't exist.[5] The result was a large "lawless" arena for the interactions between March inhabitants on opposite sides of the Anglo-Scottish border. This erected a substantial obstacle for addressing intergroup crime along the frontier, because neither England nor Scotland

---

[3] As Fraser (1995: 30) notes, wardens were really only the "nominal overseers of the community." Within each March there were domestic courts occasionally used to deal with treason. However, "attempts to enforce the ordinary laws were somewhat intermittent," and March domestic courts met only a few times a year (Tough 1928: 163–164).

[4] On various occasions the English king Edward I declared his "overlordship" over Scotland, in effect claiming the right of jurisdiction over certain cross-border conflicts. In a few cases such disputes were adjudicated according to English common law in English courts. However, these instances were rare.

[5] Nominally, traditional English common law courts remained an option for English borderers seeking justice against cross-border criminals. In practice, however, securing justice against a border inhabitant from the other realm was exceedingly difficult, if not impossible in many cases, so borderers overwhelmingly relied on the international justice system created by the *Leges Marchiarum*.

had the authority to do so.[6] In this way the border "formed almost a lawless state within, or between, two countries" (Fraser 1995: 5).

Threatening Chaos: The Anglo-Scottish Reiving System

The borderers were peculiar in many ways. But perhaps their most striking peculiarity was how many of them embraced banditry as a way of life.[7] This peculiarity was largely the result of the near-constant conflict between their broader societies. Frequent war left both border areas decimated, and inhabitants had little incentive to establish productive enterprises that would only be destroyed in the next violent outburst between their nations. In response to this situation, many borderers turned to thievery directed at their enemies in the opposite realm.

"The border thieves were no ordinary thieves," however (Tough 1928: 48). Unlike common bandits, for them, "raiding, arson, kidnapping, murder and extortion were an important part of the social system" (Fraser 1995: 3). These activities composed a system they called "reiving." Those who took part in it were called the "border reivers." These are the notorious "steel bonnets" whose exploits and personages are memorialized in the prose of Sir Walter Scott (1802–1803, 1814–1817).

The reivers thieved and raided professionally. Reiving involved the usual sorts of behavior one would expect to attend violent theft. These included killing, maiming, kidnapping and ransoming, and other typical means of banditry. More exotic reiving activities included "black meale," the medieval equivalent of the protection racket, and a custom called the "deadly feud." Black meale grew directly out of border anarchy. Our word "blackmail" derives from this border institution, although its meaning has evolved over time. The border institution referred to agreements between reivers and other borderers for property protection or, as one borderer called them, "compacts for their private safety" (Fraser 1995: 191).[8]

---

[6] In 1603 the Union of the Crowns placed England and Scotland under the same monarch. The countries remained separate, each retaining its own parliament and sovereignty in domestic affairs. However, Scotland effectively lost sovereignty in international affairs, especially those related to England. In 1707 the Acts of Union joined England and Scotland fully, placing them under the same parliament.

[7] In fairness to the border people, some of their notorious cross-border raiding was instigated, supported, and encouraged by the English and Scottish governments, which, as I noted earlier, were frequently in conflict.

[8] The practice was officially prohibited in 1587, not long before the union of England and Scotland, but remained widespread. Writing in 1593, for instance, one warden complained of some English gentlemen who paid blackmail to reivers on the other side of the border,

Deadly feud was the custom of killing the clan members of one's rivals, ostensibly in response to a violent act perpetrated against the feud initiator, propelling the deadly back-and-forth to its next turn, and so on. As one border observer described it (Fraser 1995: 170; see also, *The Border Papers* 1583: vol. 1, no. 197):

> The people of this countrey hath had one barbarous custom among them; if any two be displeased, they expect no lawe, but bang it out bravely, one and his kindred against the other and his; they will subject themselves to no justice, but in an inhumane and barbarous manner fight and kill one another. This fighting they call their feides, or deadly feides, a word so barbarous that I cannot express it in any other tongue.

Of course, the borderers didn't exclusively reive. Someone needed to produce something for others to steal. So, although many borderers regularly engaged in reiving, most were also part-time agriculturalists, raising crops such as oats and rye, as well as livestock. "Thieving, for instance, was a recognized occupation, but the professional thief could and did occupy his spare time . . . in farming of one kind or another" (Tough 1928: 47).

Seasonal concerns dictated much of this activity. The prime reiving season was between fall and spring and tended to be concentrated most heavily between Michaelmas (September 29) and Martinmas (November 11). Most reiving was reserved for the fall because during this season nights were relatively long, and livestock – a primary target of violent plunder – was both accessible and strong enough to drive from the victim's home to the thief's. During the winter cattle and sheep were weak. And during the summer borderers moved their livestock to higher pastures where they were comparatively difficult to access (Fraser 1995: 93). Because of these practical constraints, at least the season in which one could most reasonably expect to be plundered was predictable, even if the particular month, week, or day wasn't.

Reiving's focus on livestock both influenced and was influenced by these considerations. Stealing cattle required cattle healthy enough to steal, which in turn required agricultural production sufficient to raise healthy animals. This fact had a predictable effect on agricultural production. Often it didn't make sense for reivers to direct their thievery at agricultural products. Doing so would only diminish their ability to steal livestock later in the year.

Further, because the reiving season didn't interrupt agricultural production, this had the pleasant effect of enabling border inhabitants to raise

or as he called them, "inconvenient kindnes and assauraunces enterteigned between the gentlemen and the ryding borderers" (*The Border Papers* 1593: vol. 1, no. 893).

enough crops to feed their livestock and themselves, permitting at least a low level of production and consumption despite seasonal reiving. On the other side of things, the borderlands were far from fertile lands ideal for agricultural production. Thus shifting from livestock to predominantly agricultural production wasn't an option. The infertility of the soil, in turn, is partly what dictated productive activity devoted to livestock, helping focus reiving activity on the theft of cattle.

The "Lawles and Disobedient Disposition of the most part of the Inhabitants" of the border posed a serious threat to social order (Nicolson 1747: 104). As English warden Robert Carey described the problem, "we are macht with a people without laues, and we are bound to keepe laues" (Tough 1928: 258). Carey's exasperation reflected the futility of trying to provide order to the border people through "the Queenes lawes which they dare not answer" (*The Border Papers* 1583: vol. 1, no. 197).[9]

The lawlessness these observers expressed, however, doesn't mean the borderers didn't have laws. In the absence of government to create and enforce laws that could govern interactions between the members of hostile social groups on both sides of the border, the borderers' interactions gave rise to an independent body of customary rules that regulated reiving and created a self-governing, intergroup legal system for this purpose. That system was called the *Leges Marchiarum*, or laws of the Marches.[10]

LEGES MARCHIARUM: THE LAWS OF LAWLESSNESS

The *Leges Marchiarum*'s customary rules developed organically from cross-border interactions. "[T]hey are ancient and loveable custumis, ressavit and standing in force as law, be lange use, and mutual consent of the Wardanis and subjectis of baith the realms" (Balfour 1754).[11] Eventually English and Scottish peace commissioners codified "these Laws," which "have long kept in our . . . Borders," as treaties between the kingdoms (Nicolson 1747: vi).

Because no supranational government existed, this cross-border cooperation was forged without the benefit of an overarching central authority to facilitate the process. The individuals acting on behalf of each kingdom who set down in writing and subsequently modified the *Leges Marchiarum* had no recourse to a formal agency that could establish laws governing

---

[9] Carey was one of the few March wardens who actually endeavored to administer his kingdom's domestic law in his March.

[10] The name, *Leges Marchiarum*, comes from Nicolson (1747) whose compilation of international border law bears this title.

[11] Quoted in Fraser (1995: 149).

cross-border crime or compel either side to enforce the substance of the laws agreed on for this purpose. Thus, while the codified *Leges Marchiarum* was the product of cooperation between governments, like all such agreements, it had no government to create or enforce its terms.

Codified border law didn't replace the customary law that preceded it. It simply enshrined these customs in writing, including changes to these customs that evolved over time.[12] We know this because the written *Leges Marchiarum* explicitly identifies its basis in the ancient customary usage of the border people, "that Heavy Yoke which hung so long upon the Necks of their Ancestors" (Nicolson 1747: A). The written versions we have refer repeatedly to "the ancient Laws and Customs of the Borders" (Nicolson 1747: 79–80).[13]

The first written version of the *Leges Marchiarum* was set down in 1249 and periodically altered or amended and reconfirmed by both sides until the last written version in 1597, which governed intergroup crimes until the Union of the Crowns in 1603. The *Leges Marchiarum* spanned more than three centuries and underwent numerous changes over that period. My discussion focuses primarily on the laws of the Marches as they existed during the second half of the sixteenth century. Even during this much shorter time period, however, border law experienced substantial alterations that are impossible to recount fully here. I therefore consider only "snapshots" of this law at particular points in time with a view to analyzing some of its core, general features.

The *Leges Marchiarum* regulated all aspects of cross-border interaction, including killing, wounding, and maiming; robbery or theft; "over swearing" – falsely declaring the value of goods stolen or otherwise perjuring oneself; seeking unapproved revenge against a transgressor; arson; farming, pasturing cattle, felling trees, or hunting/fishing through trespass; entering into the other realm without permission; receiving and harboring outlaws from the other realm; taking "unlawful prisoners;" impeding a warden; bawling and reproaching; and breaching assurance at days of truce.

In light of the reiving system, laws dealing with physical violence and theft were especially important. Early border law relied on a form of *wergild*, called

---

[12] This chapter uses the term "border law" to refer to the system of international law that England and Scotland forged to deal with the problem of international crime. This border law should not be confused with the domestic border law both England and Scotland established to govern their March territories internally.

[13] Some of "the customs contynuallie used on the borders" were "not comprehended in the foresaid lawes and treatises" (Bell 1605: 6, quoted in Tough 1928: 95). Thus the codified *Leges Marchiarum* is far from complete.

manbote, which required any person convicted of unjustified cross-border killing to financially compensate, or to enter himself as a prisoner to, his victim's family (Neville 1998: 6). In the latter case the victim's family had the option of executing the aggressor or, more profitably, ransoming him to his relatives. According to the *Leges Marchiarum* circa 1398, for instance, if an inhabitant from one realm engaged in "slauchteris or mutilatioun" against an inhabitant of the other, his warden delivered him to the injured party (or his kin in the event of murder) on the other side of the border to "sla or raunsoum at thair lyking" (Rymer 1739–1745: vol. 3, pt. 4, 150).[14]

Manbote was barbaric. But it was also efficient. Costs the law imposed on aggressors were enjoyed as benefits by aggressors' victims. This contrasts with modern, state-based criminal punishments, such as execution or imprisonment, which often impose costs on criminals that victims don't correspondingly enjoy as benefits (Friedman 1979).[15] Mid-sixteenth-century border law moved away from straight *manbote* to capital punishment. Notably, however, the new law retained many of its efficiency properties from the earlier law by retaining a *manbote* element. In addition to punishing murderers with death, the 1556 law, for example, also required "all the moveable goodes of the committor or committors of any slaughter or slaughters in tyme comminge be tayne . . . to the use and profit of the wife and children" of the victim, "and in default of the wife and children, to the next of his or their blood" (Armstrong 1883: 28).[16]

Border law treated other forms of illegitimate cross-border violence similarly, punishing legal violations in ways that converted aggressors' costs into victims' benefits. According to the *Leges Marchiarum* circa 1553, for example, if an aggressor "mutylate and maymed" a border inhabitant in the opposite realm, his warden was to deliver him to the opposite warden to be held in "straight Prison" for six months. However, in addition, any borderer who "shall unlawfully bodily hurt or wound any of the Subjects of the other Realm . . . shall [pay] . . . the Damage so being set and esteemed to be two doubles, as in the case of Theft and Spoil is used, and deliverance to be made to the Warden of the Marche where the party grieved inhabiteth, to be kept with him until redress be made thereof accordingly" (Nicolson 1747: 80).

---

[14] Quoted in Armstrong (1883: 27).
[15] On the economics of the private enforcement of law, see Becker and Stigler (1974) and Landes and Posner (1975).
[16] Any person who harbored such a criminal – an act called "resetting" – was liable for the same punishment as the actual offender.

Analogous rules applied to theft, though later incarnations emphasized direct financial compensation as opposed to ransoming the aggressor
(Bowes 1551: ff. 84, 84b):

If any of the subjectes of ether realme, ether by violence or force, robbe or spoyle
the goodes or cattalles of any subjectes of the opposyte realme, or by night or day
steale the goodes of any suche subjecte forthe oof the sayd opposite realme upon
the complaynantes herof tryed and founde to be trewe, the offendour or offendours
shall redresse or restore unto the partie offended the *dooble and sallfye* of such
goodes or cattelles as were them ether robbed, spoyled, or stolen.[17]

The term "dooble and sallfye" in this passage refers to borderers' custom
of compensation. It entailed twice the value of what was stolen, plus compensation for the time and trouble of the victim equal to the value of the
item, making total compensation due equal to three times the stolen goods'
value (Bowes 1551: ff. 84b, 85).[18] Border inhabitants commonly used this
formula, also variously called "two double and sawfey" and "doble and
salffie," to determine fines and penalties.

The double-and-sawfey rule speaks to two important concerns that often
arise regarding self-governing systems. These are that such systems will
evolve draconian punishments in response to victims' demands for retribu-
tion, and that the resulting criminal law, having no formal mechanism for
enforcing punishments, will go unenforced.

Rather than being draconian, as the double-and-sawfey custom suggests,
border law developed a more efficient proportionality of punishment practice. If punishments are excessive and independent of the magnitude of the
crime committed, marginal deterrence is undermined. In contrast, proportionality, which the *Leges Marchiarum* enshrined, retains a penalty substantial enough to deter some crime, but simultaneously ensures that criminal
penalties for more minor infractions aren't so costly as to encourage more
egregious infractions.

The moderation of the double-and-sawfey compensation rule also suggests that cross-border criminals were often brought to justice under border
law (I discuss how later). If few criminals were brought to justice because
of enforcement's ineffectiveness, to make the expected punishment of committing a crime sufficient to deter it, the stipulated penalty would need to

[17] Quoted in Armstrong (1883: 2). In 1563 the *Leges Marchiarum* included a three-strikes rule
that punished the third offense with death. The *Leges Marchiarum* also punished knowing
receipt of stolen property and declared thief resetters liable for the same punishment as
the thieves.
[18] Quoted in Armstrong (1883: 32).

be very large to offset the extremely low probability of its enforcement. The moderation of border law punishment thus suggests that in many – albeit, for reasons I consider later, not all – cases, this law was enforced.

Hot Trod, Cold Trod, Hue and Cry

The border justice system provided mechanisms for restitution for cross-border thefts under the law just described. However, as is often the case with recourse to adjudication, the wheels of justice could grind slowly. In many cases of theft, if action was prompt, it was possible to recover stolen property and apprehend the criminals without delay simply by counter-riding on the bandits with one's own posse. To prevent this from degenerating into simple reprisal raids that would only exacerbate intergroup conflict, certain regulations on such self-help were important.

To empower self-help but prevent its abuse, the *Leges Marchiarum* established specific rules for how the victim of a reiving expedition on one side of the border could proceed against his raiders on the other side. The primary institution for this purpose was called "hot trodd." Under this institution a victim of robbery could pursue his thief into the opposite realm to recover his stolen goods with deadly force. If he caught his thief "reed hand," the pursuer could execute him on the spot. Alternatively, and more profitably, however, he might ransom the thief to his clan. According to the *Leges Marchiarum* circa 1549 (Nicolson 1747: 63–64):

If any the Subjects . . . have stolen any thing, or things, or committed any Attempts within the Marches of Land of the other Prince . . . and, after the said Theft so committed, flying, doth return to the Marches or Land to whom he is subject, it shall be lawful for him, against whom it hath been so done and attempted, freely (within six days, to be accounted from the time of the said Fault so committed or attempted) . . . to enter safely and freely the Marches or Land into which the same Evil-doer is gone; so that so soon as he hath enter'd the said Marches or Land for that case, he go unto some honest Man, being of good Name and Fame, inhabiting in the Marches which he hath enter'd, and declare unto him the Cause of his Entry: That is to say, to follow his Goods stolen.

As part of the hot trod, pursuers sometimes used a "hue and cry," sounding their horns to announce the trod and rally others to their aid. Border law permitted "Parties grieved to follow their lawful Trodd with Hound and Horn, with Hue and Cry and all other accustomed manner of fresh Pursuit, for the Recovery of their Goods spoiled" (Nicolson 1747: 89). To facilitate the recovery process, addenda to the law prevented interference with another's trod (Bowes 1551: ff. 86, 86b; see also, Lansdowne 1450–1500: No. 262):

If any man interrupte suche persone in his saide pursute, he shall answerre hym to the bill of goodes spoyled or taken. And onely for the troublance of the partie spoyled in his trod (as the termes of the border be) the trobler shall be condempned to make redresse to the partie of his goodes stolen or spoyled with doble and salffie as aforne is mentioned.[19]

Additional amendments required individuals in pursuit of hot trod to notify the first person or community they encountered on the opposite side of the border that they were in pursuit of trod and stipulated punishment for those who refused to help pursuers track down their stolen goods. By requiring pursuers to declare their purpose and intentions in the neighboring country, the first of these amendments created a way for March inhabitants to determine whether individuals were pursuing cross-border justice under the *Leges Marchiarum* or initiating intergroup crime. By requiring domestic inhabitants to aid international trod pursuers against cross-border criminals, the second created intergroup reciprocity and facilitated intergroup cooperation in the pursuit of international lawbreakers.

In addition to hot trod, the *Leges Marchiarum* provided for a "cold trodd" – any such pursuit taking place after six days. Cold trod operated similarly but required warden approval. Using deadly force to apprehend or punish the thief in this case was also a shakier proposition and could lead to punishment for the executor. The longer an individual waited to recover his stolen property, the more doubt emerged about whether he was in fact recovering stolen property or mounting a thieving expedition himself. To prevent this, and thus minimize the chances for a violent outbreak between opposing borderers, cold trod rules restricted pursuers more than hot trod.

The rules of the *Leges Marchiarum* distinguished between trod, which might involve justified killing, and straight revenge. This line was often unclear, but at least in principle, border law permitted the former and prohibited the latter. Similarly, the trod institution didn't license pursuers to slaughter innocents on the opposite side of the border. Doing either could jeopardize a borderer's ability to pursue his goods, or worse yet, result in charges against him at the "day of truce."

Days of Truce

The day of truce was an ingenious court institution the borderers developed to ask violators of border law to answer for their offenses and to resolve cross-border conflicts. According to custom, wardens from either side of

---

[19] Quoted in Armstrong (1883: 47).

the border held prearranged meetings "at a sett daie and place indifferent" to settle their inhabitants' disputes (*The Border Papers* 1585: vol. 1, no. 343).[20] Wardens announced an upcoming day of truce in their Marches in market towns on either side of the border. Borderers with grievances against those in the opposite realm then notified their alleged offenders of their intent to file a "bill of complaint" at the day of truce, a process called "arresting." Alternatively, a grieved borderer could notify his warden, who then sent notification of intent to "arrest" an inhabitant of the other realm to this inhabitant's warden.

Customary proceedings on the day of truce highlight the delicate status of Anglo-Scottish relations in the late medieval period resulting from the fact that these two groups were enemies, as well as how these proceedings developed to ameliorate this tension. Days of truce involved hundreds, and sometimes thousands, of individuals from both sides of the border (Tough 1928: 144). As the first order of the day, each warden took an oath to proceed on the day of truce honestly and amicably, to "speir, fyill, and deliver upone his honour, he shall search, enquire, and redrese the samin at his uttirmost power" (Rymer 1739–1745: vol. 6, pt. 4, 120; see also, Nicolson 1747: 88).[21] After this the wardens created English and Scottish juries called "assizes" or "inquests" to hear their fellow borderers' bills of complaint.[22] The English warden selected six Scottish jury members and the Scottish warden chose six English jury members.

This jury selection process was an institutional response to the distrust and animosity each side felt toward the other, which facilitated cooperation between members of enemy groups in applying cross-border justice. The custom of each side selecting the other's jurors created the conditions required to apply a tit-for-tat strategy. This provided strong incentives for "reasonableness" on both sides' part, given that if one side selected the other sides' jurors unfairly, the other side could reciprocate with its own unfair selection, leveling an otherwise stacked jury.

---

[20] By custom the meeting place was usually somewhere in Scotland. However, Northham ford on the Tweed, Wark, Carharm, Redenburn, Cocklaw, Reideswire, Kershipefoot, and others became focal meeting spots depending on the Marches involved (Fraser 1995).

[21] Quoted in Armstrong (1883: 19).

[22] There were two other ways that bills could be decided: on the honor of the warden or by admission of the accused. According to the first "manner of triall of any person ... the warden shall, upon his owne knowledge confesse the facte and so deliver the partie offending" (*The Border Papers* 1584: vol. 1, no. 343). After a warden had taken his oath, borderers considered his word sufficient to determine the veracity of bills of complaint when he had direct knowledge of the guilty.

Both sides also agreed to basic rules governing the selection of jurors to help ensure a fair selection and, as I discuss later, to coordinate enforcement of the border law that punished lawbreakers by diminishing or eliminating their standing and protection under the law. For example, "No tratour, murderer, fugitive, infamous person, convict upon assize, nor betrayer of one parte or other" was "allowed to passe on any assize, to beare any office, not to beare any witnes, but only good and lawfull men deserving credite and unsuspected" (Lansdowne 1450–1500: No. 263, f. 4b, No. 9).[23]

As the *Leges Marchiarum* circa 1553 described the day of truce process, anyone with a grievance against a party from the other realm shall

> make a Bill of Complaint upon the persons so offending them at the *days of Trewes*; and the party Offender to be arrested to answer such Bill, and be compelled to answer thereto after like manner as is used by Robbers, Thieves, and Spoilers; and such like proof and Tryal to be had, of every behalf, until either the Bill be acquitted or fyled, and the Damage thereof to be set down by six Gentlemen of Worship and Good Name of Scotland, to be named by the warden of England; and other six like Gentlemen of England to be named by the Warden of Scotland. (Nicolson 1747: 80)

All assize members took oaths pledging to uphold border law: "Yow shall cleare no bills worthie to be filed, yow shall fyle no bill worthie to be cleared, but shall doe that which appeareth with a truth for the maintenance of peace and suppressing of attempts. So helpe you Gode, &c." (Bell 1605).[24] The wardens then looked over their bills of complaint and agreed on how many to settle that day. To preserve the slate-cleaning nature of the day-of-truce process and to avoid upsetting the delicate balance of intergroup relations, they made an effort to hear an equal number of bills from each side (Fraser 1995).[25]

The English assize heard the Scottish bills of complaint and the Scottish assize the English bills of complaint. This cross-hearing of complaints provided an additional check on the honesty and reasonableness of both sides similar to the custom of cross-selecting the assize members.[26] If an

---

[23] Quoted in Armstrong (1883: 20).

[24] Quoted in Tough (1928: 141–142).

[25] All complainants took a public oath of honesty for bills they filed to "truth say what your goods were worth at the tyme of their taking to have been sold in a market" (Bell 1605, quoted in Tough 1928: 142). In addition, in 1553 the *Leges Marchiarum* was amended such that in the event of suspected gross overstatement the warden or assize reserved the right to modify the value considered.

[26] As a final mechanism for preventing wrongful convictions, the border trial process relied on "vowers." Vowing meant "confronting of a man of the same nation to averre the fact" of the crime alleged by the victim. The assize's decision alone wasn't enough to convict an accused criminal. But if a countryman of the accused – a vower – would also support the

assize acquitted an individual, he was "cleared." If it found him culpable, the bill was called "fyled" and the guilty "foull." Arrested individuals who didn't appear at the day of truce were "fyled condytionally, which meant, if he, at the next daye of trewce, be not redy lawfully to answerre the sayd compleynante against hym, and to excuse his former defaulte, he shalbe adjuged culpable or foull by his own defaulte" (Bowes 1551: f. 86).[27] After deciding the bills, the sides exchanged prisoners in cases where border law called for the delivery of offenders to the opposite warden, wardens set up the next day of truce, saluted and embraced each other, and the participants departed.

ENFORCING BORDER LAW

An obvious potential problem plagued cross-border dispute resolution: refusal to comply with day of truce decisions or otherwise participate in the justice process established by the *Leges Marchiarum*.[28] What ensured that an arrested individual would appear at the day of truce for his trial? If an arrested borderer didn't appear, he was conditionally filed – found guilty for nonappearance unless he appeared at the next day of truce with a legitimate excuse for his absence. But being filed by the assize would mean little for a borderer if he could perpetually avoid justice by never attending a subsequent day of truce. Furthermore, what if a fouled borderer refused to pay the compensation required by border law? If day-of-truce decisions couldn't be enforced, the system of cross-border criminal law was threatened, and with it successful self-governance.

Borderers used several mechanisms to ensure participation in days of truce and compliance with day-of-truce decisions. The first of these was

---

victim's allegation, the conviction was secured. "Then is hee by the law guilty; for except the warden him self knowing, shall acknowlege the fact, or a man of the same nation found that voluntarilie will avonche it (the ordinarie and onlie waies of triall), be the facte never so patent, the delinquent is quitt by the lawes of the Borders" (*The Border Papers* 1585: vol. 1, no. 343). Fraser (1995) and Armstrong (1883) both refer to vowing as a separate method of trial. However, as Armstrong's discussion indicates, vowing was not really a separate method but rather worked in conjunction with the assize method of trial.

[27] Quoted in Armstrong (1883: 17).

[28] An additional mechanism of border law enforcement, not discussed here, was outlawry. Refusal to make recompense could place one outside the bounds of border law, leaving him without the protection against violence established in the *Leges Marchiarum*. According to border law circa 1249, this was achieved through "Banishment by the Sound of a Trumpet" (Nicolson 1747: 17). A public declaration of outlawry in this fashion communicated the outlaw's status to the border community, effectively announcing that he and his possessions were fair game for the taking.

bonds, which the borderers called "borowis" or pledges. If, for instance, an accused party didn't appear on the day of truce as he promised during the arresting process, his warden delivered a human hostage to the other side until he did.[29]

In principle bonds could be any member of the accused individual's social group – his fellow countrymen. In practice a subset of this larger group – his family members and fellow clan members – typically performed this role. Bonds weren't always used in an ex post fashion. To ensure that arrested individuals appeared at impending days of truce, wardens sometimes also sought accused borderers' bonds – members of their family or clan – ex ante, who were released when their accused relatives appeared at the day of truce.

Immediate family or clan members provided the stronger bond, because failure to appear at a day of truce jeopardized the fate of an individual's loved ones or members of his closest support network. However, fellow countrymen bonds also provided an incentive to appear at days of truce, because borderers lived among their group members, including the bond's family. These persons could exert considerable pressure on their noncompliant compatriots to attend days of truce to which they were summoned per border law.

Borderers also used bonds to produce compensation from fouled parties who lacked the means to repay their victims. In this case the fouled party himself might enter the custody of the aggrieved or his warden at the day of truce until his payment was forthcoming. Or he might be able to cajole a family member to take his place for this purpose instead.

Borderers similarly used bonds to ensure compliance with assize decisions. If a fouled individual didn't satisfy the assize's decision by the next day of truce,

The Wardens of both Marches (at the next day of Trewes ensuing or following the Fileing of the said Bills) shall make Deliverance of such other Persons, by the Assent of the Opposite Warden; as he will undertake to be sufficient for the said Bill. The Person so delivered, to remain with the Party offended until he be fully satisfied, and lawfully and fully redressed, according to Justice, and the Laws of the Marches. (Nicolson 1747: 73)[30]

---

[29] In 1563 border law also required lords to ensure that their tenants, if arrested, appeared per this summons at the day of truce. For failing to do so, such a lord could be found liable for his tenant's crime (but he couldn't be executed even if this was the corresponding punishment his tenant should receive).

[30] On rare occasions when no suitable bond could be found, the fouled borderer's warden or one of his deputies offered himself for this purpose.

In addition to family, clan, or fellow country members, professional bonds-men also performed this role (Fraser 1995). Professional bondsmen were hostages for hire. By permitting a market for human hostages as sureties, the border system ensured that this mechanism for enforcing border law was carried out relatively cheaply. Because fouled borderers who valued their freedom more highly could compensate their victims by purchasing the services of other individuals who valued their freedom less highly to fulfill the bonding function, victims (or their wardens) secured their bonds at a lower social cost.

Bonds were helpful in enforcing the *Leges Marchiarum*. They created a strong incentive to participate in, and comply with, day-of-truce decisions. But they didn't provide a bulletproof remedy. For example, if a fouled bor-derer hired a professional bondsman to be delivered to the aggrieved in his stead while he accumulated the repayment he owed, what prevented him from stopping the process there? Why repay the victim? The victim had his bond, and could ransom or execute him if the fouled borderer defaulted on compensation. Unless the professional bondsman was a fellow group mem-ber, the fouled borderer had little incentive to make good on his promise. And on the other side of the transaction, what compelled bond recipients to release bonds once their offenders had completed compensation?

To deal with these problems and strengthen compliance with the *Leges Marchiarum* more generally, borderers employed a peculiar custom called "bawling." Bawling provided a means to reproach noncompliant individuals publicly. Sir Robert Bowes, warden of the East and Middle English Marches, described this practice as follows (1551: f. 83b):

Thais, if anye Englisheman or Scottesman be bounde to another of the opposite realme for ransomes, entry of prysoners, or any other just cause, for whiche he byndethe hym by his faythe and truthe, and dothe not accordingly perfourme and accomplishe the same, after reasonable monytions thereof given to the partie, and request to perfourme his sayde bande and promyse, it hate bene used between the realmes that the partie offended wolde beare a glove or a picture of hym [on the tip of one's sword] that had so broken his truthe, and, by the blast of a horne, or crye, to give knowledge to the hole assembly that suche a person is an untrue and unfaithfull man of his promysse, to his reproch, which is as muche in the lawe of armes as to give unto hym the lye, and appealle to fight with hym in the quarrell, and, indede, the partie soe reproched may (if he will) defende his cause and truthe by singuler battaille, which the other partie can not honestly refuse.[31]

---

[31] Quoted in Armstrong (1883: 58).

In this manner borderers denounced and shamed any man who "crakit his creddence" along the frontier (Leslie 1888–1895: 101).[32] The practice of publicly questioning one's honor and challenging him to a customary, duty-bound duel served as an important check on borderer compliance. Individuals used it most widely at days of truce to call out those who had broken their promises of repayment, bonding, and so on.[33]

Bawling's reliance on dueling reduced the potential for large-scale, intergroup violence between borderers – a critical feature in light of Anglo-Scottish enmity. As Posner (1996: 1737) points out, in the absence of government for enforcing social rules, dueling may be an efficient enforcement mechanism because it "prevents disputes from exploding into feuds by formalizing and channeling the means of enforcement." The Anglo-Scottish borderlands, which had no government to create or enforce laws governing intergroup interactions and which were home to individuals with a penchant for feuding, were precisely the sort of environment in which dueling would be efficient.[34]

Beginning in 1553, an amendment to the *Leges Marchiarum* required warden permission for "bauchling and reproving" at days of truce: "no Person or Persons of either said Realms, shall, at any Day of Trewes . . . bear, shew or declare any sign or token of Reproof or *Baughling* against any Subject of the opposite Realm, unless he be thereunto licensed by the Wardens of both the Realms" (Nicolson 1747: 81). This amendment was to ensure that overzealous bawling didn't create disorder at days of truce. "Reproofing"

---

[32] Quoted in Tough (1928: 105).

[33] The following is an example of a duel contract between borderers: "It is agreed between Thomas Musgrave and Lancelot Carleton, for the true trial of such controversies as are betwixt them, to have it openly tried by way of combat before God and the face of the world, to try it in Canonby holme before England and Scotland, upon Thursday in Easter week, being the 8th day of April next ensuing, A.D. 1602, betwixt nine of the clock and one of the same day; to fight on foot; to be armed with jack, steel cap, plaite sleeves, plaite breeches, plaite frocks, two baselard swords, the blades to be one yard and half a quarter length, two Scotch daggers or dorks at their girdles; and either of them to provide armour and weapons for themselves according to the indenture. Two gentlemen to be appointed on the field to view both the parties, to see that they both be equal in arms and weapons according to this indenture; and being so viewed by the gentlemen, the gentlemen to ride to the rest of the company, and to leave them but two boys, viewed by the gentlemen to be under 16 years of age, to hold their horses. In testimony of this our agreement, we have both set our hands to this indenture, of intent all matters shall be made so plain as there shall be no question to stick upon that day" (Armstrong 1883: 74).

[34] For further discussion of the efficiency of dueling as a rule enforcement mechanism under such circumstances, see Schwartz, Baxter, and Ryan (1984).

without permission resulted in the acquittal of the individual charged with
not fulfilling his promise.[35]

No doubt at least partly because of the prospect of bawling, despite
their preoccupation with reiving, border inhabitants took their promises
seriously. "Infamy fell on any Borderer who broke his word, even to any
enemy" (Tough 1928: 36). Consequently, although "they would not care
to steal...yet they would not bewray a man that trust in them for all
the gold in Scotland and France" (Sadler 1809).[36] Testimony from border
observer John Leslie, Bishop of Ross, suggests this as well. "[H]aving once
pledged their faith, even to an enemy," he remarked, "they are very strict in
observing it, insomuch that they think nothing can be more heinous than
violated fidelity." In the words of one English warden of the East and later
Middle Marches, the border reivers "will rather lose their lives and livings,
than go back from their word, and break the custom of the Border" (Fraser
1995: 45).

The *Leges Marchiarum* regulated and limited cross-border violence.
But they didn't eliminate it. The first factor contributing to some violence's persistence was imperfect enforcement. Enforcement under the *Leges
Marchiarum* couldn't have been wholly ineffective given that, as previously
discussed, the punishments stipulated under its terms weren't exorbitant.
But neither could have enforcement been perfect, or there wouldn't have
been any violence, which there was.

Enforcement was imperfect for several reasons. First, some corruption
plagued the Anglo-Scottish Marches. If, for example, a member of a powerful
clan violated the *Leges Marchiarum*, but this clan was important to his March
warden – for instance, because the warden was also a member of his clan, or
because the clan supported the warden in some other capacity – the warden
might do his best to avoid bringing this borderer to justice at the day of
truce. The corrupt warden could, for example, swear an oath of the accused
borderer's innocence, officially excuse his absence at the day of truce, or
otherwise help get the accused borderer off the hook in answering for his
crime. Second, the arresting process itself was crude, and wardens didn't
always have the time, energy, or resources required to track down an accused
borderer or even one of his clan members to hold in his stead.

---

[35] Border law treated perjury at days of truce in a somewhat related fashion. A perjurer could
   be imprisoned for three months but, far worse, following his term, at the next day of truce
   he was "openly denounced and proclaimed a Perjur'd man; after which time he shall not
   be reputed to be a Man able to give further Faith or Testimony in any Case or Matter"
   (Nicolson 1747: 83).

[36] Quoted in Armstrong (1883: 83).

Another reason some cross-border violence persisted despite the *Leges Marchiarum* system was the difficulty of extracting full compensation from violators and, as a result, fully compensating victims in a timely fashion. While in principle days of truce were held monthly, in practice, sometimes long periods could elapse between them. This was most likely to occur in the period immediately preceding the outbreak of official warfare between England and Scotland, during war itself, or immediately following war's conclusion, when cooperation between wardens turned to hostility. When days of truce were suspended, cross-border crimes couldn't be addressed until days of truce recommenced. Lawbreakers thus enjoyed additional time without facing punishment and victims incurred the cost of a longer wait before receiving justice.

An additional factor contributing to delayed compensation was a filed borderer's inability to come up with compensation. Human hostages, which could be ransomed, and bawling helped reduce this problem. But they did so imperfectly. There was no guarantee, for instance, that in the event a hostage had to be ransomed he would fetch a price sufficient to offset fully the victim's loss or sufficient to equal the payment stipulated by the *Leges Marchiarum*.

Further, recall that at days of truce wardens made an effort to hear an equal number of complaints from each side so as not to upset the delicate balance of Anglo-Scottish relations. This helped preserve the slate-cleaning nature of the day of truce process. But it also meant that if one side had accumulated more bills of complaint than the other side since the last day of truce, the next day of truce might be put off until the balance was equalized.

According to Fraser (1995: 163), together these factors meant that borderers sometimes had to wait years before lawbreakers actually incurred their punishments and victims actually received compensation. Delayed compensation operated to shrink the effective cost of crime for the aggressor and shrink the effective compensation for crime received by the victim, reducing the *Leges Marchiarum*'s effectiveness in addressing cross-border crime.

Finally, and perhaps most important, some violence persisted under the borderers' system of self-governance because many borderers derived utility from the act of reiving itself. These borderers didn't desire the elimination of violence. It's therefore unsurprising that scope for some violence remained, and indeed was permitted by the system itself.

The *Leges Marchiarum* wasn't the only mechanism of self-governance that helped reduce and control cross-border violence in the Anglo-Scottish Marches. Several other mechanisms aided this purpose as well.

For example, to bring potentially long-lasting and bloody feuds to a faster and more peaceful conclusion, competing clans sometimes intermarried their members, placing once-hostile borderers on cooperative terms with one another. Officially, both England and Scotland prohibited cross-border intermarriage. But this prohibition was difficult to enforce, especially in the face of the peace-promoting effects it had for border inhabitants.

Through such intermarriage "'international families' like the Grahams" extended across the Anglo-Scottish border (Fraser 1995: 65). This intermingling had another conflict-reducing effect for some borderers: it dulled the otherwise sharp distinction between Englishman and Scotsman. Intermarriage functioned as a costly social-distance-reducing investment of the kind described in the previous essay. As a result of such investments, an English warden complained of border "people that wilbe Scottishe when they will, and Englishe at theire pleasure" (*The Border Papers* 1583: vol. 1, no. 197). In this way intermarriage contributed to the ambivalent attitude some borderers displayed toward citizenship and facilitated the idea of a "border people," distinct from either English or Scottish citizenship, which reduced intergroup mistrust and hostility.

Cross-border intermarriage and fuzzy views about citizenship help explain why the more numerous English borderers didn't simply annihilate their less populous Scottish neighbors. Together with the *Leges Marchiarum*, they also help explain why cross-border violence, though present, didn't decimate the border population over years of conflict and hostility. If reiving was continually killing off larger numbers of men and women, we would expect the population on one or both sides of the border to decline precipitously over time. A dearth of population data prevents a direct evaluation of this issue. However, we know at the very least that violence wasn't so rampant as to have brought the border population to ruins since at the end of the sixteenth century it was nearly 170,000 persons strong (Tough 1928: 26–28).

At least one other mechanism of self-governance helped reduce cross-border violence: the discipline of continuous dealings between the English and Scottish governments. It didn't behoove the English crown, for instance, to send soldiers to the border to exterminate the Scottish borderers. Neither government cared deeply about the welfare of its March inhabitants, but because the border region was strategically important to both, a move such as this by the English crown would have simply prompted the Scottish crown to repopulate its border, perhaps sending along with these new citizens an army sufficient to exterminate the English Marches. Recognition of this fact likely prevented both governments from overzealously attacking the border inhabitants of the other.

In 1603 England and Scotland joined together under a single monarch. The Union of the Crowns signified the end of the Marches, of intergroup anarchy, and of the Anglo-Scottish laws of lawlessness. In the early seventeenth century, England disbanded the March wardens and applied its common, formal domestic law throughout the old borderlands (renamed the Middle Shires), unifying the formerly separate English and Scottish social groups and drawing the self-governing, Anglo-Scottish intergroup justice system to a close.

The English and Scottish border reivers were socially distant enemies. But rather than this situation preventing institutions of self-governance from emerging to regulate them, if anything, it seems that these persons' animosity *enhanced* the importance of developing a system of self-governance to oversee intergroup interactions, and thus both groups' incentive to devise institutions for limiting their predatory inclinations. The resulting system left ample scope for border society's members to indulge those inclinations. But the emergence and operation of intergroup self-governance among English and Scottish hostiles devoted to violently raiding one another makes what regulation the *Leges Marchiarum* did manage to achieve that much more remarkable. In 1598 border visitor John Udall noted precisely this. "Considering the weakness of their governors," Udall "did not marvel at the many outrages, factions, thefts, and murders committed, but rather wondered that there were not many more" (Tough 1928: 32).

PART II

SELF-GOVERNANCE AND THE PROBLEM OF VIOLENCE

4

Trading with Bandits*

No sane person would argue that it's possible to trade with bandits. We have all learned that private institutions alone are insufficient to prevent the strong from plundering the weak. Indeed, the threat of violence is perhaps the oldest, most well-accepted justification for government. Even Adam Smith believed this was true. As he put it: "It is only under the shelter of the civil magistrate that the owner of . . . property . . . can sleep a single night in security. He is at all times surrounded by unknown enemies, whom, though he never provoked, he can never appease, and from whose injustice he can be protected only by the powerful arm of the civil magistrate continually held up to chastise it" (Smith 1776: 670).

Self-governance, however, might be better at negotiating threats of violence than conventional wisdom suggests. The border reivers provided some evidence for this possibility. But in their case, self-governance had much more than ordinary threats of violence to negotiate. The Anglo-Scottish border population consisted of socially distant persons, many of whom, moreover, were committed to a system of intergroup violence as a way of life. It's difficult to tell in such an environment how much of self-governance's imperfect ability to prevent violence reflects inherent limitations on its ability to do so or rather the fact that many of the persons involved enjoyed violence per se. This essay considers an environment that isolates the potential for violent theft as the problem that individuals under anarchy confront. It examines persons for whom social distance wasn't a pressing issue and for whom violence, as is usually the case, was solely a potential means rather than also an end.

* This chapter is based on and uses material from Leeson, Peter T. 2007. "Trading with Bandits." *Journal of Law and Economics* 50(2): 303–321 [© 2007 The University of Chicago].

Most discussions of self-governance focus on commitment problems that involve potential for what might be called peaceful theft in that recourse to physical violence isn't used to take advantage of the wronged party. For peaceful theft, a separation of payment and provision, not a difference in actual strength, accounts for an individual's ability to defraud his exchange partner. Equally important when government is absent is what might be called violent theft. Here the perpetrator is a bandit who uses physical force to overwhelm his victim. His superior strength gives him the ability to deprive others of their property.

We have seen that under some conditions, at least, the discipline of continuous dealings can support cooperation in the face of the prospect of peaceful theft. But it's much harder for it to do so in the face of the prospect of violent theft. The reason is simple: weaker persons can eternally boycott stronger ones who behave violently toward them, but boycott doesn't prevent stronger persons from simply taking what they want from weaker ones.

There are exceptions to this statement, of course. If the stronger party is stationary but the weaker one is mobile, boycott can be effective. However, in situations where individuals have disparate strengths *and* stronger persons are mobile while weaker ones aren't, multilateral punishment breaks down. Weaker individuals may refuse to interact with stronger ones who behaved violently toward them in the past. But if they can't run and stronger individuals can, their refusal won't prevent them from being plundered again. Something other than the threat of lost revenue from future interactions is needed to create cooperation.

One possible solution to this problem is for physically weaker persons to invest in becoming stronger. When both parties can transform their resources into coercive power, the otherwise weaker party may be able to improve its property protection against stronger ones (see, for example, Bush and Mayer 1974; Umbeck 1981; Hirshleifer 1988, 1995, 2001; Skaperdas 1992, 2003; Anderson and McChesney 1994; Anderson and Hill 2004; Skaperdas and Syropoulos 1997; Neary 1997; Grossman 1998; Grossman and Kim 2002; Bates, Greif, and Singh 2002).[1] But significantly improving one's strength isn't always an option for weaker parties. For instance, if one party has a monopoly on the technology of greatest violence, the other may be severely limited in its ability to invest in strength for the purpose of defense or aggression. Introducing severe limitations on some persons' ability

---

[1] For a discussion of the emergence of property rights and their defense in the absence of formal enforcement, see Anderson and McChesney (2002).

to invest in additional strength leads to a situation in which those who aren't so constrained plunder those who are. Permanently weak persons can't avoid violent theft in equilibrium (see, for instance, Hausken 2004).

With both multilateral punishment and investment in greater strength eliminated as means for coping with the threat of violent theft, it would seem that there's no way for permanently weak individuals to exchange with stronger ones. Despite this, this essay demonstrates that trade between permanently weak and permanently strong individuals without government is indeed possible. Weaker individuals' inability to rely on mechanisms described by the discipline of continuous dealings and to invest in force for defense or aggression doesn't prevent them from making exchange with bandits self-enforcing in the face of threats of violent theft.

To illustrate this, I examine west-central Africa in the second half of the nineteenth century.[2] During this period, European settlers on the west coast of Africa employed middlemen to collect the goods they needed for export from producers in the remote interior of central Africa.[3] In addition, some Africans operated as middlemen on their own account, connecting European exporters and others with producers in the interior. Caravans of traveling middlemen were frequently stronger than the communities of producers with which they interacted. They were therefore tempted to overwhelm these communities with force and steal the goods they desired rather than trading for them.[4]

Communities of producers used two mechanisms of self-governance to transform middlemen's equilibrium strategy from banditry to peaceful trade. First, I discuss producers' use of credit as a means of facilitating producer-middleman exchange relations. Second, I look at producers' demands for tribute from middlemen as a kind of risk premium promoting producers' ability to interact peacefully with traveling traders.[5]

---

[2] For a classic treatment of West African trade in the colonial period through the early 1950s, see Bauer (1954).

[3] As Serpa Pinto (1881: 22) summarized it, "trade in Africa was divisible into two branches, viz. the purchasing of goods from the whites and selling them the produce of the country, and purchasing such produce from the blacks and selling to them the aforesaid goods." This trade was conducted by traveling middlemen.

[4] The problem I consider here is somewhat analogous to a violent version of the traditional hold-up problem discussed by Williamson (1975, 1985), Klein, Crawford, and Alchian (1978), and Hart and Moore (1988), among others.

[5] Olson (1993) and McGuire and Olson (1996) consider the case when the stronger party finds it in his interest to establish permanent hegemony over the weaker individuals. If his interest is stable and encompassing, and the stronger party is sufficiently patient,

To examine these strategies I use primary source materials regarding interaction between middlemen and producers in west-central Africa in the latter half of the nineteenth century. These sources consist of in-depth reports from about twenty European travelers to the area during this period. Many of these travelers were themselves traders, while others were explorers interested in learning more about the state of African trade for their home countries and spreading the word of Christianity.

PRODUCER-MIDDLEMAN RELATIONS IN LATE
PRECOLONIAL AFRICA

The persons in the anarchic episode this essay considers are the nineteenth-century inhabitants around the Upper Zambezi and Kasai, Portuguese-speaking settlers along the Angolan coast, and the middlemen they employed.[6] Middlemen typically traveled in caravans and were constantly on the move.[7] These caravans consisted of other free middlemen, guards charged with protecting the caravan on the road, and often a great number of slaves who carried the items for sale. Caravans ranged in size from tens to thousands of persons, but based on the evidence available in travelers' reports, the modal caravan consisted of about seventy or eighty people (Miller 1988: 191; Cameron 1877: 251; Soremekun 1977: 87; Capello and Ivens 1969: vol. 1, 17–18; Dias de Carvalho 1890: 186, 192, 193, 700; Harding 1905: 214; Johnston 1893: 34).

Common imports that traveling traders carried to the interior included tobacco and gin, beads, shells, and brass used as body ornaments, cloth, and firearms. As the sole suppliers of firearms to interior communities, middlemen controlled the weaponry reaching producers and thus typically had the upper hand when it came to implements used in fighting.[8]

---

he can make more this way than by sporadically pillaging weaker parties. This chapter considers the use of informal mechanisms that create a cheaper means for stronger agents to credibly commit to not plunder weaker ones than establishing government over them. For a pioneering discussion of institutions of credible commitment in the context of violent conflict, see Schelling (1960).

[6] Interaction between middlemen and producers in the interior of west-central Africa appears to have begun around 1790 (Botelho de Vasconcellos 1844).

[7] Capello and Ivens (1969: vol. 1, 103), for example, described the middlemen of Bihe as "eminently devoted to traveling."

[8] I have found no evidence to suggest that middlemen were cartelized or in any way coordinated their actions to prevent arms from reaching producers. Nevertheless, they appear to have infrequently supplied firearms to producers.

Producers consisted of village chiefs/headmen and their citizens in the remote interior. These individuals rarely traveled far beyond the bounds of their communities where the resources they used in production were found.[9] Specialization contributed to their stationarity. It was expensive to spend significant time away from home, especially given that traveling for the purpose of trade wasn't producers' comparative advantage. The goods that producers supplied to middlemen consisted mainly of ivory, beeswax, and wild rubber. Further, even though slave trading was prohibited in Angola in 1836, slaves also continued to be a source of profit to traveling traders who sought them for illegal sale both to coastal traders and to other African communities.[10]

In the nineteenth century most of interior west-central Africa consisted of scattered communities ruled by chiefs who adjudicated disagreements between their citizens, including those that dealt with credit and exchange. The relationship between rulers and citizens in these communities was largely informal.[11] As Livingstone (1963: 410) observed, for example, "So far as I can at present understand, there are no such things as nations or kingdoms in the interior of Africa." Or, in the words of two other European travelers to the African interior, "it is only in extraordinary cases that one can suspect that such a thing as a law exists" (Capello and Ivens 1969: vol. 2, 242; see also, vol. 1, 183).[12]

On the European side, crown-established governors ruled Portuguese settlements on the coast and oversaw trade posts they set up slightly further inland. These settlements' laws didn't bind Africans in the interior. Nor did interior African communities' customs bind these settlements' inhabitants. The result was a formally ungoverned arena involving interactions between them.

---

[9] While some indigenous persons in the remote interior of west-central Africa migrated within the areas composing this region, very few migrated outside of it and these weren't producers. According to Capello and Ivens (1969: vol. 1, 225; see also, Serpa Pinto 1881: 255; Harding 1905: 307), "The natives of T'Chiboco," for instance, "seldom travel beyond their own country, and it is a rare sight to behold a caravan of Ma-quioco journeying westward for the purposes of trade."

[10] According to Crawford (1914: 28), for instance, the Governor at Benguela allowed illicit slave trading to go on under his watch.

[11] See also Capello and Ivens (1969: vol. 2, 49, 242).

[12] Even where colonial outposts had been established, formal authority often wasn't effective. For instance, as Arnot (1889: 111; see also, Harding 1905: 306; Johnston 1893: 59) commented, "Though Bailundu and Bihe are within the province of Benguella, Portuguese authority has not very much influence there."

The Threat of Violent Theft

To profit, middlemen needed to obtain goods from producers in the interior of central Africa and bring them to outlying communities and coastal exporters. They could obtain these goods in two ways: peaceful trade or violent theft. In connecting stationary producers with people outside the narrow bounds of their communities, middlemen had the capacity to enable producers to realize significant gains from exchange they would have been otherwise unable to capture.[13] Unfortunately, the fact that middlemen tended to be stronger than the communities of producers they interacted with created a situation in which middlemen were tempted to use force rather than trade to realize their ends (see, for instance, Harding 1905: 93, 108, 124, 138; Cameron 1877: 226, 253, 292, 331, 472; Johnston 1893: 40–41; Gibbons 1904: vol. 1, 67; Livingstone 1874: vol. 2, 29; Livingstone 1857: 180, 297; Livingstone 1960: 277; Livingstone 1963: vol. 1, 12). As Cameron (1877: 393) observed, for example, left unchecked, caravans "profited by rapine and robbery in passing through countries where people did not possess guns."[14] Thus a potentially highly beneficial situation for producers could easily turn into a massively harmful one.

Like all behavior, the decision to engage in banditry versus trade is guided by the relative marginal cost and marginal benefit of these alternative modes of action. Sufficiently superior strength lowers the marginal cost of plunder below that of trade as a means of obtaining desired goods. Where an individual is strong enough to take what he wants with little or no resistance, it's cheaper to steal than to pay for the objects of his desire. His payoff-maximizing strategy is to violently overwhelm weaker individuals.

Two features of middlemen accounted for the fact that they were often the stronger force in their interactions with interior producers. First, as previously noted, middlemen were producers' sole source of modern weaponry, namely guns. By controlling the quantity and quality of firearms reaching

---

[13] As two travelers to the interior put it, "Commerce, by obliging them [traveling traders] to make repeated journeys, carries with it, as a necessary consequence, the establishment of relations and the making of contracts with distant peoples" (Capello and Ivens 1969: vol. 2, 18).

[14] Caravan leaders often made this bad situation worse by encouraging their groups to steal from the villages they traveled to. Leaders were usually responsible for providing their group's provisions on the road. And provisions became very costly when caravans were large (see, for instance, Serpa Pinto 1881: vol. 1, 165). Theft was thus sometimes promoted as a cost-cutting measure. As Cameron (1877: 259) observed, for example, "At Kwakasongo there is an Arab settlement of some size . . . they send out their caravans. . . . These fellows get no pay, but are allowed to loot the country all round in search of subsistence and slaves."

interior communities, middlemen could secure their strength superiority, giving them a decisive advantage should they decide to attack these communities. Heightening this advantage was the fact that, often, "in the interior . . . the villages are open and unprotected" (Serpa Pinto 1881: vol. 1, 177). This made producers easy targets for better-armed middlemen. Middlemen's weapons advantage wasn't always sufficient to ensure victory if they attacked. If a caravan was sufficiently small and the community it attempted to plunder was sufficiently large, better weaponry was meaningless. But overcoming this potential obstacle to banditry wasn't hard. Middlemen simply needed to be selective about the communities they attacked.

Second, middlemen were highly mobile and producers were highly stationary. This meant two things for middleman success in plundering expeditions. On the one hand, middlemen could always return to the coast or their home bases near the coast and gather additional members if greater numbers were needed to succeed in violently plundering communities of interior producers. More important, producers' relative immobility meant middlemen could escape from conflict with their booty by fleeing to the coast without concern that bands of producers would later locate them, track them down, and forcibly recover from them what the middlemen had stolen.[15]

Analyzing the Threat of Violent Theft

To understand the threat of violent theft that middlemen posed for producers, it's useful to examine their interactions in the context of a simple game. Consider an economy of complete and perfect information with one community of producers and one caravan of middlemen. Because it's stationary and sufficiently weaker than the caravan of middlemen, the community of producers doesn't have a choice about whether it will interact with the middlemen. If the caravan approaches the community of producers, the community can't avoid interaction. Thus multilateral punishment, which requires the ability to terminate future interaction in the event of

---

[15] According to Crawford (1914: 22–23), persons in west-central Africa at this time also frequently changed their names. This, of course, would have contributed to the difficulty of tracking down violent middlemen. However, it remains unclear how pervasive this practice was. A third reason for middlemen's strength superiority could also be added. Namely, the fact that they were mobile and producers were stationary meant that middlemen had the ability to initiate surprise attacks on communities of producers. This may help explain Serpa Pinto's (1881: vol. 1, 178) comment: "It is a noteworthy circumstance connected with wars in this part of the Africa, that the attacking party is ever the victor."

uncooperative behavior, isn't an effective strategy for preventing banditry here. However, the community of producers does control a different variable of the game: how much it produces.

Producers move first and decide whether to produce for trade or for subsistence. Producing for trade means producing a large quantity of goods that producers may consume or trade with the caravan if it approaches them. Producing for subsistence means producing a small quantity of goods barely larger than what producers need for consumption. Production for trade therefore involves a surplus stock of goods that affords producers additional consumption and trade, whereas production for subsistence involves a stock just large enough to sustain the community and permits only a minimal level of trade.

The caravan of middlemen moves second and decides whether to stay home – that is, to not travel to the community of producers at all – to travel to the community of producers and trade, or to travel to the community of producers and plunder. For reasons described earlier, the caravan's attempt to plunder is always successful and met without resistance such that the community loses all it has produced when it's plundered.

If producers produce for trade and middlemen stay home, producers receive H_p and middlemen receive H_m – what each can earn without interacting with the other. If middlemen trade, both producers and middlemen earn a higher payoff from exchanging, E_p and E_m respectively, where E_m is middlemen's payoff net of traveling expenses. If middlemen plunder, they receive a still higher payoff, which, when travel expenses are deducted, yields them P. Producers, in contrast, receive their lowest payoff in this case, $-H_p$.

The situation is similar if producers produce for subsistence, but the payoffs change because a smaller stock of goods is available for producers to consume, middlemen to violently take if they choose to plunder, and producers to trade with middlemen if middlemen decide to exchange. Only middlemen's payoff from staying home, which is unaffected by the stock of goods producers keep on hand, doesn't change when producers produce for subsistence. Thus if producers produce for subsistence and middlemen stay home, middlemen continue to earn H_m. Producers, however, earn less. Because the inconvenience of producing just enough to sustain the community is costly, producers receive a payoff of only h_p, where h_p is equal to H_p minus the value they place on the foregone stock in consumptive uses.

If middlemen plunder, producers receive $-h_p$, which is their smallest payoff when they produce for subsistence but larger than what they receive when middlemen plunder and they produce for trade $(-H_p)$. Middlemen in

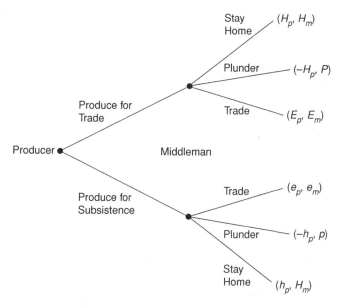

Figure 4.1. The Threat of Violent Theft

this case earn p, which is more than they earn by trading but, because there's so little to steal, is smaller than the payoff of staying home (H_m). Finally, if middlemen trade, producers earn e_p, which is smaller than what they earn from trade when they produce for trade (because there's a smaller stock available for trading), but still their highest payoff when they produce for subsistence. Middlemen in this event earn e_m, their smallest payoff, which includes the cost of travel.

To summarize, then, for producers: $E_p > H_p > e_p > h_p$. And for middlemen: $P > E_m > H_m > p > e_m$. $E_p + E_m > P - H_p$, which is to say that the higher level of trade is efficient. Figure 4.1 depicts this game.

The unique subgame perfect Nash equilibrium of this game involves producers producing for subsistence and traveling traders staying home. If producers produce more, they increase middlemen's payoff from banditry by making more available to steal. This entices middlemen to plunder, generating losses for producers.

To avoid these losses, producers produce only what's needed to sustain themselves. As a result there's little available for theft, creating a situation for middlemen in which staying home yields a higher return than plundering. In equilibrium, producers earn h_p and middlemen earn more, H_m. Producers "pay" for their strength inferiority by incurring the cost associated with reducing stocks to a level that prevents middlemen from engaging in banditry.

In discouraging middlemen from interacting with them, producers also forego significant potential gains from trade. However, the threat of being plundered didn't prevent trade between middlemen and producers in the late precolonial period. Indeed, legitimate exports supplied by remote interior producers leaving Angola alone amounted to close to $4 million per year by the end of the nineteenth century (Vellut 1979: 101). How did producers overcome the threat of violent theft posed by trading with bandits?

A CLEVER USE OF CREDIT

To capture the gains from trade with middlemen, producers required a strategy that could keep middlemen's payoff from plunder below the payoff from staying home, like when they produced for subsistence, but raised middlemen's payoff from trade above the payoff from staying home, like when they produced for trade. Credit made these two seemingly incompatible goals possible. Although middlemen couldn't steal goods that didn't yet exist, credit enabled producers to trade with goods that didn't yet exist. You can't steal what's not there, but you can trade with it. By keeping current stocks low but exchanging with middlemen on credit, producers could produce for subsistence, deterring plunder, while still enabling trade, allowing both sides to reap the benefits of cooperation.

To see how the use of credit arrangements enhanced producer-middleman exchange, consider the game in Figure 4.2. This game is like that in Figure 4.1, only now when producers produce for subsistence, middlemen's trade strategy is to trade on credit rather than simultaneous exchange. This modification makes the game dynamic. When trade on credit is chosen, each round is composed of two subperiods: one in which middlemen provide credit and another in which, if producers have produced, exchange takes place and, if they haven't, they're plundered to clear off as much of the debt as possible.[16]

The payoffs on the Produce for Trade branch of the tree are the same as before. Likewise, the payoffs from {Produce for Subsistence, Stay Home} and {Produce for Subsistence, Plunder} are the same. However, because it

[16] For instance, when the traveling trader "Hassani of Dugumbe got [a] chief into debt" and the chief could not repay, Hassani "robbed him of ten men and ten goats to clear off the debt" (Livingstone 1874: vol. 2, 35).

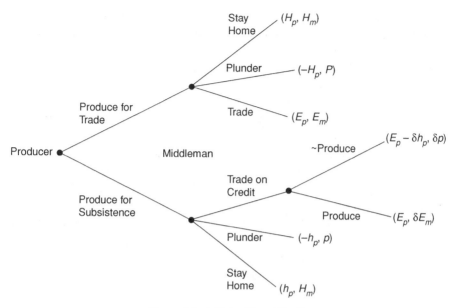

Figure 4.2. A Clever Use of Credit

now involves trading on credit, which increases the volume of exchange possible, the payoff of trade under subsistence production rises.

Because middlemen provide credit in the first subperiod, they only receive what they're owed in the second subperiod if producers have produced. If middlemen provide credit and producers subsequently produce, producers receive the same payoff as when they produce for trade and middlemen trade under the Produce for Trade branch of the tree, E_p. Middlemen, in contrast, earn δE_m, where δ is the caravan's discount factor and $\delta \in (0, 1)$.

The reason for discounting middlemen's payoff is straightforward. Because trade in this case is conducted on credit in the first subperiod, middlemen only receive all or part of the gains from exchange via repayment in the second subperiod. If after receiving credit in the first subperiod the caravan arrives to receive payment in the second subperiod but producers haven't produced, middlemen punish them by plundering what's available. When this happens, producers receive $E_p - \delta h_p$: what they received on credit in subperiod one, less the discounted value of what's taken from them in subperiod two. Middlemen, in contrast, receive δp: the discounted value of what they're able to take as compensation in subperiod two.

What course of action the caravan of middlemen now finds most profitable depends on its discount rate and the credibility of producers' promise to produce in subperiod two. Where $\delta > H_m/E_m$ and producers can credibly commit to produce, trade is more profitable for the caravan than staying home. Where δ doesn't satisfy this inequality or producers can't credibly commit to produce, the caravan finds staying home more profitable.

Because $E_p > E_p - \delta h_p$ for any $\delta \in (0, 1)$, and $E_p > h_p > -H_p$, producers can credibly commit to produce for repayment in subperiod two. Given this, for middlemen whose discount rates satisfy $\delta > H_m/E_m$, trading on credit is the payoff-maximizing strategy. For middlemen whose discount rates don't satisfy this inequality, staying home is payoff maximizing. In equilibrium the caravan only travels to the community of producers if it's going to trade (on credit), and stays home if it poses a threat of violence. Plunder is avoided and producers and middlemen who are sufficiently patient realize the gains from exchange.

The use of credit for this purpose in nineteenth-century producer-middleman exchange was ubiquitous. As the traveling trader Henrique Augusto Dias de Carvalho (1890: 700) put it, "[T]he trader sees himself forced to give credits, and this is indispensable for anyone who takes the risk of trading in such a region, if he wants to do it with any success."[17] Producers' efforts to keep stocks of thievable goods low was eased considerably by the fact that the main goods middlemen desired – for instance, ivory, rubber, and wax – required harvesting before they were available in exportable form. These goods remained in the ground, so to speak, until producers collected them.

To keep stocks perpetually low, producers protracted the debt repayment process (see, for instance, Cameron 1877: 47; Livingstone 1874: vol. 1, 305; Dias de Carvalho 1890: 699). Consider the observation of European traveler to the Upper Zambezi and Kasai, Paul Pogge (1880: 16):

The native would be little inclined to gather the products of his country, were he not given the payment in advance... [*Ambaquista* middlemen – A.v.O.] can buy some products in the interior, these being brought to them by the natives and paid [immediately].... In general, however, they cannot purchase very many commodities in this way but instead give the native credit. Where rubber occurs in the forest, and where the elephant occurs, the Baptist [*Ambaquista*] gives payment in advance to the elephant hunter for so and so many tusks, and to the one who wants to bring rubber or beeswax payment for so and so many pounds of rubber or wax. *These people then have to wait for months and years until their debtors satisfy them* [emphasis added].[18]

---

[17] Translation from Oppen (1994).
[18] Translation from Oppen (1994). See also, Buchner (1883: 82).

The goods producers desired that middlemen extended to them on credit – for instance, alcohol, cloth, and tobacco – were typically the kind producers consumed shortly after receiving them. Thus middlemen weren't able to extend goods to producers on credit and then retake them by force when they returned to a village to receive an installment of debt repayment. Obviously, however, producers couldn't reduce their stocks of goods to zero. They needed to keep some provisions on hand to survive. Additionally, some goods traveling traders desired – for instance, slaves – couldn't be made unavailable in the way that others could. Consequently, there was always something available for stronger middlemen to steal if they wanted.

Still, by significantly reducing their holdings, producers could concomitantly reduce violent theft's benefit for middlemen bent on banditry. Moreover, it was unnecessary for producers to reduce their stock of goods to zero to have the desired effect. As long as producers kept stocks low enough such that the value of the goods available for plunder was lower than middlemen's payoff from trading on credit, middlemen would trade with producers rather than plunder them.

The pattern of historical references to middleman-producer credit agreements closely tracks the declining importance of slaves and the rising importance of ivory, rubber, and wax from the 1840s and 1850s onward, following the abolition of Angolan slave trading in 1836 and then slavery itself in 1858. In the first half of the nineteenth century credit agreements are rarely mentioned.[19] In the second half of the century they're common. This reflects the fact that, as previously pointed out, the credit mechanism wasn't especially effective in preventing plunder by middlemen seeking slaves, but was highly effective in preventing plunder by middlemen seeking other goods.

While the game presented earlier is bilateral, in actuality multiple caravans of middlemen interacted with multiple communities of producers.[20] The presence of multiple communities of producers and caravans introduced the possibility of one caravan plundering the goods producers harvested to repay another caravan as part of a previous credit agreement. However, it seems unlikely that caravans could have pursued this strategy effectively, for two reasons. First, for such theft to be effective, caravans would require specific knowledge of when the goods produced to repay other caravans were available for stealing before they had been collected. Second, caravans had

---

[19] Where credit is mentioned, producers rather than middlemen were the creditors. See, for instance, Baptista (1873).

[20] See, for instance, Buchner (1883: 62), who refers to Mwant Yav's "business relations with a number of traders from the coastal areas" (translation from Oppen 1994: 360).

strong incentives to ensure that other crews of middlemen wouldn't plunder the goods owed to them. The use of credit created a stake for middlemen in producers' well-being. By indebting themselves to middlemen, producers transformed their status in these traders' eyes from targets of violence to productive assets. To produce the goods necessary to repay their debts, producers needed to be alive and well. So it was in middlemen's interest to ensure the health and safety of those to whom they made loans. One way middlemen protected their valued investments was by punishing other middlemen who wronged them. For example, according to Arnot (1889: 179), "three Garganze caravans had been plundered and many men killed – one at Bihe, another in the Lovale country, the third in the Lunda country, but all at the instigation of Bihe chiefs and traders, who thought that they had been unjustly dealt with in certain business transactions they had with Msidi."

It's not clear whether some caravans were able to establish monopoly control over some areas. Securing an effective monopoly would require a significant and lasting strength disparity between caravans such that stronger caravans could forcibly exclude potential competitors from trading with particular villages. Such a disparity may have existed in some instances, but it clearly didn't in many others. A monopoly caravan would create less favorable terms of trade for producers. In principle, monopoly middlemen could get away with paying producers just above their payoff of producing for subsistence and not trading on credit (producers' equilibrium payoff from Figure 4.1). Thus, if competition were absent, it would be reasonable to expect poor bargaining power among producers and near-subsistence wages. However, the historical record indicates that, for some producers at least, just the opposite prevailed. As one traveler complained about villagers he encountered, for instance, "the people being satiated with cloth, owing to their constant intercourse with the coast, would sell us nothing, or asked higher prices than we could afford" (Cameron 1877: 390).

TRIBUTE AS A RISK PREMIUM

In communities where producers held wealth predominantly in the form of humans (slaves) and livestock, producers were constrained in their ability to reduce the size of their thievable stocks. As long as those stocks weren't so large as to make banditry more profitable than trading on credit regardless of a caravan's discount rate, sufficiently patient caravans continued to find trading on credit the most profitable course of action. To see this, consider a community that, because it holds much of its wealth in the form of humans and livestock, can't reduce its stock of goods as low as others who don't hold most of their wealth in these forms. The benefit of plundering this community is therefore higher, Ψ, where $\Psi > H_m$. Despite this, if $\Psi < E_m$, there exists some caravan that will continue to find the payoff from trading on credit (δE_m) greater than the payoff from plundering (Ψ). Specifically, where $H_m < \Psi < E_m$, caravans with discount rates that satisfy $\delta > \Psi/E_m$ will trade on credit.

However, caravans with discount rates where $\delta < \Psi/E_m$ won't. In fact, because $\Psi > H_m$, some caravans that would rather stay home than trade on credit with producers who can reduce their stock of thievable goods sufficiently would rather plunder producers who can't do this than stay home. For these middlemen, banditry is the most profitable course of action. Thus, while producers who could reduce their stocks sufficiently were safe from plunder and could trade with bandits, those who held their wealth in the form of humans and livestock couldn't. Sufficiently patient middlemen would trade with them on credit, but impatient ones would plunder them.

To address this problem, communities of vulnerable producers demanded tribute from traveling traders who approached them for exchange. Typically community headmen were gatekeepers to their community's producers and required middlemen to meet their tribute demands before they would consummate trade relations.[21] As the prominent middleman Antonio Francisco Ferreira da Silva Porto (1885: 580) recorded, tribute payment "*was necessary*

---

[21] Tribute was sometimes kept and consumed by the headman or chief who received it. This didn't inhibit tribute's usefulness as compensation for the cost imposed on them by violent middlemen, however. Occasionally, local rulers would declare a monopoly right to trade with middlemen who approached them. In this event tribute functioned as a premium offsetting the ruler's risk of trading with the outsider. Additionally, tribute consumed by local leaders indirectly reached villagers in the form of public investments undertaken by the ruler, for which tribute was his pay. For instance, resolving community disputes (via arbitration) was a common duty of rulers, as was generally maintaining community order. Likewise, rulers could be charged with providing food in the event the community encountered hard times – a form of social insurance. Tribute collected and consumed by a chief functioned as payment for performing such public services, indirectly compensating community members for the risk posed by impatient middlemen. As noted previously, some chiefs/headmen had coercive power. When this power was greater than that of a visitor, he could use this to coerce tribute payment. However, for reasons described already, more often than not, it seems that this wasn't the case. Instead the power of chiefs was in preventing access to their community. This was the case, for instance, if a river separated his community and persons desiring to visit him and the canoe was on his side of it (see, for instance, Cameron 1877: 266). Chiefs also had power in their ability to refuse to furnish guides/assistants to visitors who didn't know the area or how to safely get to the next village, or who required additional protection when traveling between villages.

to open the door! We tried to find the solution to this enigma and found
out that it was necessary to give some pannos [yards of cloth – A.v.O.] to
obtain permission for the people of the caravan and of the country to buy
and sell provisions and other commodities, without which nothing could
be done."[22]

The way tribute worked is straightforward. Suppose that caravans of middlemen are heterogeneous in discount rates such that ρ is the proportion
of caravans with discount rates that satisfy $\delta > \Psi/E_m$ and $1 - \rho$ is the
proportion of caravans with discount rates that don't satisfy this inequality.
If a caravan of middlemen was excessively impatient and so intended to
plunder a community, demanding tribute was worthless. The stronger caravan would simply overwhelm the community, refuse tribute payment, and
go about violently stealing what it desired. For those caravans that weren't
too impatient, however, demanding tribute was effective. These middlemen
found peaceful exchange more profitable than plunder and so were willing
to pay for the opportunity to trade.

Where producers can't reduce their stocks sufficiently and the resulting
benefit from plunder is Ψ, their expected payoff of producing for subsistence
and trading on credit is $\rho(E_p) + (1 - \rho)(-h_p)$, which is greater than
producers' expected payoff of producing for subsistence and not trading on
credit for any $\rho > 0$. Sufficiently patient middlemen earn $\delta E_m > \Psi$ when
producers agree to trade on credit and Ψ when they don't. Because of this,
producers could demand tribute T from sufficiently patient middlemen in
order to exchange with them on credit, where $T \leq \delta E_m - \Psi$, and these
middlemen would pay it (beside those others cited here, see, for instance,
Arnot 1889: 71, 80, 102, 135–137, 151, 159, 204; Arnot 1893: 26; Harding
1905: 81, 95–96, 142, 148, 290; Serpa Pinto 1881, vol. 1, 67–68, 90, 175,
228–229; Graca 1890; Johnston 1893: 111; Capello and Ivens 1969: vol. 1,
87, 116–117, 137–138; Livingstone 1963: vol. 1, 9, 33, 98; Cameron 1877:
77).[23] Thus "it is not surprising that tribute is paid to the [every] village
headman where one sets up the camp" (Silva Porto 1885: 577).[24]

Tribute demands acted as a risk premium that communities of vulnerable producers charged middlemen. Those demands helped protect producers against the risk of interacting with traveling traders who, as a general
class, were comprised of some patient and some impatient members. More

[22] Translation from Oppen (1994). See also Crawford (1914: 118) and Harding (1905: 148).
[23] As the proportion of impatient caravans in the population increases, the credibility of
producers' threat to not trade on credit with those who refuse to pay tribute increases too.
As $\rho \to 0$, the gains producers forego by adhering to this strategy fall.
[24] Translation from Oppen (1994).

specifically, tribute acted as a tax on patient middlemen used to subsidize impatient middlemen's banditry. By taxing middlemen who expressed a desire to exchange, producers could extract compensation from patient middlemen who traded with them to cover losses that impatient middlemen imposed on them when the latter plundered them.[25] This helps explain Francois Coillard's (1897: 611) remark about the Luvale chief – Chief Kakenge – when he noted the "homage or rather a tax he exacts from black Portuguese traders who enter his country."

Tribute frequently took two forms: goods that producers consumed immediately or shortly after receiving them, for instance, an ox that would be slaughtered and eaten right away, alcohol or tobacco, or European novelties (for example, a watch) that weren't sought by middlemen to bring to coastal European traders for export. The reason for this is straightforward: to avoid tribute payments contributing to vulnerable communities' stocks of thievable goods. If tribute was either consumed quickly or consisted of goods middlemen weren't looking for, producers didn't need to fear losing it to a violent caravan's banditry.[26]

Key to its usefulness as a risk premium, tribute also needed to constitute a net gain to recipient producers. This ruled out the possibility of present reciprocation, as was practiced in gift-exchange arrangements between some villages and which, as the discussion in this book's first essay suggests, may have reflected social-distance-reducing signaling.[27] Thus, although

---

[25] Where the total population of middlemen is θ, producers generate $\rho\theta T$ in revenue from demanding tribute, which is used to help offset losses in the amount $(1 - \rho)\theta(-h_p)$. To completely offset the losses imposed by impatient middlemen, $T = -[(1 - \rho)(-h_p)]/\rho$. As already noted, however, the amount producers could demand in tribute was bound at the upper limit by $\delta E_m - \Psi$. Whether or not full compensation was possible therefore depended upon how much greater the payoff of trade was over the payoff of plunder for patient middlemen (which in turn depended on how patient patient middlemen were), the proportion of impatient middlemen in the population, and the value of the stock lost in the event of plunder (which, of course, depended on the extent to which producers were able to reduce their stocks).

[26] The fact that thievable goods were sometimes demanded as tribute is attributable to two possible factors. On the one hand, this may reflect that some communities of producers assigned a relatively low probability to being plundered by a caravan of violent middlemen. On the other hand, even though the tribute a community received – say, a slave – would ultimately be stolen by a violent caravan, in the time between when the community received it and the time it was stolen, the employment of the slave yielded some benefit to the community. If the slave were needed enough, this benefit could outweigh the benefit of a non-thievable tribute even though its employment wouldn't be permanent. In this case the slave would be preferred as tribute to say, an ox, even though the former was at risk for theft while the latter wasn't.

[27] For an analysis of the gift exchange system, see Landa (1994).

communities of producers often offered traveling traders food or temporary shelter after receiving tribute, these "gifts" were worth substantially
less than those they demanded, leaving a large effective premium in place
(Miller 1970: 193). As Livingstone (1963: 253; see also, Harding 1905: 192,
290) complained, for example, "the Negroes do not seem to have the smallest
idea of presents being reciprocal."

Considering where we started from, producers' use of tribute highlights
a surprising result of their interaction with middlemen. That starting place,
recall, was this: without government, stationary and permanently weak
persons are at the violent whim of mobile and permanently strong ones.
In late-nineteenth-century west-central Africa, however, it was stationary
and permanently weak producers who ended up with the upper hand over
mobile and permanently strong caravans. The former managed to charge the
latter for the privilege of trade rather than the latter violently overwhelming
the former and stealing whatever they wanted. By altering the cost-benefit
structure of trade versus violence, weaker persons' self-governing strategies
transformed stronger persons' incentive from plunder to peaceful exchange.
Self-governance enabled trade with bandits.

5

Efficient Plunder*

No governance arrangement can preclude perfectly the prospect of stronger persons using violence to steal from weaker ones. That, of course, includes government. There always remain situations when stronger persons find it profitable to plunder weaker ones and so do. Here I consider an extreme case of such a situation under anarchy – one in which profitable opportunities for plunder are ubiquitous and, at least temporarily, there's no chance of significantly reducing them: war.

This case is instructive not because it characterizes the usual state of affairs under anarchy, but because its extremity in opportunity for, and frequency of, profitable plunder provides a chance to examine the question of just how violent and destructive – how "Hobbesian" – even a Hobbesian jungle can become. In this essay, then, the central problem that persons under anarchy confront isn't how to prevent plunder, which is already an inescapable feature of the social landscape, but rather how to limit plunder's social cost.

Everyone knows theft is socially inefficient. From society's perspective, resources thieves use to transfer others' property to themselves and resources others use to prevent thieves from stealing their property are wasted. The social costs of violent theft – of plunder – are larger still. Plunder not only produces deadweight losses in the form of wasted resources. It literally destroys resources that are obliterated in violent contests between plunderers and their victims.[1]

What's typically overlooked is that plunderers have strong incentives to engage in activities that reduce plunder's social losses – to make plunder

---

* This chapter is based on and uses material from Leeson, Peter T., and Alex Nowrasteh. 2011. "Was Privateering Plunder Efficient?" *Journal of Economic Behavior and Organization* 79(3): 303–317 [© 2011 Elsevier B.V.].

[1] For the classic discussion of the welfare costs of theft, and their similarity to the welfare costs of monopolies and rent-seeking, see Tullock (1967).

more efficient. While self-interest seeking leads plunderers to embark on violent theft in the first place, it also leads them to do so in ways that reduce their private cost. This in turn reduces plunder's *social* cost.

When contracts between plunderers and their victims are enforceable and transaction costs are low, plunderers and their victims benefit from trade that facilitates the former's ability to plunder the latter. Coasean "plunder contracts" transform part of plunder's social costs – resources invested in violent appropriation and lost in violent conflict over ownership – into private benefits for plunderers and their victims. A significant portion of the wealth that plunder would otherwise destroy is preserved instead. The result is less socially costly, and thus more efficient, plunder.

To investigate this claim I consider maritime marauding in the eighteenth and nineteenth centuries. During war privately owned and operated vessels from enemy nations called privateers plundered one another's merchant shipping.[2] Traditional plunder whereby a privateer battled a merchant-man and then hauled its prize back to port for condemnation in a "prize court" was costly to the privateer, the merchantman, and society. To reduce their costs of plunder, privateers developed a system of ransom and parole founded on Coasean plunder contracts between themselves and victim merchantmen.

Under these contracts privateers agreed to give merchantmen, their cargoes, and their crews their freedom for a price. The Coasean bargains that underlaid the ransom and parole system not only preserved merchant vessels, their cargoes, and merchant sailors' lives and freedom. They preserved privateering vessels, privateersmen's lives, and improved privateers' profit while reducing the social cost of maritime marauding. Not all privateers could capitalize on this system, but those that did facilitated more efficient plunder.

My discussion highlights the Coase theorem's relevance and operation where it's expected least: between powerful plunderers and weak victims. Traditionally, the Coase theorem's operability is confined to situations in which property rights are well defined and interactions are voluntary. However, this essay suggests that Coase's (1960) insight also applies to situations in which property rights are poorly defined and interactions are coercive.

While exchange and coercion are usually thought of as mutually exclusive, my discussion illustrates the possibility and practice of exchange *within* coercion or, more generally, cooperation within conflict. In turn, that

---

[2] Leeson (2010a) discusses mutiny on eighteenth-century merchantmen and the institutions that merchant sailors devised to overcome the collective action problem of maritime rebellions.

possibility places an upper bound on how destructive, and thus "nasty, brutish, and short," even an anarchic world populated by parties locked into violent conflict can become.

A THEORY OF (MORE) EFFICIENT PLUNDER

Plunder's social cost has three sources: resources invested to steal others' property, resources used to defend against predation, and the deadweight loss of destruction. The first two sources are socially costly because resources invested to transfer or defend property aren't used to produce wealth. The third is costly because resources are literally and irrevocably destroyed. The pie of existing wealth shrinks.

Perfectly efficient plunder avoids each of these costs completely. It constitutes a costless transfer. If no resources were required to violently steal from others or defend against violent theft, and violent theft destroyed nothing, its social cost would be zero. Plunder would be a costless reassignment of property from one holder to another.[3] Because, at a minimum, plunder requires time, it always involves a positive cost and perfectly efficient plunder is impossible.

However, more efficient plunder is possible and can, under certain circumstances, approach the perfectly efficient ideal. More efficient plunder satisfies one or more of the following conditions: (1) It economizes on resources plunderers use to steal from victims. (2) It economizes on resources victims use to prevent being plundered. (3) It economizes on resources destroyed in violent struggles between plunderers and their victims.

My theory of more efficient plunder is a special case of the theory of the gains from trade. The unique aspect of this theory's operation in the case of plunder is the source of those gains: plunder's social cost. That cost is also a private cost borne partly by plunderers. The more resources plunderers must expend to exploit their victims, the lower their return from plundering. Thus plunderers have an incentive to satisfy condition (1) for more efficient plunder – to economize on resources used to steal from victims.

Additionally, the more resources victims must expend to prevent being plundered, the lower plunderers' return will be from plundering. Resources

---

[3] For one influential model of the social cost of plunder, see Buchanan (1975). For another, see Hirshleifer (1995, 2001). For related discussions on the endogenous emergence of property rights and cooperation and conflict under anarchy more generally, see, for instance, Anderson et al. (2006), Bush and Mayer (1974), Haddock (2003), Libecap (2003), Skaperdas (1992, 2003), and Umbeck (1981).

victims use to deter plunder are resources plunderers can't steal. This gives plunderers an incentive to satisfy condition (2) for more efficient plunder – to economize on resources victims use to prevent being plundered.

Similarly, the more resources plunderers destroy in violent fights with their victims over property, the less they earn from plundering. This gives plunderers an incentive to satisfy condition (3) for more efficient plunder – to economize on resources destroyed in violent struggles with their victims.

Plunderers can conserve on resources spent to produce, to prevent, and that are destroyed during violent theft by striking bargains – forging "plunder contracts" – with their victims. In exchange for victims forgoing defensive investments to prevent being plundered and surrendering their property peacefully, plunderers agree to give some of that property back to them. Victims are worse off than if they weren't plundered at all. But conditional on being plundered in the first place, they're better off than if they don't enter this agreement. Plunderers are better off by the amount of resources they save by inducing victims to forego defensive investments and to surrender their property peacefully (less the amount returned to their victims for acquiescence). This includes the resources they would have spent producing plunder, those that victims would have consumed in preventative measures and thus would have been unavailable for the taking, and those that would have been destroyed in violent clashes with their victims. Plunder contracts transform part of plunder's social cost into private benefits for plunderers and their victims. In doing so they make plunder more efficient.

The larger plunder's social cost when plunder doesn't economize on the resources used in plunderous production, the resources victims use to prevent plunder, and the resources destroyed in the violent conflict plunder precipitates, the larger the space for mutually beneficial exchange through plunder contracts, and thus the more likely it is that plunder will be conducted more efficiently. For example, plunder is more socially costly when the means of producing it are less specific than when they're more specific. In the former case, resources spent plundering have a higher opportunity cost: they could be used to produce a wide range of other things. In the latter case, resources spent plundering don't have many – or in the limiting case, any – alternative uses. It follows that the space for mutually beneficial exchange via plunder contracts is larger when the means of plunderous production are less specific. The plunderer's benefit of achieving a Coasean agreement with his victim is bigger in this case, making it more likely that he will forge such an agreement with his victim.

Three conditions must be satisfied for plunderer-victim Coasean bargains to take place and thus for more efficient plunder to be possible. First, transaction costs must be sufficiently low to make exchange between plunderers and victims worthwhile. If a plunderer speaks English but his victim only speaks Swahili, striking such a bargain may be prohibitively costly. Transaction costs may also be prohibitively high if the bargaining process is protracted and thus the parties have difficulty reaching a mutually agreeable price because they're negotiating strategically to increase their share of the gains from trade. Similarly, if many parties must be brought into the negotiation to make Coasean plunder agreements possible, bargaining costs may exceed the gains available from forging such agreements, preventing them from coming into existence.

Second, information about the plunderer's and victim's strength must be symmetric. The plunderer and victim must agree that the plunderer is stronger. If the victim is delusional about his relative strength, he may believe he can obtain better terms than what the plunderer offers through exchange by battling him. This prevents the parties from negotiating a Coasean bargain required for more efficient plunder.

Finally, plunder contracts must be enforceable. If either party to the plunder contract expects the other to renege, Coasean agreement is impossible. There are several ways that plunderers and their victims can make their contracts self-enforcing. A Williamsonian (Williamson 1983) hostage exchange is one example. A plunderer and/or his victim may give his counterparty a hostage that's valuable to him but not to his counterparty to ensure contractual compliance. Or he may give such a hostage to a third party who destroys or releases it to his counterparty if he reneges. Further, while the discipline of continuous dealings is typically unable to prevent plunder, it may nevertheless be able in some cases to support Coasean plunder agreements. A plunderer who violates his agreement with a victim may find future victims unwilling to contract with him. If the plunderer is sufficiently patient, the shadow of the future can enforce his plunder contracts today. The specific ways in which plunderers and their victims make their contracts self-enforcing depend on the particular situations in which they find themselves. In some cases hostage swapping without resorting to a third party may be effective. In other cases a third party may be needed. In still others reputation may be most effective, and so on.

PRIVATEERING AND MARITIME PLUNDER

Privateering in the eighteenth and nineteenth centuries provides a useful case for exploring this theory of more efficient plunder. Privateering began in the twelfth century as a form of self-help against maritime muggers.

Several centuries later privateering's self-help role had given way to one as the means for cash-strapped nations to prosecute war against enemies at sea. Even into the eighteenth century, by which time European governments had grown their public navies considerably, their navies remained too small and weak to conduct warfare effectively on the water alone.[4]

Privateering remedied this situation by calling private initiative to the war effort. Although, as I discuss later, privateers were commissioned by their respective governments and operated within the constraints of rules these governments created, interactions between privateers of one nation and the vessels of another were formally ungoverned and thus anarchic. There wasn't in the eighteenth and nineteenth centuries, as there isn't today, a formal supranational agency with the authority to oversee and control interactions between foreign countries, let alone belligerents. Foreign sovereigns and their citizens dealt with one another in an anarchic international arena.

Privateering was a form of maritime plunder. I focus on British and North American privateering, but the system worked similarly elsewhere. The way it did so is straightforward.[5] A group of investors sought a "letter of marque" from their government. This licensed them to send a private warship to sea over a stipulated time to plunder the merchant ships of an enemy nation (see, for instance, Admiralty Court Prize Papers 39, 1691; Admiralty Court Prize Papers 90, 1693; Admiralty Court Miscellanea 862, 1694; Admiralty Court Prize Papers 118, 1742; Admiralty Court Prize Papers 115, 1746; Admiralty Court Letter of Marque Declarations 12, f. 1, 1760).[6] Investors earned a pre-negotiated share of any "prizes" their crew captured. Until the first decade of the eighteenth century, in return for commissioning the privateer, the British government entitled itself to a share of prizes as well. To encourage privateering, it generously left off this practice in 1708.

There were two sorts of privateers: letters of marque and private men-of-war. The former was a merchant ship engaged in trade but also licensed "to annoy the enemy and take their ships, as occasion shall offer" (P.C. Register 76, f. 142, 1695). Letters of marque were primarily traders. Their crewmen earned fixed wages like typical merchant sailors. But they also

---

[4] On the history and development of privateering, see Starkey (1990).

[5] For excellent descriptions of the privateering system in the economics literature, see Anderson and Gifford (1991), Sechrest (2004), and Tabarrok (2007). For descriptions of the privateering system in the historical literature, see, for instance, Crowhurst (1989), Garitee (1977), Petrie (1999), and Swanson (1991).

[6] Unless otherwise noted, all seventeenth- and eighteenth-century documents cited in this essay are from Marsden (1915–1916: vol. 2).

earned shares of any prizes their vessels might plunder while engaged in commercial activity.

Private men-of-war were private warships fitted specifically for the purpose of plundering enemy merchant shipping.[7] Private men-of-war didn't engage in commercial activity. Their crewmen were paid exclusively in shares and only if they plundered successfully. Because private men-of-war engaged only in plunder, they were typically smaller and without the large cargo-carrying capacity of merchant ships. This made them faster and more agile than merchantmen, even though they carried more crewmembers and guns per ship tonnage.

Upon application to the Admiralty for a privateering commission, a privateer's owners signed a performance bond to secure its good conduct. The bond's value depended on the proposed vessel's or crew's size (see, for instance, Admiralty Secretary In Letters 3878, April 12, 1744; Admiralty Secretary In Letters 3878, June 30, 1744; Admiralty Court Letter of Marque Declarations 12, f. 1, 1760).[8] As the instructions for a privateer that James II commissioned after his abdication read, "Before the ship put to sea, security is to be given to our . . . agent or his deputy for the due performance of the above articles" (Hist. MSS Commission, Stuart Papers, i, 92, 1694). If the privateer went about seizing neutral vessels or other ships not permitted under the terms of its commission, or operated outside the area or time frame specified in this commission, it could forfeit its bond.

A privateer could also forfeit its bond if it was later discovered that its crew had misused enemy prisoners. The "law of nations" – the international law of war that European and North American governments respected and enforced on their citizens – protected prisoners.[9] As American privateer owner George Stiles's bond read for the *Nonsuch*, a ship he fitted out during the War of 1812, the bond was to ensure that the "said armed vessel shall observe the treaties and laws of the United States, and the instructions which shall be given to them according to law for the regulation of their conduct."

The instructions referred to here, issued to every privateer when it received its commission, instructed the privateer "to pay the strictest regard to the rights of neutral powers, and the usages of civilized nations. . . . Towards enemy vessels and their crews, you are to proceed, in exercising

---

[7] A bit confusingly, these vessels were also commissioned via a document called a letter of marque.

[8] Sureties were also required for the performance bond.

[9] This chapter considers the international law of war only insofar as it influenced the constraints privateers confronted in plundering merchantmen. For a discussion of this law, its emergence, and its enforcement, see Anderson and Gifford (1995).

the rights of war with all the justice and humanity which characterizes the nation of which you are members" (Garitee 1977: 94, 97–98). As the instructions George II issued to British privateers in 1739 read, "no Person or Persons, taken or Surprized in any Ship or Vessell as aforesaid, tho' known to be of the Enemy's Party, shall be in Cold Blood killed, maimed, or by Torture and Cruelty Inhumanely Treated, contrary to the Common Usage and just Permission of War," under the threat of severe punishment for violating these instructions (Jameson 1923: 349).

When a privateer overtook an enemy merchant ship, it was entitled to take its prize back to port in the commission-issuing country or, in some cases, a port in a friendly foreign nation (see, for instance, Admiralty Court Libels 117, No. 82, 1676; Letter of Marque Declarations I, f. 23, 1689; Hist. MSS. Commission, Stuart Papers, i, 92, 1694; Admiralty Court Prize Papers 118, 1742). In these ports were "prize courts" that determined the seized merchant vessel's status. If the court adjudged the prize legitimate – that is, an enemy-owned vessel – the ship and its cargo were condemned and auctioned, and the proceeds were divided according to the terms established in the privateer's contract between its owners and crew. The prize court received an administrative fee. The government received its share (if any), and import duties on the receipts of the vessel's and cargo's sale were appropriated by the commissioning government, the privateer "duely and truly pay[ing] or caus[ing] to be paid . . . the usual customes due His Majestie for all ships and goods so as aforesaid taken and adjudged for prize" (Admiralty Court Prize Papers 63, 1719).[10]

The most common reason a prize court adjudged a prize illegitimate was that the prize wasn't in fact an enemy-owned merchantman. Rather, it was owned by citizens of a neutral power whose ire the commissioning government was eager not to raise, "it being our royal intention," a letter to the Lords of the Admiralty explained, "that . . . all engagements which subsist between us and our said good friends and allies should be most carefully and religiously observed" (S.P. Dom. Naval 60, April 30, 1744; see also, S.P. Foreign, Foreign Ministers, &c, 22, April 7, 1705; S.P. Dom. Naval 34, f. 265, 1744).[11] Like privateers, commercial vessels in the Age of Sail

---

[10] Such duties could be extremely high, in some cases consuming 30–40 percent of a prize's value (see, for instance, Garitee, 1977: 183; see also Lydon, 1970: 91). However, to further encourage privateering, at various times some colonial governments exempted privateer-obtained booty from onerous customs (Swanson 1991: 15).

[11] This wasn't the only reason a prize may be adjudged "bad," but it was the main one. The British government also prohibited its privateers from "breaking bulk," that is, disposing of plundered cargo before a prize court had adjudged it legitimate (although exceptions for unusual circumstances were permitted). This was another ground on which a prize may be

carried a variety of false flags and papers to prevent enemy privateers or navy warships from seizing them. Thus it wasn't always easy for privateers to discern whether a prospective prize was legitimate or not. If a mistake arising from such difficulty appeared honest to the adjudicating prize court, the vessel and its crew were released and the privateer received nothing. If the mistake was the result of negligence, the privateer's owners could be ordered to pay damages to the offended neutral vessel's owners. In cases of willful illegitimate seizure, or if mistakes became common, the offending privateer could forfeit its bond and lose its commission.

In addition to prohibiting privateers from mistreating merchant sailors they overwhelmed or killing such sailors in cold blood, the law of nations imposed some positive obligations on privateers. Privateers couldn't seize a merchant ship and dump its crewmembers in the water to fend for themselves. To condemn a captured vessel, prize courts required testimony from two or three merchant sailors from the vessels a privateer seized – typically the captain and a few officers.

Privateers had two choices for other members of a quarry's crew: they could release the sailors if a vessel was available to send them home in, or they could take the sailors with them, requiring the privateers to provide for the sailors until they could be sent home via a prisoner cartel arranged in port or at sea. Under the rights the law of nations afforded prisoners, privateers were "bound for fair and safe custody [of captives], and . . . liable for any loss occasioned by their neglect or want of proper care. . . . In cases of gross misconduct on the part of private captors, the [captors' government's] court will decree a revocation of their commission" (Upton 1863: 393).

Prisoner cartels were belligerent nations' means of exchanging prisoners in wartime. To ease the burden of providing for captured enemies and to get one's own prisoners back, warring nations traded prisoners – man for man of equal rank – throughout (and sometimes following) conflict. Thus if Britain sent fifteen French merchant sailors who British privateers had recently captured and returned to port with for adjudication to France, France would send fifteen British merchant sailors of the same status to England.[12]

adjudged illegitimate. According to a letter of marque issued to an East Indiaman in 1694 for plundering French merchant shipping, for example, "you are to keep in safety all such ships, vessels, and goods, which shall be taken in your voyages outward or homeward, and not break bulk, sell, wast, spoil, or diminish the same before judgment be first given in our Admiralty court in England or the East Indies respectively" (Admiralty Court Miscellanea 862, 1694; see also, Admiralty Court Prize Sentences 21, No. 140, 1697).

[12] Alternatively a privateer could place its prisoners on a ship and send them home after having them sign a declaration certifying their capture and release, which the privateer's

The law of nations, which governed such arrangements, amounted to promises between sovereigns about prisoner treatment and related matters described earlier. But European governments enforced this law on their own citizens, threatened by the discipline of continuous dealings. So it was generally upheld. A privateer that misused prisoners taken into custody by starving them, or dispatching them outside one of the accepted methods described previously, jeopardized its prize, which the prize courts might release, as well as its bond, which the courts might seize.[13]

Indeed prize courts sometimes ruled against privateers in the case at hand based on their past mistreatment of prisoners when this was discovered. The British privateer *Minerva* captured the *Anna* at the mouth of the Mississippi River in 1805. The justice presiding in this prize case, Sir W. Scott, discovered that before capturing the *Anna*, the *Minerva* captured a Spanish vessel named the *Bilbao*. The privateersmen of *Minerva* set the *Bilbao*'s prisoners ashore on an uninhabited island near the mouth of the Mississippi. Justice Scott considered this "an act highly unjustifiable in its own nature." Because of it, he refused to condemn the *Anna* (Roscoe 1905: 399).

PRIVATEER-MERCHANTMAN COASEAN BARGAINING

Ransom and Parole

The potential social losses of privateer-committed maritime plunder are familiar: resources privateers devoted to transferring foreign merchant ship owners' wealth to themselves, resources merchantmen devoted to attempting to prevent privateer capture, and resources destroyed in violent conflict with merchantmen in privateers' efforts to appropriate their vessels and cargo. However, provided their interactions satisfied the conditions

---

government could then present to its enemy along with a request for the release of an equivalent number of its citizens held prisoner. For an example of this, see Fanning (1912: 187). For an example of an impromptu arrangement for prisoner exchange between a French privateer and its British prize, see Admiralty Secretary in Letters (3382, April 12, 1747).

[13] Besides the fact that governments punished their citizens who violated rules about prisoner treatment, privateers were also encouraged to comply with these rules through the use of bounties in certain cases. Governments sometimes offered "head money" for each sailor on an enemy merchant ship (or navy vessel) that a privateer overwhelmed. Returning home with prisoners was the most convincing (albeit not the only) way to evidence what head money was due and thus to collect bounties owed. In addition to this, recall that prize courts relied on the two or three merchant sailors taken captive by a privateer to testify at its prize hearing. If privateers hoped for favorable testimony, it behooved them not to mistreat these prisoners.

discussed earlier in this essay, my theory predicts that privateers and merch-antmen would enter Coasean contracts, facilitating more efficient plunder.

As that theory suggests, central to this possibility was the costliness of producing plunder for privateers. Privateers' cost of producing plunder had several sources. The first was violent conflict with a merchantman. This cost of producing plunder resulted from privateers' failure to use Coasean bar-gains to induce potential victims to forego making defensive investments – a failure that in turn resulted from a failure to satisfy one of the three con-ditions required for such bargains to come into existence, identified earlier: sufficiently low transaction costs.

In principle privateers could have struck agreements with merchantmen not to arm or undertake other defensive measures in consideration for receiving a larger fraction of the goods privateers would otherwise seize from them if they overwhelmed them. Both parties had an incentive to create such an agreement. If, say, a merchantman could save $150 worth of goods from being plundered by making a defensive investment that cost it $100, both parties could benefit by forging an agreement in which the merchantman agreed to not spend anything on defensive investments in exchange for the privateer agreeing to seize $60 worth of goods less when it plundered the merchantman.

Such bargains proved impossible in practice, however, because privateers' strengths varied. The price a privateer would be willing to pay to a merchant-man in the form of more returned goods following plunder depended on its strength. Stronger privateers would have a lower maximum willingness to pay to induce victims to forgo defensive investments. Weaker privateers would have higher ones.

Because a Coasean bargain inducing victims to forgo such investments would have be to forged ex ante – that is, before merchantmen took to the water – this would have required each merchantman to strike a separate agreement with each privateer. Given the many privateers that might attack them, such agreements were prohibitively costly. Alternatively, if every pri-vateer could agree with every other privateer to take to the water with the same vessel, number of guns, men, and so on, such that all would have the same strength, merchantmen would only have to conclude one contract with all privateers. But in this case prohibitive transaction costs would have entered through another door: that of each individual privateer contracting with all others.

Because of the prohibitive transaction costs of doing so, privateers and merchantmen were unable to create Coasean bargains that could preclude the latter's defensive investments, leaving this source of plunder's social cost unmitigated. Merchantmen invested in defensive measures capable of preventing some privateer plunder.

Those measures took several forms. First, merchantmen invested in guns for their ships. As I discuss later, the average merchantman in the mid-eighteenth century of some 240 tons carried 28 guns (Swanson 1991: 61, 71). Similarly, they could employ vessel shapes/sizes that made them faster for battle maneuvering. Second, merchantmen sometimes sailed along outlying or less desirable routes where privateers were less prevalent or didn't sail.[14] Third, merchantmen sailed together in convoys instead of individually, which made them harder for privateers to attack (see, for instance, Martens and Horne 1801). Closely related, to reduce the threat privateers posed, merchantmen resorted to "direct voyages," which ran to a single port and back, instead of engaging in more lucrative "multilateral voyages," which involved visits to several ports before returning home (see, for instance, Morgan 1989).

These defensive investments were costly to merchantmen and society. They hindered merchantmen's capacity to serve as merchant ships, reducing their profits, and in doing so retarded merchant shipping's ability to produce wealth. Canon took up room that cargo would otherwise occupy. Their added weight slowed the carrying vessel down. A sharper-built vessel could reduce the merchantman's cargo capacity and undermine its stability for long cargo-carrying expeditions.

Similarly, an outlying route was a longer one or undesirable for other reasons, such as being harder to sail. Using it cost a merchantman precious time and could increase the odds of a wreck, delay, or damage resulting from less favorable waters and weather. Convoys were also costly. They required multiple merchantmen to coordinate their sailing dates, routes, and stops, creating a "package" whose elements differed from those that convoy members would choose individually if they were unconstrained by the need to sail in consort with others. These defensive investments not only reduced wealth by diverting resources that could otherwise be used for productive purposes to the prevention of plunder. They reduced wealth by raising the cost of merchant shipping, which reduced the number of merchant ships engaged in trade.

A fourth "defensive investment" of sorts to which merchantmen resorted might also be added to those just mentioned: insurance. Insurance didn't prevent or deter privateer attacks, but it partly reflected merchantmen's

---

[14] Still another social cost of privateering plunder manifested in the form of defensive investments by merchantmen was the cost of training merchant sailors to be adept at seaborne conflict.

attempts to mitigate the losses of privateer plunder.[15] And higher insurance premiums because of privateer threats contributed to merchant shipping's cost and thus the associated reduction in wealth-creating merchant shipping activity that higher shipping costs engendered.

Because transaction costs prevented Coasean bargains that would have ensured merchantmen disarmament, most merchantmen were armed. If a merchantman resisted a privateer's advances, running or engaging its attacker, a bloody melee was likely to ensue. This contributed to plunder's cost for privateers. Although privateers were typically much stronger than the merchant vessels they attacked, even a significantly weaker merchantman was capable of putting up a fight. A merchantman couldn't only damage the privateering vessel. It could injure or kill its crewmembers. Captain Harriot's St. Kitts-based privateer discovered this when it engaged a French merchantman near the Calicos Islands in 1744. The merchantman fought back, killing eighteen of Harriot's privateer crew and injuring many more (Swanson 1991: 198). Even if a merchantman wasn't strong enough to significantly damage its attacker, if the two came to blows, damage to the merchantman and its cargo hindered the privateer's ability to bring its prize safely to port and reduced what the prize could fetch at auction. In extreme cases the entire prize might be lost, leaving the privateer with nothing to show for its efforts.

Privateers confronted two other costs of producing plunder: the cost of bringing the victim to a prize court to adjudge its legitimacy and the cost of carrying and providing for captured merchant sailors. Privateers could and did seize prizes considerable distances from the nearest prize court. Even when they didn't, the nearest prize court located at the port where their plundered goods had the greatest market could be far. A privateer that had to return to shore after taking each prize lost considerable time in transit that could be spent plundering instead. More important, traveling any distance back to port was a risky endeavor. At some point every privateer needed to return home. But the more trips a privateer made between port and its cruising ground, the greater were the risks it would never make it back.

The high risk of additional back-and-forth trips had several sources. One was the unavoidable chance of seaborne travel, such as the prospect of shipwreck or a related nature-driven tragedy. But the most significant risk of such trips was manmade: the possibility of destruction or capture by the enemy. This danger was especially high when to return with a merchantman to the nearest prize court a privateer had to break through an enemy blockade

---

[15] On the contrary, insurance could actually encourage privateer attacks because it made merchantmen more likely to acquiesce in the face of a privateer attack.

(see, for instance, Crowhurst 1989: 36). If it negotiated the blockade unsuccessfully, the privateer stood to lose not only its prize to the enemy but its freedom as well.

If a privateer had enough crewmembers, it could place some of its men on the prize to create a "prize crew" to return to port for consideration by a prize court, allowing the privateer to remain at sea. However, some privateers were too small to do this. "Many of the [French] corsairs . . . in the eastern half of the English Channel" in the late eighteenth and early nineteenth centuries, for example, "carried a handful of men which was barely adequate to sail the ship and provide prize crews" (Crowhurst 1989: 53).

Even for larger privateers that had enough men to form prize crews, delivering victims to prize courts remained costly. Putting enough men on a captured quarry to create a prize crew weakened the privateer, reducing its ability to take future prizes and defend itself against attack. The British privateer *Sheerness* had to let five potential French prizes escape because its crew remained too small for the task, most of its members having departed previously on prize crews (Swanson 1991: 63). Further, prize crews, like the privateers that created them, faced the threat of capture en route to port. In the War of 1812 less than one-third of American prize crews made it to port (Garitee 1977: 170). Many of these lost their freedom to British privateers and navy ships on their way to prize courts.

The third important cost of producing plunder for privateers was carrying and providing for the merchant crews they overtook. The law of nations required privateers to care for their captives until they were brought to port or could be exchanged via a prisoner cartel. Provisions used to support prisoners reduced those available to privateer crewmembers, shortening the duration of plundering cruises because reprovisioning became necessary more often.[16]

Taking on prisoners posed another problem: the prisoners might revolt. This prospect was most significant on a prize crew. During the American Revolutionary War, the American privateer *Yankee* captured two British merchantmen and put prize crews aboard both. The *Yankee*'s crew must have been severely disappointed when British prisoners overwhelmed both prize crews and managed to seize control of the *Yankee*, making the American privateersmen the captives (Coggins 2002: 68).

To avoid these costs of plunder, which not only constituted social costs but also private costs for privateers, many privateers resorted to plunder

[16] The merchantman's provisions could be seized to help address this problem. But any provisions that had to be used to support captured merchant sailors were provisions the privateer couldn't enjoy the revenues of from being sold at auction at a prize court.

contracts with merchantmen they overwhelmed. As I describe later, unlike Coasean contracts that could have induced victims to forego defensive investments to prevent plunder, Coasean contracts that could induce victims to surrender their goods peacefully once attacked, which permitted privateers to avoid the costs of plundering described earlier, could in some cases satisfy the conditions required for such bargains to come into existence, and thus were possible. In these cases privateers and merchantmen forged them. The resulting contracts formed the basis for the system of "ransom and parole."

After overwhelming a merchantman, such a privateer offered its victims the following bargain: for a price it would allow the merchant vessel, its cargo, and its crewmembers their freedom. If the price was right, this arrangement was mutually beneficial. Provided the price agreed on in the plunder contract was higher than what the privateer expected to earn if it plundered its victim traditionally and thus had to incur the costs discussed earlier, it was happy to enter such a contract.

Consider French privateer captain Nathaniel Fanning's reasoning, whose crew aboard the *Comte de Guichen* "ransomed ... two [British merchant] ships ... for three thousand two hundred guineas; and the brig and cargo for five hundred." Although "these two sums were not more than half the value of these vessels," Fanning noted, "we thought it more prudent to ransom them for this sum than to run the risque of sending them to France" (Fanning 1912: 139). Or consider the reasoning of privateer captain William Ashion who sought to avoid the cost of creating a prize crew when he entered a plunder contract with the *Wife of Sable d'Ollone*: "the Master thereof proposing to Ransom ... considering the number of men they had on board, and that he could not send her for this Island, without coming allong with her, which should have been a great hindrance to him," Ashion was pleased to negotiate a plunder agreement with his victim instead (Bromley 1987: 344).

Provided the price agreed on in the plunder contract was lower than what the merchantman expected to lose if the privateer plundered it traditionally – lower than the value of the ship, its cargo, and the value the merchantman's crewmembers attached to their freedom – it was also happy to enter such a contract. As Fanning describes in his case, the merchantmen got an excellent deal, paying only half the value they would have lost without the plunder agreement. Such an arrangement benefited both parties by preventing the destruction of valuable vessels, cargo, and men. The possibility of such an offer lowered merchantmen's cost of being plundered, encouraging them to submit to stronger privateer attackers. This permitted the plunder process to proceed peaceably rather than through violence, avoiding the deadweight losses of violent conflict.

If a mutually agreeable ransom price could be arrived at, the merchantman and privateer drew up a written contract in duplicate called a "ransom bill," stating the agreement's terms. Under these terms the merchant ship captain obligated his ship's owner – and failing that, himself – to pay the privateer upon presentation of the bill. In return the agreement entitled the merchantman to safe passageway, or "parole," without plunder by other privateers from the ransoming privateer's nation or allies, to a specified port within a proscribed period of time and in some cases via a proscribed route. If the merchantman were approached by another privateer from that nation or one of its allies en route, it needed only to produce the ransom bill and the privateer would customarily allow the ship to continue on its way.

Consider the ransom bill contracted between a British privateer, the *Ambuscade*, and its French merchant ship victim, *Le Saint Nicolas*, circa 1711 (Admiralty Court Prize Papers 91, 1711):

Whereas on the seventh day of October, old style, 1711, the ship called St Nichola of Sable d'Olone, near Rochelle, whereof Jacque Ayreau is commander, together with her cargo as follows, viz. nine thousand Bank fish, and forty hogsheads of salt, and four hogsheads of oyl, or thereabouts, was taken prize by the Ambuscade of Bristol, a private man of war, Robert Summers commander, by virtue of a commission bearing date in London the twenty ninth day of March 1711. And whereas the said Robert Summers is willing, at the instance and request of the said Jacque Ayreau, together with the said ship and cargo, to proceed on his intended voyage to Nants, or any first port in France, upon condition that the aforesaid Jacque Ayreau shall pay or cause to be paid unto the said Robert Summers, or his executors, administrators, or assigns, the full sum of eleven thousand five hundred livres tournis, French money, which makes nine hundred and fivety sterling money of England, at twelve livres the pound, to be paid in London for the Ransom of the above ship and cargo.... And I Jacques Ayreau to hereby bind myself, my heirs, executors, and assigns, for the true payment of the said sum as above... as before agreed on, unto the said Robert Summers, his heirs, executors, or assigns. In Witness whereof we have set our hands and seals this seventh day of October 1711, old stile.

[signed] Joachim Bruneteau.

[signed] Andre Caillaud.

Signed, sealed, and delivered in the presence of us,
Testes, Richard Pym, Fran. Gandouet.

Memorandum. I, Jaque Ayreau, do acknowledge and confess that no Barbarous or Uncivil Treatment has been used to me of any of my Men, nor no Imbezlement nor Pilferage have been actually done to my ship or cargo by the said Robert Summers, his officers or Company, since the aforesaid Agreement; And that it is agreed between me and the said Robert Summers that I shall be allowed seventy Days to accomplish my Voyage afterward, and no more; And that I do well and truly understand the Bargain and Agreement as aforesaid.

Je recognois avoir ransomme ledit navire Le Saint Nicolas pour la somme de vinze mil cinq livres tournois argent et monnois de France.

[signed] Jacques Ayreau.

As my theory highlights, this kind of Coasean plunder contract is most likely when the means of plunderous production are relatively nonspecific and thus the gains of negotiating such an agreement are largest. Privateering was close to the ideal in this respect because privateers' plunderous capital was highly nonspecific. Most privateers were simply modified merchant vessels. As Rajan and Zingales (1998) point out, asset owners have incentives to develop their assets in ways that retain their value in alternative uses – to avoid making specific investments. This is as true for plunderers, such as privateer owners, as it is for anyone else. Privateer owners benefited by investing in vessels that were useful in non-plunder-related production, such as commercial voyages, in addition to being useful for producing plunder. Privateer owners accomplished this by modifying existing merchantmen to build their ships or, when seeking purpose-constructed private men-of-war, by building privateers generically enough to be useable in merchant shipping when not plundering.

Recall the two types of privateers: merchantmen with a commission to plunder (letters of marque), which differed from ordinary merchantmen only by virtue of their raiding license and the fact that they might carry a few extra guns; and private men-of-war, which were often smaller and had less cargo-carrying capacity than typical merchantmen. Nearly all other basic elements of private men-of-war were the same as typical merchantmen. Thus they could be easily converted to regular merchantmen when not employed for plunderous purposes. Indeed, "the majority" of private men-of-war were merely "merchantmen converted for the task" (Starkey 2001: 72; see also, Swanson 1991: 57, 120).

Converting private men-of-war back to merchantmen when war ended was equally straightforward. More than 90 percent of the privateers that went to sea from America's chief privateering port in Baltimore in the War of 1812 were schooners – vessels identical to the brigs preferred in merchant shipping save their rigging.[17] Similarly, 50 percent of Massachusetts' early-nineteenth-century privateering fleet consisted of schooners. Sixty-six percent of New York's privateering fleet did as well (Garitee 1977: 166, 114). If they weren't already fit for a particular merchant shipping need, by simply modifying their sail setups, many "sharp-built" schooners could easily be made so. And, when war ended, this is precisely what many privateer owners, or individuals who purchased ex-privateers, did (Garitee 1977: 220).[18]

The switch was still cheaper for privateers that were letters of marque. These could be "converted" to regular merchantmen simply by taking one or two guns off them.[19] Indeed, even this "conversion" wasn't required: letters of marque *were* merchant ships. For them, costs saved through plunder contracts over producing plunder traditionally, such as the travel time involved in going back and forth to prize courts with prizes, translated directly into socially productive activity – more time spent commercial shipping – even before war ended.

Letters of marque were numerous – more numerous in many cases than private men-of-war. For instance, 7,100 of the 9,151 British vessels that sought privateer commissions between 1739 and 1815, or nearly 78 percent, were letters of marque (Starkey 1997: 130). Similarly, in the War of 1812, 114 of Baltimore's 175 privateers, or more than 65 percent, were letters of marque (Garitee 1977: 166). These vessels' capital was equally well suited for productive (commerce) and nonproductive (plundering) purposes, permitting them to quickly and inexpensively "transform" their capital's application to commerce and plunder as they found convenient.[20]

---

[17] While schooners were fore-and-aft rigged, brigs were square rigged.

[18] Anderson and Gifford (1991: 114) note that following war's end smaller privateers were often sold as merchantmen, similarly suggesting privateers' low-cost convertibility.

[19] Besides adding a few guns, the only other notable way in which a merchantman was modified to make her fit for a letter of marque was perhaps some reinforcement of the bulwarks and additional siding to make her sturdier.

[20] Contrast this situation with the situation navy warships confronted. Although these vessels were primarily concerned with handling enemy navy warships rather than enemy commercial vessels, they, too, could and occasionally did assault merchant ships. However, unlike privateers, which were often no more than slightly modified merchant ships, the plunderous capital embodied in navy ships was highly specific. These ships were designed exclusively for warfare and had no commercial use. They were massive, built to engage in and withstand heavy fire, and carried an extraordinary number of guns. Naval vessels' gains from entering Coasean exchanges with their victims were therefore smaller than that of privateers, leading them to enter them less often and engage in traditional plunder more often instead.

Conditions for Privateer-Merchantman Plunder Contracts and Their Breakdown

Earlier I highlighted several conditions that must be satisfied to make Coasean plunder contracts possible. Transaction costs must be sufficiently low, information about the plunderer's and victim's strength must be symmetric, and plunderer-victim bargains must be enforceable. Many – but, as I discuss later, not all – privateer-merchantman relations satisfied these conditions for bargains that reduced the cost of producing plunder and reduced the deadweight loss of destruction in connection with privateer-merchantman conflicts. This permitted some privateers and merchantmen to forge Coasean agreements like the one recounted in the previous section, facilitating more efficient plunder.

Two types of potential transaction costs threatened to render such privateer-merchantman contracts unprofitable by overshadowing the gains of these agreements. Both had their source in potential bargaining difficulties. The first was the simple fact that because privateers and their victims were necessarily from different countries, they spoke different languages. This meant they didn't always know the language of the other, or didn't know it well enough to negotiate contracts. If privateers and merchantmen couldn't communicate because of language barriers, they couldn't forge Coasean plunder contracts.

Privateers developed a simple solution to this problem: they created template plunder contracts in multiple languages. During the War of the Spanish Succession (1701–1714), when France was at war with Britain, Portugal, Holland, and several other countries, French privateers carried multiple, generic plunder agreements – one in French and the others translations of the French template into the their enemies' languages so their foreign victims could read them (Senior 1918: 52).

The second type of transaction cost that threatened to overwhelm the prospective gains from privateer-merchantman plunder contracts was the time required to negotiate such agreements. A privateer and its victim merchantman confronted a classic bilateral monopoly problem in which, because of the unusual monopolistic and monopsonistic nature of the market, the process of converging on a mutually agreeable price can be long and tedious. Fortunately, although the "plunder market" in which a privateer and its victim merchantman operated consisted of only a one seller and one buyer, the vessel and cargo the merchantman had that the privateer sought were bought and sold in competitive markets with many sellers and many buyers.

Because the privateer and merchantman both had an idea about the prevailing market prices for these goods, the maximum price the privateer could reasonably expect the merchantman to pay in lieu of these goods and the minimum price the merchantman could reasonably expect the privateer to accept in lieu of these goods were brought close together. Remaining haggling to influence the distribution of the surplus the agreement created was thus delimited and reflected unknowns, such as the value the different parties attached to the merchant crewmen's freedom, the odds the privateer or its prize crew would be seized en route back to the nearest prize court, and so on. Thus privateers' and merchantmen's bargaining ranges were narrowed significantly, lowering the transaction cost of negotiating Coasean plunder agreements.

The second condition privateers and merchantmen had to satisfy to enable Coasean agreements between them was symmetric information about their strengths. The most important difference between merchantmen and privateers was the larger number of crewmembers and guns (per ton) the latter carried. Between 1739 and 1748 the average privateer that plied the sea was 166 tons, carried 35 guns, and had 100 crewmembers. The average privateer victim in this same period was 45 percent bigger (241 tons), but carried 7 fewer guns and had only 11 more crewmembers (Swanson 1991: 61, 71). Thus a privateer that attacked a merchantman of equivalent size boasted significantly greater firepower and manpower. This gave privateers the upper hand in both ship-to-ship and hand-to-hand combat.

Besides knowing that the average privateer of equal size was stronger, merchantmen knew that privateers aimed to attack significantly weaker ships because doing so made their job easier. Conditional on being assaulted by a privateer, then, a merchantman also knew it was probably the weaker party and likely to lose a fight if it resisted. As privateer historian Jerome Garitee (1977: 148) put it, "The captain of a [privateer-attacked] merchant vessel [typically] knew he was confronting a heavily manned, better-armed, and swifter opponent." Thus many merchantmen found it in their interest to submit peacefully to their plunderers, particularly when they expected Coasean bargaining opportunities that could improve their post-plunder positions. Because "[m]ost merchant ships were outsailed, outmanned and outgunned by almost any privateer . . . the crew meekly surrendered when escape was impossible" (Crowhurst 1977: 36; see also, Crowhurst 1997: 156–157). Consequently, "[t]he great majority of captures were made without resistance" (Bromley 1987: 356).

Finally, recall that for Coasean plunder contracts to be possible, both privateers and merchantmen required reason to believe the other party would fulfill their end of the agreement. Privateers and merchantmen achieved this through several means. From merchantmen's perspective the central problem was ensuring that other privateers from their captor's nation wouldn't plunder them a second time while en route to their specified destination as the terms of their contract promised to protect them from. Reciprocity between privateers from the same or allied nations – a successful application of the discipline of continuous dealings – was one means of ensuring this.

Equally important was privateers' governments' unwillingness to adjudge a "doubly seized" merchantman a good prize. For much of the eighteenth century, European governments recognized privateer-merchantman plunder contracts as legally binding on the privateer that issued them and protected the privateer's right as first captor to sell parole, prohibiting subsequent captors from his nation or his nation's allies from seizing the merchantman again. The U.S. government continued to recognize such contracts' legitimacy into the nineteenth century. Governments' refusal to award doubly seized merchantmen as prizes to their captors dramatically reduced privateers' incentive to violate the terms of plunder contracts their compatriots negotiated with enemy merchantmen with whom they subsequently caught up. Because of this, merchantmen were confident the terms of their Coasean bargains with privateers would be respected.

The more significant potential enforcement difficulty was from privateers' perspective. After granting a merchantman its freedom, how could a privateer ensure it would be paid? Three mechanisms were critical to ensuring contractual compliance. First, privateers often required a hostage from their victim – typically the captain of the ship or one of his officers – who they would take with them and release only after being paid. Privateers and merchantmen negotiated the terms of such hostages, and even how they would be cared for, in their plunder contracts. Consider the hostage terms of the ransom bill entered into between the French merchantman and British privateer recounted earlier (Admiralty Court Prize Papers 91, 1711; see also, Fanning 1912: 126, 139):

And it is agreed by and between the said Roberts Summers and the said Jacque Ayreau that he the said Jacque Ayreau shall leave some Hostages or Ransomers in the possession of the said Robert Summers . . . for and till the true payment of the abovesaid sum so agreed upon for the Ransom of the said ship and cargo, and shall also bind himself, his heirs, executors, administrators, and assigns, for the true payment thereof, and the Redemption of the Hostages, with the allowance of three shillings and four pence per day for the victualling of the said Hostages from the date hereof until the time of their arrival in England and being released &c, to be likewise well and truly paid . . . with all other charges that may occur until the time of the Hostages being released. Now these Presents witness that we Jonachim

Bruneteau and Andre Caillaud, at the instance and request of the said Jacque Ayreau are willing and voluntarily oblige ourselves to become Hostages and Ransomers for the said ship and cargo, and to remain so until the abovesaid sum . . . agreed upon, with the allowance aforesaid, by fully paid and satisfyd.

The second means privateers used to enforce the terms of their plunder contracts with victim merchantmen was state courts. For much of the eighteenth and nineteenth centuries, governments recognized plunder contracts as legally binding. Britain forbade alien enemies, such as foreign privateer owners, from directly initiating legal action against their citizens in their courts. A privateer owner couldn't sue a British merchantman that violated its plunder contract with the aid of Britain's courts.[21] However, British law recognized a merchant captain's right to enter a plunder contract that obligated his ship's owners to a privateer: "He is the agent of these owners, lawfully authorized to enter into such contracts. . . . His signature therefore binds them as debtors of the ransom" (Wheaton 1815: 236).

When a merchant ship captain signed a ransom bill, he also obligated himself to pay his captor the agreed-on sum if his ship's owners failed to. Crucially, the law granted him a right of action *in rem* against the owners' vessel in this case to recover the ransom sum he paid the privateer to gain his freedom in lieu of the owners or, more likely, given that most hostages didn't have the funds required to pay this sum, to recover his freedom by compelling the owners to pay the privateer. Because of this, privateers were able to initiate action against nonpaying merchantmen indirectly through their hostages whose incentive was aligned with privateers'.

For example, in 1696 British merchant ship captain John Munden of the *Reyner* entered a plunder contract with French privateer captain Louis Daincon of the *Phillipicene*. According to their contract, Munden promised to "pay, or cause to be paid, to Daincon the sum of £170 sterling, and give himself up as a prisoner for the payment of that sum." However, the *Reyner's* owners "never paid the bill." Munden sued the *Reyner* from his St. Malo prison, as the law entitled him to, and succeeded. The *Reyner's* owners were compelled to uphold their end of the plunder contract. The *Phillipicene* received the payment it was due, and Munden recovered his freedom (Admiralty Court Libels 126, No. 107, 1698; see also, Admiralty Court Libels 130, No. 237, 1713).[22] In this way a privateer could rely on its hostage's incentive

---

[21] Although, for a discussion of an exception, see Senior (1918: 54).

[22] If the hostage wasn't the ship captain, the captain might be tempted to ransom the ship fraudulently to secure its release – that is, to enter a plunder contract for a price that exceeded the ship's and its cargo's value without intending to honor the agreement.

to use the law to compel nonpaying merchant ship owners to comply with the terms of their plunder contracts, ensuring contractual enforcement.

The third method privateers used to enforce plunder contracts with victim merchantmen was repossession. Privateers chiefly resorted to repossession after Britain and France banned their citizens from partaking in plunder contracts, which I discuss later. The way repossession worked was simple. If a known, nonpaying merchantman was spotted in a foreign port, its privateering creditors, or someone on their behalf, would seize it (Petrie 1999: 23). Although after 1782 Britain and France no longer viewed plunder contracts entered into by their merchantmen as legally binding, the rest of Europe's governments and those of North America did. These governments permitted repossession enforcement in their ports. As an early-nineteenth-century legal digest describing the law of maritime capture and prizes stated, although "no [plunder] contract can be enforced against a British subject in the courts of his own country[,] . . . There is no such prohibition by the municipal laws of other states, and the contract may therefore be enforced in them" (Wheaton 1815: 232). Repossession was the chief means of doing so.

Many privateer-merchantman interactions satisfied the conditions required for Coasean plunder agreements that reduced the cost of producing plunder and the deadweight loss of destruction, thus enabling more efficient plunder. According to historian of privateering Carl Swanson (1991: 204), while "[i]t is difficult to determine how often prizes were ransomed," before Britain and France outlawed plunder contracts they were common. Indeed, this is why the British and French governments had to resort to legislation to curb the practice in the first place.

Eager to realize the benefits of entering plunder contracts, some merchant ship owners encouraged their captains to seek ransom if privateers seized them. Before merchantman owner John Reynell sent his ship the *Bolton* to Antigua, he instructed its captain that, "In case of being taken," the captain should "Endeavour to ransom if thou cans't for Twelve Hundred Pounds Sterling (if Sugar Loaden, may'st advance as much more as thou thinks Reasonable) and draw for the same on Birkett and Booth of Antigua, on Elias Bland of London, or on us here and the Bills shall be honourably paid and the Hostage fully Satisfied for his time, Expences, etc." Similarly, Gerard

---

However, this was prevented by two factors. First, as I discussed previously, privateers had an idea of the market value of ships and their cargoes, limiting merchant captains' ability to get away with such fraud. Second, the hostage had a right of action against his captain for fraud if his captain did this (see, for instance, Marsden 1915–1916: vol. 2, 398).

Beekman, owner of the *Dolphin*, advised his ship's captain: "As you[r] Vessell is Loaded only with Lumber and is very old Can be of Lettle worth to an Enimy. in Case you Should be taken Which God forbid you may Give them fifty Pounds Sterling as a ransom for her again for She will not be worth that to them" (Swanson 1991: 204).

Although little systematic data exist to measure precisely the popularity of Coasean plunder contracts in eighteenth- and nineteenth-century privateering, what data are available suggest that while such contracts weren't the rule, neither were they exceptional. Between 1776 and 1783, when the American Revolutionary War was waged, foreign privateers captured 3,386 British merchantmen. Of these, privateers ransomed 507, approximately 15 percent. In three of these years no ransoms were recorded. When these years are excluded, the percentage of British merchantmen that entered plunder contracts with their captors rises to nearly 19 percent. To put this in perspective, the Royal Navy succeeded in retaking only 495 British merchantmen seized by privateers (Wright and Fayle 1928: 156). Thus plunder contracts "saved" more British merchantmen than the government's official navy. According to Senior (1918: 57), in the same war French privateers ransomed more British merchantmen than they returned to prize courts with.

Other data on the frequency of plunder contracts suggest they were still more common. Between 1688 and 1697, during the War of the Grand Alliance, French privateers leaving from St. Malo, one of France's major privateering ports, ransomed more than 30 percent of all merchantmen they captured. Between 1702 and 1712, during the War of the Spanish Succession, these privateers ransomed nearly 24 percent of all prizes they captured (Crowhurst 1977: 18–19). In these same years Dunkirk and Calais privateers ransomed more British and Dutch merchantmen than they took to prize court, nearly 56 percent of those they seized. All told, during the War of the Spanish Succession, French privateers entered plunder contracts with 2,118 merchantmen, almost 30 percent of the total number they captured (Bromley 1987: 67, 223).

Although plunder contracts were a common feature of eighteenth- and nineteenth-century maritime marauding, they were less common than traditional plunder was. Many privateers chose to plunder their victims in the usual way instead of through Coasean bargains. These privateer-merchantman interactions failed to satisfy the previously discussed conditions required for plunder contracts to be formed. Privateers and merchantmen misjudged each other's strength, plunder contracts proved unenforceable, the transaction costs of bargaining proved prohibitively high, and privateers' cost of producing plunder traditionally was sometimes low, shrinking the benefit of plunder contracts.

Coasean agreements weren't possible in these cases, so privateers plundered without them. Because of this, conflict between privateers and merchantmen that destroyed valuable resources occurred, privateers expended resources dragging every captured merchantman back to shore for prize court adjudication, and merchantmen lost their vessels, cargoes, and crewmembers' freedom. Plunder's social losses in such cases stood where conventional wisdom suggests they always are: at their maximum.

In some cases merchantmen fought their privateering aggressors because they misjudged their strength. Although in many cases a merchantman could conclude by virtue of coming under attack that it was weaker and likely to lose in a violent contest, privateers could miscalculate their own strength leading them to mistakenly assault stronger vessels. The average privateer was much stronger than the average merchantman. But owing to the variation in privateer strengths noted earlier, that didn't preclude some privateers from being weaker than some merchantmen. If the former erred in which ship they attacked, a fight was likely to result.

In February 1815 Captain Boyle's American privateer, the *Chasseur*, spotted an innocent-looking schooner with only three gun ports and made for her. Imagine the *Chasseur*'s surprise when, upon closing on her, the schooner revealed seven hidden gun ports. The formidable ten-gun quarry proved to be His Majesty's *St. Lawrence*. The *Chasseur* prevailed that day but was prizeless for her efforts. The *St. Lawrence* was "a perfect wreck in her hull and had scarcely a Sail or Rope Standing" (Garitee 1977: 161). The *Chasseur*, too, sustained damage to her rigging and sails from the battle beside losing five men and having seven injured.

Merchantmen were capable of making their own mistakes, wrongly believing they were stronger than their assaulter, in which case they may hazard a conflict rather than negotiating a Coasean agreement, again preventing more efficient plunder.[23] In January 1813 Captain Stafford's American privateer, the *Dolphin*, engaged two merchantmen off the coast of St. Vincent. The merchantmen didn't yield to the *Dolphin*'s advances, believing their joint strength was enough to overwhelm the *Dolphin*. They were wrong. Although the merchantmen's joint forces were in fact superior to the privateer's, the *Dolphin* proved more effective with 10 guns and 60 men than the

---

[23] On the ways in which pirates sought to overcome the informational asymmetry regarding their strength and identity vis-à-vis merchantmen in the eighteenth century, see Leeson (2010b).

merchantmen did with more than twice as many guns and five more men (Coggeshall 1856: 128). Unfortunately the merchantmen didn't realize their mistaken judgment until after the bloody battle that led to their capture.

In other cases Coasean plunder agreements weren't created because they couldn't be enforced. In 1782 the British government legally barred its merchantmen from entering plunder contracts with privateers. In 1793 it prohibited British privateers from entering plunder contracts with their merchantman victims. Similarly, in 1756 France began restricting its citizens' use of plunder contracts. First the government forbade French privateers from ransoming merchantmen until they had brought at least three prizes to port. Then in 1782 the French government prohibited its citizens from entering plunder contracts as plunderers or victims. After these years neither the British nor French government could be relied on to help enforce plunder contracts against their citizens.

Because they benefited from them, some British and French merchantmen continued to enter plunder contracts with privateers despite their governments' ban. British merchantmen continued to offer ransom bills to American privateers throughout the War of 1812, a full thirty years after parliament criminalized such contracts (see, for instance, Garitee 1977: 272; Petrie 1999: 22–23). And American privateers continued to accept them, relying on the threat of repossession for enforcement.

Privateers remained "justified in their expectations of payment" from British and French victims even after their governments criminalized plunder contracts "because the vessels were merchant ships." As noted earlier, "A merchant ship owner who didn't pay his obligations simply couldn't trade in foreign ports in the future or his vessel would be seized there by his creditors" (Petrie 1999: 23). Because of this, Britain's and France's plunder contract prohibitions had a muted effect on foreign privateers' ability to enforce the terms of their bargains with British and French merchantmen. But they did have some effect, namely in those cases in which repossession was insufficient to ensure contractual compliance. Some assaulted commercial vessels, such as Arctic whalers, had no occasion to ever dock at a foreign port where they could be seized on behalf of the privateer to whom they were indebted, rendering this enforcement mechanism useless (see, for instance, Petrie 1999: 23–24).

Although problems relating to asymmetric information and enforcement are responsible for why some Coasean plunder agreements were never negotiated, problems relating to the benefit of such agreements in certain cases, and the transaction cost of creating them in others, are probably the reasons most privateer-merchantman plunder agreements failed to get off the ground. A privateer confronted a trade-off when deciding how to proceed with a captured merchantman. As my theory highlights, negotiating a plunder contract with a victim merchantman had value to the privateer because it could avoid certain costs of producing plunder by doing so. These costs resulted from the time and risk associated with going back and forth between sea and prize court, giving up men to form a prize crew, and carrying and providing for a captured merchantman's sailors.

However, several of these costs were minimized if the privateer was seizing its final prize for the expedition. Even a well-provisioned privateer couldn't plunder forever. Many privateers couldn't last longer than the time it took to seize a single prize, especially considering that many weren't full-time plunderers but were employed in commerce instead. Because privateers had to return to port after seizing their final prize, the time and risk they hazarded in traveling home, and the men they sacrificed to form a prize crew, were costs they incurred whether they contracted with victim merchantmen or not. Only the cost of providing for the captured merchant crew's sailors could be avoided by negotiating such an agreement. In these cases the gains from a plunderer-victim Coasean bargain were small.

In March 1815 Captain Matthews's Baltimore privateer, the *Ultor*, was cruising when Matthews heard from a passing American ship that the war was over (Garitee 1977: 155). The *Ultor* could plunder vessels on its way back to Baltimore, but in couldn't resume plundering after that. Because the victims the *Ultor* encountered on its way home at war's end would be its last, the privateer couldn't save time that could be spent plundering, travel costs of going back to port, or avoid the dangers of venturing to a prize court with its prizes by entering plunder contracts with these victims. So Matthews plundered the foreign merchantmen he encountered on his return home in the tradition fashion: without a Coasean contract.

In addition to the smallness of privateers' potential gains of using plunder contracts in some cases, the transaction costs of negotiating plunder agreements could be large. Earlier in this essay I discussed how high transaction costs of negotiating Coasean agreements prevented privateers and merchantmen from using such agreements to reduce the cost of defensive investments by merchantmen. In some cases high transaction costs also precluded Coasean contracts that could reduce the cost of producing plunder and the deadweight loss of destruction.

Recall the bargaining problem created by the bilateral monopoly situation that privateers and victim merchantmen confronted. The market for vessels and cargoes that merchantmen carried helped narrow privateers' and merchantmen's bargaining range, reducing these costs. But in other cases the vessel and cargo were worth little. In these situations the majority of the price a privateer could extract from its victim merchantman was based on the value the merchant crewmembers' attached to their freedom.

Here there was no market to narrow the bargaining window. The transaction costs of negotiation in these cases threatened to be large – large enough to trump the potential gains from plunderer-victim exchange, particularly if such gains were small in the first place because the privateer was heading home anyway. Indeed, when a captured vessel and cargo were worth little, even traditional plunder could be more costly than it was worth, leading the captor to simply release its victim. When the *Yankee* overwhelmed the British schooner *Ceres*, the privateersmen were disappointed to find she was carrying only produce. "As this vessel was of little value she was released after some articles of value to her captors had been taken out" (Maclay 1900: 271; see also 272).

It's impossible to reduce plunder's social cost to zero. Thus a world of perpetual plunder necessarily fares worse than one without it. But this doesn't mean the former world faces unbounded violence and destruction. Plunderers have strong incentives to engage in activities that minimize plunder's social cost. In doing so they promote more efficient plunder, limiting how Hobbesian even a Hobbesian jungle can become.

This has important implications for how we think about even "worst case" anarchy. It suggests that even if the Hobbesian prediction that without government individuals will be locked into a state of war with another were right, the welfare implications ordinarily drawn from that prediction will often be wrong. Life in an anarchic world of warfare will be nasty, brutish, and short. But it will often be less nasty, less brutish, and less short than Hobbes or conventional wisdom following him suggests.

PART III

SELF-GOVERNANCE AND THE PROBLEM OF "BAD APPLES"

6

Pirates' Private Order*

The previous chapters considered self-governance among persons who earned at least part of their living, and thus spent at least part of their time, in peaceful, productive economic activities. Privateersmen were only part-time plunderers. When their countries weren't at war, most of them worked in merchant shipping. Even the Anglo-Scottish border reivers, who, as we saw several chapters ago, had a penchant for raiding one another, spent at least part of their time producing something to steal. And not every borderer engaged in reiving. Here I consider a different and, in at least one important sense, more difficult problem situation for anarchy – one in which society consists exclusively of "bad apples": persons who choose to earn a living solely by theft, murder, and violating other important social rules.

Bad apples may be "bad" because they lack the internal constraints, the cooperation-enhancing "moral compasses" most other people have that prevent them from taking advantage of every opportunity for privately profitable but socially destructive behavior. All persons are tempted to behave opportunistically when material costs and benefits make doing so profitable. But within some bounds, at least, most persons are also guided by nonmaterial, "internal" costs and benefits that depress the ultimate payoff of, for example, stealing from others and increase the ultimate payoff of behaving honestly toward them. Moral compasses increase the likelihood of cooperative behavior even where uncooperative behavior has no chance of being detected, and thus no chance of being punished, by others. Feelings of guilt or, on the other side, self-respect, for example, can produce some

* This chapter is based on and uses material from Leeson, Peter T. 2007. "An-*arrgh*-chy: The Law and Economics of Pirate Organization." *Journal of Political Economy* 115(6): 1049–1094 [© 2007 The University of Chicago].

degree of cooperation whether other governance mechanisms exist or not. Bad apples may also be "bad" because they're excessively impatient. Criminal punishments sufficient to deter more patient persons from seeking a living by breaking social rules, or to deter persons "naturally" more inclined to behave cooperatively along the previously discussed lines from doing so, may be insufficient to deter persons with exceptionally high discount rates from seeking to earn a living this way.

There are surely other reasons why some persons may be willing to earn their livings through theft and murder. But these two are sufficient to highlight the daunting challenge that the most notable societies composed exclusively of bad apples confront in trying to achieve social order through self-governance: outlaw societies. Outlaw societies tend to be composed of the very sorts of people that any governance arrangement has the most difficulty controlling: persons whose moral compasses are nonexistent or deficient from the perspective of cooperation, and persons who are extraordinarily myopic. How, then, can we expect individuals committed to stealing and killing to secure social order? From where might so-called honor among thieves spring?

Clearly not from government. Outlaw societies are outside the laws and means of enforcement enjoyed by legitimate persons in legitimate societies governed by states. Yet, like societies composed mostly of legitimate persons, those consisting exclusively of bad apples require governance too. Their criminal enterprises require social cooperation, albeit for the purpose of exploiting others, no less than legitimate persons' enterprises do. If societies of bad apples fail to govern themselves, their very livelihoods, which depend on their ability to coordinate for profitable theft and violence, evaporate. Thus even the members of criminal societies have strong incentives to make self-governance work. And they do.

To see how, I examine history's most notorious outlaw society: that of Caribbean pirates. Pirates are known for raucousness, recklessness, and chaotic rapine. But pirate reality is quite another picture. Real-life pirates were highly organized criminals. Unlike the swashbuckling psychopaths of fiction, historical pirates displayed sophisticated organization and coordination.

These "most treacherous rogues" terrorized the Caribbean and the Atlantic and Indian oceans during the seventeenth and eighteenth centuries. Pirates formed a loose confederation of maritime bandits outside the law of any government. Despite this, they successfully cooperated with hundreds of other rogues. Amid ubiquitous potential for conflict, pirates rarely fought, stole from, or deceived one another. In fact, piratical harmony was as common as harmony among their lawful contemporaries who relied on government for social cooperation. As one pirate contemporary put it (Johnson 1726–1728: 527): "Nature, we see, teaches the most Illiterate the necessary Prudence for their Preservation . . . these Men whom we term, and not without Reason, the Scandal of human Nature, who were abandoned to all Vice, and lived by Rapine; when they judged it for their Interest . . . were strictly just . . . among themselves."

To organize their banditry effectively, pirates required mechanisms of self-governance to prevent internal predation, minimize crew conflict, and maximize piratical profit. Pirates devised two institutions for this purpose. First, I analyze the system of piratical checks and balances that crews used to constrain captain predation. Second, I examine how pirates used democratic constitutions to minimize conflict and create piratical law and order. Remarkably, pirates adopted both of these institutions before seventeenth- and eighteenth-century governments did.

My discussion draws on a series of historical documents that provide a firsthand glimpse into their organization.[1] The first of these is Captain Charles Johnson's *General History of the Pyrates* (1726–1728), which contains reports on several of history's most notorious pirates, related by a pirate contemporary. I also draw on Alexander Exquemelin's (1678) invaluable account of the seventeenth-century buccaneers. Exquemelin was a surgeon who sailed with the buccaneers, and he provides a detailed, firsthand account of their raids, system of rules, and social organization. The buccaneer William Dampier (1697–1707) also published a journal relating to his maritime exploits, of which I make use as well.

Buccaneers differed from "pure" pirates in that they frequently plundered ships with government sanction. However, many other times they plundered without official permission, as full-blown pirates. These proto-pirates, many

---

[1] "Captain Johnson" is a pen name used by the author of *A General History of the Pyrates*. His true identity remains unknown. In 1932 John R. Moore claimed that Johnson was in fact Daniel Defoe. However, in the late 1980s this view was overturned (see Furbank and Owens 1988), and today many pirate historians reject the view that Defoe is the author of this important book (see, for instance, Cordingly 2006; Rediker 2004; Woodard 2007; for the opposing view, see Rogozinski 2000). Whatever Johnson's true identity, it's agreed that he "had extensive first-hand knowledge of piracy" (Konstam 2007: 12). While it's widely acknowledged that Johnson's work contains some errors and apocryphal accounts (such as the community of Libertalia), "Johnson is widely regarded as a highly reliable source for factual information" on pirates (Rediker 2004: 180) and remains a definitive source that historians rely on in constructing their accounts of seventeenth and eighteenth-century piracy. As eminent pirate historian David Cordingly (2006: xx) puts it, this book "is the prime source for the lives of many pirates of what is often called the Golden Age of Piracy."

of whom turned to pure piracy when governments stopped issuing licenses for plunder, influenced and anticipated the organization of pure pirates in the late seventeenth and early eighteenth centuries. Buccaneer records are therefore important for understanding the institutions and organization of seventeenth- and eighteenth-century pirates.

In addition to these sources, the Calendar of Colonial Office Papers, which contains correspondence between colonial governors and their central governments relating to piracy, and records from the trials of various pirates, such as testimony from individuals taken prisoner by pirate ships and the testimony of pirates themselves, form an important part of the historical record on which this essay relies.[2] Finally, a few pirate captives, such as William Snelgrave (1734), whose captors ultimately released them, published longer works describing their harrowing captivity by pirate crews.[3] I also draw on these accounts, which provide important firsthand records describing piratical governance and organization.[4]

A "NEST OF ROGUES"

Seventeenth- and eighteenth-century pirates occupied the waterways that formed major trading routes.[5] These included the waters surrounding the Bahamas that stood between ships traveling from Central America to Spain, the waters connecting Europe and the North American sea coast, those between Cuba and Haiti, which separated ships traveling from Europe and the west coast of Africa to Jamaica, and the waters around Madagascar traveled by ships sailing to and from India (Cordingly 2006: 88). These areas encompass major portions of the Atlantic and Indian oceans, the Caribbean Sea, and the Gulf of Mexico. The trade routes connecting the Caribbean,

[2] Jameson (1923) has edited an excellent collection of such records. Unless otherwise noted, all depositions and examinations quoted in this chapter are from his collection.
[3] Importantly, drawing on the historical episode of pirates helps overcome the problem of "getting inside" criminal organizations, whose criminality often precludes inside views. Records from individuals who had direct experiences with pirates, as well as those that shed light on piratical governance mechanisms from pirates themselves, allow me to view pirates' criminal organization "from the inside."
[4] Additionally, this essay relies on and is greatly indebted to a voluminous modern literature covering all aspects of piracy, including those considered here, written by contemporary historians. Some of the best discussions belong to Rediker (1981, 2006), Cordingly (1996, 2006), Gosse (1946), Rankin (1969), Pringle (1953), Konstam (2002), and Rogozinski (2000).
[5] The "nest of rogues" terminology in this section's heading comes from Governor William Spotswood who, in a letter to the British Lords of the Admiralty, complained of the growing pirate problem in New Providence (Spotswood 1882: vol. 2, 168).

North America's Atlantic sea coast, and Madagascar consequently formed a loop called the "Pirate Round" that many pirates traveled in search of prey.

The "Golden Age" of piracy, when pirates were at their strongest, extended from 1690 to 1730 (Konstam 2002: 94).[6] The years from 1716 to 1722 mark the height of the Golden Age. "This was at a Time that the Pyrates had obtained such an Acquisition of Strength, that they were in no Concern about preserving themselves from the Justice of Laws" (Johnson 1726–1728: 87). The pirates of this era include many well-known sea robbers, such as Blackbeard – whose real name was Edward Teach – Bartholomew Roberts, "Calico" Jack Rackam, and others.

Pirates were a diverse lot.[7] A sample of 700 pirates active in the Caribbean between 1715 and 1725 reveals that 35 percent were English, 25 percent were American, 20 percent were from West Indies, 10 percent were Scottish, 8 percent were from Wales, and 2 percent were from Sweden, Holland, France, and Spain (Konstam 2002: 9). Others came from Portugal, Scandinavia, Greece, and East India (Marx 1996b: 103).

Pirate crews were also racially diverse. Based on data available from twenty-three pirate crews active between 1682 and 1726, the racial composition of ships varied between 13 percent and 98 percent black. If this sample is representative, 25–30 percent of the average pirate crew was of African descent (Kinkor 2001: 200–201).

The pirate population is difficult to measure precisely, but by all accounts it was considerable.[8] According to the reports of contemporaries and estimates of pirate historians, in any one year between 1716 and 1722, the loop that formed the Pirate Round contained between 1,000 and 2,000 sea

---

[6] The dates historians give to mark the Golden Age of Piracy vary. Cordingly (2006) provides a slightly larger range, from about 1650 to 1725. Still others, such as Rankin (1969), date the great age of piracy as encompassing the years between 1630 and 1720. The further back in this range one goes, the more one is dealing with buccaneers, as opposed to pure pirates.

[7] Pirates also exhibited some diversity in social standing. Although most pirates were uneducated and from the lower classes of society, a few were well educated and came from higher stations in life.

[8] Pure pirates should be distinguished from buccaneers, privateers, and corsairs. Pure pirates were total outlaws and attacked merchant ships indiscriminately for their own gain. Privateers and corsairs, in contrast, were both state-sanctioned sea robbers. Governments licensed the former to attack enemy ships in times of war. Governments licensed the latter to attack the ships of other nations on the basis of religion. "Buccaneering was a peculiar blend of piracy and privateering in which the two elements were often indistinguishable" (Marx 1996a: 38). Often times, buccaneers plundered with official sanction, making them more like privateers than pirates. Many other times, however, they didn't. In these cases they were acting as pure pirates.

bandits (see, for instance, Konstam 2002: 6; Marx 1996b: 102, 111; Pringle 1953: 185; Johnson 1726–1728: 132; Rediker 2006: 256).[9] The buccaneering community of the seventeenth century must have been even larger than this; as I discuss later in this chapter, some firsthand observers report single expeditions of 2,000 men (Exquemelin 1678: 171).

Contrary to most people's images of pirate crews, they were quite large. Based on figures from thirty-seven pirate ships between 1716 and 1726, the average crew had about eighty members (Rediker 2006: 256; see also, Deposition of Simon Calderon 1682, Public Record Office, Colonial Office Papers I: 50, no. 139). A number of pirate crews were closer to 120, and crews of 150–200 weren't uncommon (see, for instance, Snelgrave 1734: 199; Examination of John Brown May 6, 1717, Suffolk Court Files, no. 11945, paper 5; Deposition of Theophilus Turner June 8, 1699, Public Record Office, Colonial Office Papers 5: 714, no. 70 VI; Examination of John Dann, August 3, 1696, London, Public Record Office, Colonial Office Papers 323: 2, no. 25; Deposition of Adam Baldridge, May 5, 1699, Public Record Office, Colonial Office Papers 5: 1042, no. 30 II; Johnson 1726–1728: 442; Cordingly 2006: 165).

Several pirate crews were larger than this. For example, Blackbeard's crew aboard the *Queen Anne's Revenge* was 300 men strong (Public Record Office, Colonial Office Papers 152/12, no. 67, iii; see also, Marx 1996b: 112).[10] Even a sixth-rate Royal Navy ship in the early eighteenth century carried more crew members than the average pirate vessel (about 150). But compared to the average merchant ship, which carried only thirteen to seventeen men, pirate ships were extremely large (Rediker 2006: 107). Furthermore, some pirate crews were too large to fit in one ship. In this case they formed pirate squadrons. Captain Bartholomew Roberts, for example, commanded a squadron of 4 ships that carried 508 men (Cordingly 2006: 111).

In addition to this, pirate ships sometimes joined for concerted plundering expeditions. The most impressive fleets of sea bandits belong to the buccaneers. Alexander Exquemelin (1678: 171), for example, records that Captain Morgan commanded a fleet of 37 ships and 2,000 men

---

[9] These numbers are especially large when one puts them in historical perspective. The Royal Navy, for example, employed only 13,000 men in any one year between 1716 and 1726, making the pirate population in a good year more than 15 percent of the Navy population (Rediker 2006: 256). In 1680 the total population of the American colonies was less than 152,000 (Hughes and Cain 1994: 20). In fact, as late as 1790, when the first U.S. census was taken, only 24 places in the country had populations greater than 2,500 (Hughes and Cain 1994: 28).

[10] Quoted in Cordingly (2006: 165–166).

sufficient to attack coastal communities on the Spanish Main. Elsewhere he refers to a group of buccaneers who "had a force of at least twenty vessels in quest of plunder" (Exquemelin 1678: 69; see also 85, 105, 93). Similarly, William Dampier records a pirating expedition that boasted 10 ships and 960 men (Dampier 1697–1707: 62).[11] Although their fleets weren't as massive, eighteenth-century pirates also "cheerfully joined their Brethren in Iniquity" to engage in multi-crew pirating expeditions (Snelgrave 1734: 198).

MERCHANT SHIP ORGANIZATION

Although some pirates came from the Royal Navy, most sailors who entered piracy came from the merchant marine. Merchant ships were organized hierarchically.[12] On top was the captain, below him were his officers, and far below these were ordinary seamen. This hierarchy empowered captains with autocratic authority over their crews. The captain's authority gave him control over all aspects of life aboard his ship, including victual provision, wage payment, labor assignment and, of course, crew member discipline.

Merchant ship autocracy reflected a sensible institutional response to the specific economic situation these ships confronted and, in particular, the ownership structure of merchant vessels. Merchant ships were owned by groups of typically a dozen or more landed merchants who purchased shares in various trading vessels and financed their voyages.[13] In addition to supplying the capital required for ships' construction and continued maintenance, owners outfitted their vessels, supplied them with provisions, advanced sailor wages, and, most importantly, solicited customers (who were other landed merchants) and negotiated terms of delivery and freight.

---

[11] In the South China Sea, Cheng I commanded a pirate confederacy that may have boasted an astonishing 150,000 members (Konstam 2002: 174). Chinese pirates sometimes sailed together in fleets of 500 ships or more.

[12] Navy ships were also organized autocratically. Their captains were commissioned by the Admiralty (typically on the recommendation of superior commissioned officers) and had command over crew activities, power to physically punish sailors (or to direct/authorize lower-ranking officers to do so), and so forth. Captains of larger naval ships didn't, however, have control over victuals, which were instead controlled by a warrant officer called the "purser." The purser's logs, which documented victuals distributed, were often approved by the captain.

[13] Ownership groups were sizeable because of the need to diversify the risk of merchant shipping. Each merchant purchased a small share in many ships rather than being the sole owner of one.

Merchant ship owners were absentee owners of their vessels. They didn't sail on their ships.[14] They were landlubbers. Most merchant ship owners didn't want to take their chances with brutal life at sea, and in any event could earn more by specializing in their area of expertise – investment and commercial organization – hiring seamen to sail their ships instead.[15] Because of this, merchant ship owners confronted a principal-agent problem with respect to the crews they hired. Once a ship left port, it could be gone for months.[16] At sea the owners' ship was beyond their watchful eyes or reach. Thus ship owners couldn't monitor their sailors directly.

This situation invited various kinds of sailor opportunism. Such opportunism included negligence in caring for the ship, carelessness that damaged cargo, liberality with provisions, embezzlement of freight or advances required to finance the vessel's voyage, and outright theft of the vessel itself. To prevent this, ship owners appointed captains to their vessels to monitor crews in their stead. Centralizing power in a captain's hands to direct sailors' tasks, control the distribution of victuals and payment, and discipline and punish crew members allowed merchant ship owners to minimize sailor opportunism. Because merchant ships tended to be quite small, captains could cheaply monitor sailors' behavior to prevent activities (or inactivities) that were costly to ship owners and secure sailors' full effort.[17]

Admiralty law facilitated captains' ability to do this by granting them authority to control their crews' behavior through corporal punishment. The law empowered captains to beat crew members with the infamous (and ominous) cat-o-nine-tails, imprison them, and administer other forms of harsh physical "correction" to sailors who disobeyed orders or shirked their duties. It also permitted captains to dock sailors' wages for damaging or stealing cargo and for insubordination.

To align owner-captain interests, owners used two devices. First, they hired captains who held small shares in the vessels they were commanding or, barring this, gave small shares to their captains who didn't. Merchant

---

[14] Because most merchant ships were owned by groups of investors, even in cases when a merchant captained his vessel himself, there remained absentee owners: his co-investors.

[15] Absentee ownership was further assured by the fact that the members of merchant vessel ownership groups engaged in many commercial activities beside their concern in a particular merchant ship. These other commercial activities often required merchants to be on land to tend to their affairs rather than at sea.

[16] Although merchant ships engaged in coastal trade were at sea for shorter periods, merchant ships engaged in long-distance trade could be gone for periods of nine months or more.

[17] In addition to using autocratic captains to cope with this principal-agent problem, merchant ships also held back a portion (or sometimes all) of sailors' wages until a voyage was complete.

ship captains continued to draw regular fixed wages like the other sailors on their vessels.[18] But unlike regular sailors, captains became partial residual claimants of the ships they controlled, aligning their interests with those of absentee owners.[19] Second, whenever possible, absentee owners appointed captains with familial connections to one of the members of their group (Davis 1962: 128). This ensured that captains didn't behave opportunistically at the absentee owners' expense because, if they did, they were more likely to face punishment.[20]

The reason merchant ship owners required *autocratic* captains to effectively serve their interests is straightforward. A captain who didn't have total authority over his crew couldn't monitor and control sailors' behavior successfully. Reducing the captain's power over victuals, payments, labor assignment, or discipline and vesting it in some other sailor's hands instead would have concomitantly reduced the captain's power to make sailors behave in the absentee owners' interest.

Similarly, if merchant ship owners didn't appoint their captains as the permanent commanders of their voyages, but instead permitted a ship's sailors to popularly depose the captain and elect another member of the

---

[18] A few merchant ships engaged in part-time fishing used a share system of payment similar to the one privateers, whalers, and pirates used. The overwhelming majority of merchant ships used a fixed-wage system. In vessels engaged in coastal shipping, sailors were paid lump-sum wages. In vessels engaged in long-distance shipping, sailors were paid monthly wages.

[19] The owner-sailor principal-agent problem couldn't have been overcome by converting every crew member's fixed wage to a profit-sharing scheme. Even under profit sharing, sailors would still have an incentive to consume cargo, liberal provisions, and so on and then blame the loss on the uncertainties of the sea, such as pirates or wreck. Although this opportunism would reduce each sailor's share of the voyage's net proceeds, because the cost of such behavior is borne partially by the absentee owners, sailors have an incentive to act opportunistically. Further, converting sailor wages to shares wouldn't have deterred the crew from the most costly kind of opportunism – absconding with the ship and its freight. Because the benefit of such theft would exceed the crew's fraction of a successful voyage's proceeds, which are shared with the absentee owners under a profit-sharing scheme, absent an authority to monitor and control their behavior, crews would still have an incentive to steal the ships on which they sailed. This is why both privateers and whaling ships, for instance, which used a pirate-like profit-sharing system, but also had absentee owners, still required and used autocratic captains. On the efficiency of the fixed-wage system for the merchant marine and efficiency of the share system for privateers and whalers, which also applies to pirates, see Gifford (1993).

[20] A third device owners used for this purpose, though of declining importance over time, was that of the supercargo – an agent hired by the ship's owners who sailed on the ship and managed commercial aspects of the voyage, such as buying and selling cargo at port, and sometimes deciding what ports the ship should stop at, when the captain could not be trusted in these capacities (Davis 1962).

crew to this office at their will, the captain's capacity as acting manager of the ship's absentee owners would cease to exist. To see this, simply imagine the kind of captain merchant sailors would elect if given the power to select him democratically. Sailors' interests were best served by a lax, liberal captain who let them do as they pleased – exactly the opposite sort of captain that best served the owners' interests. Merchant ship autocracy was therefore essential to overcoming the owner-crew principal-agent problem, and thus to merchant ship profitability.

Merchant ship autocracy worked quite well in this respect. While some sailors still managed to steal from the ships on which they sailed, disobey command, and in several cases mutiny and abscond with the owners' ship, these were relatively unimportant exceptions to the general rule whereby merchant sailors, under the authority of autocratic captains, served their absentee owners' interests.

The Problem of Captain Predation

Although merchant ship autocracy largely overcame the principal-agent problem that absentee owners confronted with respect to their crews, in doing so it created potential for a different kind of problem: captain preda-tion. The trouble was that a captain endowed with the authority required to manage his crew on the ship owners' behalf could also easily turn that authority against his seamen for personal benefit. As British marine com-mander William Betagh (1728: 41) characterized the problem, "unlimited power, bad views, ill nature and ill principles all concurring" "in a ship's commander," "he is past all restraint."

Betagh's opinion of some captains' "ill-nature" notwithstanding, mer-chant captains weren't necessarily bad men. But they were rational and thus responded to the incentives their institutional environment created. Endowed with autocratic authority over their crews, some merchant cap-tains used the power their employers and Admiralty law gave them to prey on their sailors. As a result of merchant ships' autocratic organization, one eighteenth century observer remarked, "a Captain is like a King at Sea, and his Authority is over all that are in his Possession" (Bishop 1744: 78).[21] Cap-tains "had absolute authority over the mates, the carpenters and boatswain, and the seamen." They had the power to "make life tolerable or unbearable as they wished" (Davis 1962: 131–132). Unfortunately for seamen, more than a few captains opted for the latter.

---

[21] Quoted in Rediker (2006: 208).

Merchant captain mistreatment of ordinary seamen was largely responsible for driving sailors from this profession into the arms of sea bandits. The pirate John Archer's last words before being put to death testify to this. As he lamented, "I could wish that Masters of Vessels would not use their Men with so much Severity, as many of them do, which exposes us to great Temptations" (Johnson 1726–1728: 351). In 1726 the pirate William Fly pleaded similarly at his death sentence. "Our Captain and his Mate used us Barbarously. We poor Men can't have Justice done. There is nothing said to our Commanders, let them never so much abuse us, and use us like Dogs" (Rediker 1981: 218).

Captain predation took several forms, each the result of abusing the autocratic power captains had at their disposal. Predatory captains cut sailors' victual rations to keep costs down or to leave more for them and their fellow officers to consume. As one sailor testified, for example, although the members of his crew "were att short allowance and wanted bread," the officers "were allowed . . . their full allowance of provisions and liquors as if there had been no want of scarcity of any thing on board" (*Babb v. Chalkley* 1701, High Court of Admiralty Papers, 24/127).[22] Predatory captains also fraudulently docked sailors' wages or paid sailors in debased colonial currency (Morris 1965: 237; Rediker 2006). They might also voyage to locations where the crew hadn't contracted to sail (Gifford 1993: 144).

To keep their hungry and uncomfortable men in check, abusive captains could and did use all manner of objects aboard their ships as weapons to punish insolent crew members. They hit sailors in the head with tackle or other hard objects on board, crushing their faces, and used other barbaric tactics to discipline seamen (*Jones v. Newcomin* 1735, High Court of Admiralty Papers, 24/138).[23] As merchant ship captain Nathaniel Uring (1726: 176–177) described how he dealt with a "seditious Fellow" on his ship, for instance, "I gave him two or three such Strokes with a Stick I had prepared for that purpose . . . the Blood running about his Ears, he pray'd for God's sake that I not kill him."

Besides preventing dissension, captains also used their kingly power to settle personal scores with crew members. Admiralty law considered interfering with captain punishment mutinous and thus prohibited crew members from doing so (Morris 1965: 264–265). Given that captains effectively defined when punishment was legitimate, they were free to abuse seamen at will. As one seaman warned a newcomer, "There is no justice or injustice on

---

[22] Quoted in Rediker (2006: 247).
[23] Quoted in Rediker (2006: 216).

board ship, my lad. There are only two things: duty and mutiny – mind that. All that you are ordered to do is duty. All that you refuse to do is mutiny" (Rediker 2006: 211).[24]

PIRATE SHIP ORGANIZATION

Like merchant ship organization, the particular economic situation pirate ships confronted crucially shaped their organization. Most notably, pirates didn't confront the owner-crew principal-agent problem that merchant ships did. The reason for this is simple enough: pirates didn't acquire their ships legitimately. They stole them.[25]

Because of this, pirate ships had no absentee owners. On a pirate ship the principals *were* the agents. As one historian described it, in this sense a pirate ship was like a "sea-going stock company" (Pringle 1953: 106). Thus, unlike merchant ships, pirate ships didn't require captains to align the crew's interests with those of the ship's absentee owners.

But they did require captains. Many important piratical decisions, such as how to engage a potential target, the method to pursue when "chasing" a target or being chased by authorities, and how to react if attacked, required snap decision making. There wasn't time for disagreement or debate in such cases, and conflicting voices would have made it impossible to undertake the most essential tasks. Furthermore, pirate ships, like all ships – indeed, more than other ships – needed some method of maintaining order, distributing victuals, payments, and administering discipline to unruly crew members.

The office of captain overcame such difficulties by vesting control over these matters in the hands of an authority. In this sense, although pirate ships differed from merchant ships in requiring captains to solve an owner-sailor principal-agent problem, pirate ships were similar to merchant ships in requiring some kind of authority for their undertakings' success. While a pirate ship's activity – maritime theft – was wholly different from that of a merchant ship, both kinds of vessels shared the need to create internal order to achieve their ends.

Indeed, the difficulty pirate ships confronted in their need for authority was considerably greater than that which merchant ships confronted. While the historical record contains plenty of charges of merchant captain

---

[24] This quotation is from a late-eighteenth-century sailor, but captures the situation in the earlier part of the century as well.

[25] However, there is one eighteenth-century pirate, Stede Bonnet, who actually purchased the first ship with which he went on the account.

predation, merchant sailors, at least, could rely on government to deter some captain predation. English law, for example, included several legal protections that were supposed to insulate sailors from captain abuse. And merchant seamen could, and sometimes did, take predatory captains to court for their actions.

As outlaws, pirates were out of luck in this regard. They couldn't rely on government protection from predatory captains at all. Furthermore, pirates' captains, who were, like all pirates, professional outlaws, were men with a demonstrated willingness to use theft and violence to get what they wanted.

The need for captains therefore posed a serious dilemma for pirates. On the one hand, a captain who wielded unquestioned authority in certain decisions was critical for success. On the other hand, what was to prevent a captain with this power from behaving toward his pirate crew in the same manner that predatory merchant ship captains behaved toward their crews or, more likely, still worse?

Because pirates didn't have absentee owners but instead jointly owned the stolen ships on which they sailed, although they required captains, unlike merchant ships, they didn't require *autocratic* captains. Thus, in sharp contrast to the situation on merchant ships, pirates could and did democratically elect their captains without problem. The pirates sailing a particular ship were both the principals and the agents, so democracy didn't threaten to lead to captains who served the agents at the principals' expense. On the contrary, pirate democracy ensured that pirates got precisely the kind of captains they desired. Because pirates could popularly depose any captain who didn't suit them and elect another in his place, pirate captains' ability to prey on crew members was greatly constrained compared to merchant ship captains.

Similarly, because pirates were both principals and agents of their ships, they could divide authority on their vessels to further check captains' ability to abuse crew members without loss. Unlike merchant ships, which couldn't afford a separation of power because this would have diminished the ability of the absentee owners' acting agent (the captain) to make the crew act in the owners' interests, pirate ships could and did adopt a system of democratic checks and balances.

Piratical Checks and Balances

In light of the threat of captain predation, pirates "were adamant in wanting to limit the captain's power to abuse and cheat them" (Rogozinski 2000: 174).

To do this they instituted a democratic system of divided power, or piratical checks and balances, aboard their ships. As the pirate Walter Kennedy
testified at his trial (Hayward 1735: vol. 1, 42):

Most of them having suffered formerly from the ill-treatment of Officers, provided
thus carefully against any such Evil now they had the choice in themselves... for
the due Execution thereof they constituted other Officers besides the Captain; so
very industrious were they to avoid putting too much Power into the hands of one
Man.

The primary "other officer" pirates "constituted" for this purpose was the
quartermaster. The way this office worked was straightforward. Captains
retained absolute authority in times of battle, enabling pirates to realize
the benefits of autocratic control required for success in conflict. However,
pirate crews transferred power to allocate provisions, select and distribute
loot (there was rarely room aboard pirate ships to take all they seized from
a prize), adjudicate crew member conflicts, and administer discipline to the
quartermaster, who they democratically elected (Johnson 1726–1728: 213):

For the Punishment of small Offences... there is a principal Officer among the
Pyrates, called the Quarter-Master, of the Men's own choosing, who claims all
Authority this Way, (excepting in Time of Battle) If they disobey his Command, are
quarrelsome and mutinous with one another, misuse Prisoners, plunder beyond
his Order, and in particular, if they be negligent of their Arms, which he musters
at Discretion, he punishes at his own dare without incurring the Lash from all the
Ship's Company: In short, this Officer is Trustee for the whole, is the first on board
any Prize, separating for the Company's Use, what he pleases, and returning what
he thinks fit to the Owners, excepting Gold and Silver, which they have voted not
returnable.

William Snelgrave (1734: 199–200), who observed the pirates' system of
checks and balances firsthand, characterized the relationship between captain and quartermaster similarly: "the Captain of a Pirate Ship, is chiefly
chosen to fight the Vessels they may meet with. Besides him, they chuse
another principle Officer, whom they call Quarter-master, who has the general Inspection of all Affairs, and often controuls the Captain's Orders." This
separation of power removed captains' control over activities they traditionally used to prey on crew members while empowering them sufficiently to
direct plundering expeditions.

The institutional separation of powers aboard pirate ships predated its
adoption by seventeenth- and eighteenth-century governments. France –
and the United States, for that matter – didn't experience such a separation
until 1789. The first specter of separated powers in Spain didn't appear until

1812. In contrast, pirates had divided, democratic governance aboard their ships at least a century before this. Arguably, piratical checks and balances predated even England's adoption of similar institutions. England didn't experience a separation of powers until the Glorious Revolution of 1688. But the buccaneers, who used a similar, if not as thoroughgoing, system of democratically divided power as their pure-pirate successors, had in place at least partial democratic checks and balances in the early 1680s (Rogozinski 2000).

Piratical checks and balances proved highly successful. According to Johnson (1726–1728: 423), as a result of the institution of the quarter-master, aboard pirate ships "the Captain can undertake nothing which the Quarter-Master does not approve. We may say, the Quarter-Master is an humble Imitation of the Roman Tribune of the People; he speaks for, and looks after the Interest of the Crew." As noted previously, the only exception to this was "in Chase, or in Battle" when crews desired autocratic authority and thus, "by their own Laws," "The Captain's Power is uncontroulable" (Johnson 1726–1728: 139, 214).[26]

As noted earlier, in addition to this separation of powers, pirates imposed a further check to balance captains' authority. They converted the office to a democratically elected one, "The Rank of Captain being obtained by the Suffrage of the Majority" (Johnson 1726–1728: 214). The combination of separated powers and democratic elections for captains ensured that pirates "only permit him to be Captain, on Condition, that they may be Captain over him" (Johnson 1726–1728: 213).

Crews could vote captains out of office for any number of reasons. Predation was one reason, but so was cowardice, poor judgment, or any other behavior a crew felt wasn't in its best interest. In this way pirates could be sure that captainship "falls on one superior for Knowledge and Boldness, Pistol Proof, (as they call it)" (Johnson 1726–1728: 214).

The historical record contains numerous examples of pirate crews deposing unwanted captains by majority vote or otherwise removing them from power through popular consensus. Captain Charles Vane's pirate crew, for example, popularly deposed him for cowardice: "the Captain's Behavior was obliged to stand the Test of a Vote, and a Resolution passed against his Honour and Dignity . . . deposing him from the Command" (Johnson

---

[26] Of course even pirates' democratic system of checks and balances couldn't prevent all instances of captain predation. Because he controlled battle-related decisions, a pirate captain could, for instance, still put a crew member he disliked in harm's way.

1726–1728: 139). Similarly, Captain Christopher Moody's pirate crew grew dissatisfied with his behavior and "at last forced him, with twelve others" who supported him "into an open Boat . . . and . . . they were never heard of afterwards" (Snelgrave 1734: 198).[27]

Crews sometimes elected quartermasters who displayed particular valor or keen decision making to replace less capable or honorable captains. For example, when one pirate crew "went to Voting for a new Captain . . . the Quarter-Master, who had behaved so well in the last Affair . . . was chosen" (Johnson 1726–1728: 479). This helped create competition among pirate officers that tended to check their abuses and encouraged them to serve their crews' interests.[28]

Pirates took the limitations they imposed on captains' authority through their system of checks and balances seriously. A speech made by one of the pirates aboard Captain Bartholomew Roberts's ship testifies to this. As he told his crew, "should a Captain be so sawcy as to exceed Prescription at any time, why down with him! it will be a Caution after he is dead to his Successors, of what fatal Consequence any sort of assuming may be" (Johnson 1726–1728: 194–195). This pirate was exaggerating – but only slightly. Crews quickly and readily deposed old captains and elected new ones when the former overstepped the limited power crews gave them.

The seriousness with which pirates sought to limit their captains' power is reflected in other ways as well. For instance, unlike aboard merchant vessels, on pirate ships, captains were unable to secure special privileges for themselves at their crews' expense. Their lodging, provisions, and even pay were nearly the same as that of ordinary crew members. As Johnson (1726–1728: 213–214) described it, aboard pirate ships, "every Man, as the Humour takes him . . . [may] intrude [the captain's] Apartment, swear at him, seize a part of his Victuals and Drink, if they like it, without his offering to find Fault or contest it." In other cases, "the Captain himself not being allowed a Bed" had to sleep with rest of the crew in far less comfortable conditions than a captain would otherwise be used to (Snelgrave 1734: 217). Or as one pirate fellow-traveler marveled, "even their Captain, or any other

---

[27] In some cases crews also physically punished their captains for behaviors they deemed inconsistent with their interests. Oliver La Bouche, for example, was deprived of his captain position and flogged for attempting to desert his crew (Bucquoy 1744: 103, translated and quoted in Rogozinski 2000: 177). Occasionally, crews also deserted predatory captains (Council of the Leeward Islands May 18, 1699, Public Record Office, Colonial Office Papers, 152: 3, no. 21).

[28] This competition likely explains the rarity of cases of captain-quartermaster collusion against crews.

Officer, is allowed no more than another Man; nay, the Captain cannot [even] keep his own Cabin to himself" (Downing 1737: 99).[29]

One pirate captive records an event in which the captains of a pirate fleet borrowed fancy clothes that were part of the loot their crews acquired in taking a recent prize. These captains hoped their stolen finery would attract local women on the nearby shore. Although the captains intended only to borrow the clothes, the crews became outraged at their captains who they saw as transgressing the limits of their narrowly circumscribed power. As the observer described it, "The Pirate Captains having taken these Cloaths without leave from the Quarter-master, it gave great Offence to all the Crew; who alledg'd, 'If they suffered such things, the Captains would for the future assume a Power, to take whatever they liked for themselves'" (Snelgrave 1734: 257).[30]

One can also get an idea of the effectiveness of piratical checks and balances by considering the remarks of a pirate contemporary that point to the rarity of pirate captain predation. Perplexed by an anomalous pirate captain who abused his crew, he puzzled, "The captain is very severe to his people, by reason of his commission, and caries a very different form from what other Pirates use to do . . . often calling for his pistols and threatening any that durst speak to the contrary of what he desireth, to knock out their brains" (Rogozinski 2000: 139; see also Deposition of Benjamin Franks October 20, 1697, Public Record Office, Colonial Office Papers, 323: 2, no. 124).[31]

This success helps explain why, counterintuitively, "the People [pirates overtook] were generally glad of an opportunity of entring with them" (Snelgrave 1734: 203). Indeed, pirates frequently "strengthen'd themselves with a great many fresh Hands, who most of them enter'd voluntarily" (Johnson 1726–1728: 170; see also 228; Deposition of Jeremiah Tay July 6, 1694, Suffolk Court Files, no. 3033, paper 6; Colonial Office Papers May 31, 1718, f. 18).[32]

---

[29] Quoted in Rogozinski (2000: 175).

[30] This decentralization of authority and elimination of captain privilege aboard pirate ships was a radical departure from conditions in the legitimate maritime world. Observers were therefore shocked at the incredible absence of hierarchy aboard pirate ships. Commenting on their democratic form of governance, for example, the Dutch governor of Mauritius marveled, "Every man had as much say as the captain" (Ritchie 1986: 124).

[31] The captain referred to here is William Kidd, a privateer-turned-pirate, who was ultimately executed for his crimes. Notably, Kidd's privateer ship was financed by absentee, landed-merchant owners.

[32] Many individuals ostensibly forced to join pirate crews in fact joined voluntarily. Officially, they asked to be "forced" and occasionally put up a show to their comrades to this effect

Pirate Constitutions

Pirates' system of checks and balances prevented captains from preying on their crews. But a significant problem remained. In vesting many of the powers captains typically held in quartermasters instead, what was to prevent quartermasters from abusing their authority to benefit privately at crews' expense?

As discussed earlier, quartermasters had numerous roles aboard pirate ships. They were in charge of distributing booty, provisions, conflict resolution, and crew member punishment. This gave them ample latitude to prey on crews. I already discussed one check on quartermaster predation, which also checked captain predation: democratic elections. As with their captains, pirate crews elected quartermasters and could depose them if they overstepped their authority.

But what precisely did this include? Were, for instance, quartermasters free to divide booty and provisions as they saw fit? Could they punish crew members at their discretion? Furthermore, according to what "laws" were they supposed to adjudicate disputes between those on board?

After all, pirates weren't only afraid of captain predation. They opposed any situation that threatened to jeopardize their ability to cooperate for organized banditry, including the institution of the quartermaster. To solve this problem, pirate crews forged written constitutions that specified their laws, punishments for breaking these laws, and more specifically limited the actions that quartermasters might take in carrying out their duties.

Pirate constitutions originated with "articles of agreement" followed on buccaneer ships in the seventeenth century. The buccaneers called their articles a *chasse-partie*. Those articles specified the division of booty among the officers and crew along with other terms of the buccaneers' organization. All sea bandits followed the basic rule of "no prey, no pay." Unless a pirating expedition was successful, no man received any payment.

Exquemelin (1678: 71–72) describes the *chasse-partie* that governed his crew's expedition in detail:

The buccaneers resolve by common vote where they shall cruise. They also draw up an agreement or chasse partie, in which is specified what the captain shall have for himself and for the use of his vessel. Usually they agree on the following terms. Providing they capture a prize, first of all these amounts would be deducted from the whole capital. The hunter's pay would generally be 200 pieces of eight. The

so that in the event their pirate crew was ever captured, they could claim that they were compelled as a defense (Pringle 1953; see also, Rankin 1969; Leeson 2010c).

carpenter, for his work in repairing and fitting out the ship, would be paid 100 or 150 pieces of eight. The surgeon would receive 200 or 250 for his medical supplies, according to the size of the ship.

Then came the agreed awards for the wounded, who might have lost a limb or suffered injuries. They would be compensated as follows: for the loss of a right arm, 600 pieces of eight or six slaves; for a left arm 500 pieces of eight or five slaves. The loss of a right leg also brought 500 pieces of eight or five slaves in compensation; a left leg 400 or four slaves; an eye, 100 or one slave, and the same award was made for the loss of a finger. If a man lost the use of an arm, he would get as much as if it had been cut off, and a severe internal injury which meant the victim had to have a pipe inserted in his body would receive 500 pieces of eight or five slaves in recompense.

These amounts having first been withdrawn from the capital, the rest of the prize would be divided into as many portions as men on the ship. The captain draws four or five men's portions for the use of the ship, perhaps even more, and two portions for himself. The rest of the men share uniformly, and the boys get half a man's share....

When a ship is robbed, nobody must plunder and keep his loot to himself. Everything taken – money, jewels, precious stones and goods – must be shared among them all, without any man enjoying a penny more than his fair share. To prevent deceit, before the booty is distributed everyone has to swear an oath on the Bible that he has not kept for himself so much as the value of a sixpence, whether in silk, linen, wool, gold, silver, jewels, clothes or shot, from all the capture. And should any man be found to have made a false oath, he would be banished from the rovers, never more be allowed in their company.

Over time the buccaneers institutionalized their articles of agreement and social organization. The result was a system of customary law called the Custom of the Coast, or the Jamaica Discipline.

Eighteenth-century pirates built on this institutional framework in developing their own constitutions. Pirates created them "for the better Conservation of their Society, and doing Justice to one another" (Johnson 1726–1728: 210). The basic elements of pirate constitutions displayed great similarity across crews (Rediker 2006: 261). In describing the articles on Captain Roberts' ship, for instance, Johnson (1726–1728: 213) refers to "the Laws of this Company . . . principle Customs, and Government, of this roguish Commonwealth; which are pretty near the same with all Pyrates."

Frequent inter-crew interactions led to information sharing that facilitated constitutional commonality.[33] More than 70 percent of Anglo-American pirates active between 1716 and 1726, for example, can be

---

[33] A letter from colonial Governor Alexander Spotswood to the Board of Trade highlights the effectiveness of pirates' information-sharing network. Spotswood, who having "been

connected back to one of three pirate captains: Benjamin Hornigold, George Lowther, or Edward Low (Rediker 2006: 267). Thus a significant proportion of all pirates during this period were associated with one another in some way, via traveling on the same ship, in concert with other ships, and so on.

Articles of agreement required unanimous consent. Consequently, pirates democratically formed them in advance of launching pirating expeditions. "[A]ll [pirates] swore to 'em," sometimes on a Bible or, for one pirate crew, "upon a Hatchet for want of a Bible" (Johnson 1726–1728: 342). The same was true for newcomers who joined pirate companies already under way. As one observer put it, "When ever any enter on board of these Ships voluntarily, they are obliged to sign all their Articles of Agreement" (Downing 1737: 107). Pirate captain Howell Davis's crew's articles, for instance, "were signed and sworn to by himself and the rest." In pirate captain Worley's crew, too, "they all signed Articles" (Johnson 1726–1728: 167–168, 298). Pirates recognized that "it was every one's Interest to observe them, if they were minded to keep up so abominable a Combination" (Johnson 1726–1728: 210). And because pirates unanimously agreed to their articles before sailing, the rules they established were largely self-enforcing once in place.

A crew forged its articles alongside the election of a captain, quartermaster, and occasionally other smaller officers. Pirates sought agreement on their articles ex ante "to prevent Disputes and Ranglings afterwards" (Johnson 1726–1728: 342). In the event a pirate disagreed with their conditions, he was free to search elsewhere for more satisfactory terms.[34] When multiple pirate ships joined together for an expedition, they created similar articles establishing the terms of their partnership. Upon encountering one another at Grand Cayman, for example, Captain George Lowther's and Edward Low's pirate crews forged such an agreement. Lowther "offering himself

markt as the principle object of their vengeance, for cutting off their arch pirate Thatch [a.k.a. Blackbeard]" complained of finding a place to escape to "where neither Master nor Sailors know me, & so may possibly escape the knowledge of ye plrates" (Colonial Office Papers June 16, 1724, 5/1319: ff. 190–192, quoted in Rediker 2006: 254, 134).

[34] Some pirate ships required crew members to agree to stay on until a certain sum was earned or an expedition completed. However, if a ship became too crowded or some other compelling reason came along for a crew to split, it did so. In this case new articles were drawn up and pirates had the option to sign on with the new crew or stay with the old. There don't appear to be any cases of pirate constitutions being altered or amended midcruise. The status of forced men on pirate ships seems to have varied. A few appear to have been compelled to sign the ship's articles. Others weren't compelled to do so but didn't have a vote in the company's affairs until they signed (Rediker 2004: 79–81).

as an Ally; *Low* accepted of the Terms, and so the Treaty was presently sign'd without Plenipo's or any other Formalities" (Johnson 1726–1728: 319). Likewise, crews that objected to the proposed articles or some other element of an intended multi-ship expedition were free to depart peaceably. In one such case, for example, "a Spirit of Discord" emerged between three pirate crews sailing in consort "Upon which … [they] immediately parted, each steering a different Course" (Johnson 1726–1728: 175).

Charles Johnson's records contain several examples of pirate constitutions through which, as one court remarked, these rogues were "wickedly united, and articled together" (Johnson 1726–1728: 253). Consider, for instance, the articles aboard Captain Roberts' pirate ship (Johnson 1726–1728: 211–212):

I. Every Man has a Vote in the Affairs of Moment; has equal Title to the fresh Provisions, or strong Liquors, at any Time seized, and may use them at Pleasure, unless a Scarcity make it necessary, for the Good of all, to vote a Retrenchment.

II. Every Man to be called fairly in Turn, by List, on board of Prizes, because, (over and above their proper Share) they were on these Occasions allowed a Shift of Cloaths: But if they defrauded the Company to the Value of a Dollar, in Plate, Jewels, or Money, Marooning was their Punishment. If the Robbery was only betwixt one another, they contented themselves with slitting the Ears and Nose of him that was Guilty, and set him on Shore, not in an uninhabited Place, but somewhere, where he was sure to encounter Hardships.

III. No person to Game at Cards or Dice for Money.

IV. The Lights and Candles to be put out at eight a-Clock at Night: If any of the Crew, after that Hour, still remained enclined for Drinking, they were to do it on the open Deck.

V. To keep their Piece, Pistols, and Cutlash clean, and fit for Service.

VI. No Boy or Woman to be allowed amongst them. If any Man were found seducing any of the latter Sex, and carry'd her to Sea, disguised, he was to suffer Death.

VII. To Desert the Ship, or their Quarters in Battle, was punished with Death or Marooning.

VIII. No striking one another on board, but every Man's Quarrels to be ended on Shore, at Sword and Pistol.

IX. No Man to talk of breaking up their Way of Living, till each shared a 1000 l. If in order to this, any Man should lose a Limb, or become

a Cripple in their Service, he was to have 800 Dollars, out of the
publick Stock, and for lesser Hurts, proportionately.

X. The Captain and Quarter-Master to receive two Shares of a Prize;
the Master, Boatswain, and Gunner, one Share and a half, and other
Officers one and a Quarter [everyone else to receive one share].

XI. The Musicians to have Rest on the Sabbath Day, but the other six
Days and Nights, none without special Favour.

Several important features stand out from this constitution. First, it created
a democratic form of governance and explicitly laid out the terms of pirate
compensation. This was to clarify the status of property rights aboard pirate
ships and to prevent officers, such as the captain or the quartermaster, from
preying on crew members. In particular, making the terms of compensation explicit helped circumscribe the quartermaster's authority in dividing
booty.

When booty was indivisible, or there was question as to its value and
thus how many shares it counted for in payment, pirates sold or auctioned
the troublesome items and distributed the divisible proceeds accordingly
(Rogozinski 2000: 169; Snelgrave 1734). This practice prevented conflict
between crew members. More important, it constrained the discretion of
the quartermaster who might otherwise be in a position to circumvent
the terms of compensation when loot was indivisible or of ambiguous
value.

Second, pirate constitutions prohibited activities that generated significant negative externalities and threatened the success of criminal organization aboard their ships. Thus pirate articles required crew members to
keep their weapons in good working order; on Roberts's ship, they limited
drunken raucousness to allow nonparticipant pirates to get sufficient sleep
and to "give a Check to their Debauches" (Johnson 1726–1728: 211); prohibited on-board fighting that might jeopardize the entire crew's ability to
function; and prohibited activities, such as gambling, that were likely to
lead to on-board fights. On similar grounds, crews' articles often prohibited women (and young boys), who it was thought would invite conflict
or tension among crew members aboard their ships. "This being a good
political Rule to prevent disturbances amongst them, it is strictly observed"
(Snelgrave 1734: 256–257; see also, Johnson 1726–1728: 212).

In the same way, some pirate ships forbade activities such as firing one's
guns or smoking in areas of the ship that carried highly flammable goods,
such as gunpowder. According to the constitution that governed John

Phillips's *Revenge*, for example, "That Man that shall snap his Arms, or smoak Tobacco in the Hold without a Cap to his Pipe, or carry a Candle lighted without a Lanthorn, shall suffer the same Punishment as in the former Article" (Johnson 1726–1728: 342–343).

Third, pirate constitutions contained articles that provided incentives for crewmember productivity and prevented shirking. One manifestation of this was their creation of social insurance for pirates injured during battle. As in the earlier examples from Exquemelin and Roberts, articles specified in detail what a lost arm was worth, a lost leg, and so on. They even went as far as to assign different insurance values depending on whether it was, for instance, the right or left appendage that was mutilated or lost, according to the importance pirates assigned to these body parts.

Another manifestation of these incentive provisions was the use of bonuses for crew members who displayed particular courage in battle, were the first to spot potential targets, and so on. Because pirate crews were large, quartermasters couldn't easily monitor individual pirates' effort. This is why pirates used profit sharing rather than fixed wages for payment.

The problem with a share system is that it can create incentives for free riding. Further, one team member's laziness directly reduces the income of the others. To deal with this, pirates, like privateers and whalers, who also used a share system, created bonuses. According to the rule aboard Exquemelin's buccaneering vessel, for instance, "Those who behaved courageously and performed any deed of extraordinary valour, or captured a ship, should be rewarded out of the common plunder" (Exquemelin 1678: 156). Or as Johnson (1726–1728: 191) records, "It must be observed, they [pirates] keep a good Look-out; for, according to their Articles, he who first espies a Sail, if she proves a Prize, is entitled the best Pair of Pistols on board, over and above his Dividend."

Finally, pirate articles stipulated punishments for failure to adhere to their rules. As previously discussed, for more minor infractions, crews typically delegated punishment power to the ship's democratically elected quartermaster. As Johnson (1726–1728: 213) described it, the quartermaster "acts as a Sort of civil Magistrate on board a Pyrate Ship."[35] In the case of more severe infractions, crew members voted on punishments. In both cases pirate

---

[35] Thus, the quartermaster also refereed duels between conflicting parties, which would take place on land so as not to destroy the ship (Johnson 1726–1728: 212; see also, 339): "The Quarter-Master of the Ship, when the Parties will not come to any Reconciliation, accompanies them on Shore with what Assistance he thinks proper, and turns the Disputants Back to Back, at so many paces Distance: At the Word of Command, they turn and fire

crews tended to follow the punishments for various infractions identified
in their articles. By specifying punishments in their articles, crews were able
to limit the scope of quartermasters' discretion in administering discipline,
checking quartermasters' power for abuse.

Punishments for article violations varied from physical torture, such as
"slitting the Ears and Nose of him that was Guilty," to marooning – a practice
Captain Johnson (1726–1728: 211) described as the "barbarous Custom of
putting the Offender on Shore, on some desolate or uninhabited Cape or
Island, with a Gun, a few Shot, a Bottle of Water, and a Bottle of Powder,
to subsist with or starve."[36] On Captain Phillips's ship, for example, article
violations were punished with "Moses's Law (that is, 40 Stripes lacking one)
on the bare back" (Johnson 1726–1728: 342–343).

In this sense "Pirates exercised greater cruelty in maintaining discipline
among themselves than in their treatment of prisoners" (Rankin 1969: 37).
Pirates considered theft aboard their ships especially heinous. Their articles
reflected this and frequently punished theft with torture, marooning, or
death. To help keep themselves honest, some crews used random searches
to hunt for anyone who might be holding back loot (Exquemelin 1678: 205–
206).[37] To ensure the quartermaster didn't hide booty from the crew, some
pirates prohibited their valuable plunder from being kept under lock-and-
key. As pirate captive Peter Hooff described the situation on Captain Sam
Bellamy's *Whydah*, for instance, the "money was kept in Chests between
Decks without any Guard, but none was to take any without the Quarter
Masters leave" (Rediker 2004: 67; see also Marx 1996a: 44).

Because pirate constitutions tended to be short and simple, they couldn't
cover all possible contingencies that might affect a crew. In this sense they
were always incomplete. To deal with this, when a significant issue emerged,
the crew gathered to act as a kind of judiciary to interpret or apply the
ship's articles to situations not clearly stipulated in the articles themselves
(Johnson 1726–1728: 213): "In Case any Doubt should arise concerning the
Construction of these Laws, and it should remain a Dispute whether the
Party had infringed them or no, a Jury was appointed to explain them, and
bring in a Verdict upon the Case in Doubt." Through this "judicial review"

---

immediately. . . . If both miss, they come to their Cutlashes, and then he is declared Victor
who draws the first blood."

[36] Marooning was frequently coupled with ostracism in the event that the transgressor
managed to survive. See, for instance, Exquemelin (1678: 72).

[37] Oath taking was also commonly used among pirates as a method of staking one's reputation
to help enforce piratical articles and custom. See, for instance, Exquemelin (1678: 68, 71–
72, 100, 104, 156, 161).

process pirate crews were able to further limit quartermasters' discretionary authority, restraining the potential for quartermaster abuse.

The historical record points to the effectiveness of pirate constitutions in this capacity, evidenced by the rarity of accounts of quartermaster abuse. Equally important, in the infrequent event that abuse did occur, the evidence indicates that crews successfully removed abusive quartermasters from power. For example, in 1691 quartermaster Samuel Burgess cheated his crew in the division of food. In response his crew marooned him (Rogozinski 2000: 177).

The evidence also suggests that piratical constitutions were successful in preventing internal conflict and creating order aboard pirate ships. Pirates, it appears, strictly adhered to their articles. According to one historian, pirates were more orderly, peaceful, and well organized among themselves than many of the colonies, merchant ships, or vessels of the Royal Navy (Rogozinski 2000). As one astonished pirate observer put it, "At sea, they perform their duties with a great deal of order, better even than on the Ships of the Dutch East India Company; the pirates take a great deal of pride in doing things right" (Bucquoy 1744: 116).[38] Or, as the editor of the 1699 edition of Exquemelin's pirate memoir described buccaneer society (Exquemelin 1699: Anonymous Editor's Preface), "it is very remarkable, that in such a lawless Body as these Bucaniers seemed to be, in respect to all others; that yet there should be such an Oeconomy (if I may say so) kept and regularity practiced among themselves, so that every one seemed to have his property as much secured, as if he had been a member of the most Civilized Community in the World."

An eighteenth-century commentator was even more impressed with the effectiveness of pirate self-governance in this regard, but, in his astonishment, couldn't help but misconstrue their private system of self-governance as government. Their constitutions, he argued, "which kept Peace amongst one another, and under the Title of Articles, has produced a System of Government, which I think, (considering what the Persons were who fram'd it) as excellent for Policy as any Thing in *Plato*'s Commonwealth" (*Weekly Journal* May 23, 1724). While it seems strange to think about such order prevailing among pirates, the peculiarity fades when one recognizes that their organized criminal enterprise's success depended on it.

And succeed many pirates did. Although there aren't data that would allow me to compute anything like the average pirate's wage, what evidence is available suggests that incredibly large pirate prizes weren't unheard of.

---

[38] Translated and quoted in Rogozinski (2000: viii).

Of course, this evidence must be interpreted with caution. These seizures were recorded precisely because of their spectacular size. More common were undoubtedly more modest prizes. Nevertheless, the examples we have are enough to point to the significant success of piratical plunder in some cases and the opportunity piracy offered sailors for becoming incredibly wealthy.

"At a time when Anglo-American seamen on a trading voyage to Madagascar were collecting less than twelve pounds sterling a year . . . the deepwater pirates could realize a hundred or even a thousand times more" (Marx 1996c: 141). In 1695, for example, Henry Every's pirate fleet captured a prize carrying more than £600,000 in precious metals and jewels. The resulting shareout earned each member of his crew £1,000, the equivalent of nearly forty years' income for an able merchant seaman at the time (Konstam 2007: 98). In the early eighteenth century Captain John Bowen's pirate crew plundered a prize "which yielded them 500 l. per Man." Several years later Captain Thomas White's crew retired to Madagascar after a marauding expedition, each pirate having earned £1,200 from the cruise (Johnson 1726–1728: 480, 485). In 1720 Captain Christopher Condent's crew seized a prize that earned each pirate £3,000. Similarly, in 1721 Captain John Taylor and Oliver La Bouche's pirate consort earned an astonishing £4,000 for each crew member from a single attack (Marx 1996c: 161, 163). Even the small pirate crew captained by John Evans in 1722 took enough booty to split "nine thousand Pounds among thirty Persons" – or £300 a pirate – in less than six months "on the account" (Johnson 1726–1728: 340). To put these earnings in perspective, compare them to the average able merchant seaman's wage over the same period. Between 1689 and 1740 this varied from 25 to 55 shillings per month – a meager £15–£33 per year (Davis 1962: 136–137).

Absent data for a larger number of pirate hauls, it's impossible to say whether the average seventeenth- or eighteenth-century pirate consistently earned more than the average seventeenth- or eighteenth-century merchant sailor. It's certainly possible that this was the case, however. As one pirate testified at his trial, for instance, "it is a common thing for us [pirates] when at Sea to acquire vast quantities, both of the Metal that goes before me [silver, referring to the silver oar of the Admiralty court], and of Gold" (Hayward 1735: vol. 1, 45).

This pirate's remark may reflect his desire to impress the court more than it reflects piracy's profitability. Still, what the evidence on pirate booty does clearly point to is the tremendous potential upside of piratical employment.

Unlike employment as a merchant sailor, which guaranteed a low, if more regular, income, a single successful pirating expedition could make a sailor wealthy enough to retire. This is no doubt largely the reason why, as one eighteenth-century colonial governor remarked, "so many are willing to joyn them [pirates] when taken" (Colonial Office Papers May 31, 1718: f. 18).[39]

The financial rewards of securing successful self-governance motivated pirates to do just that despite the difficulty of doing so in their societies composed exclusively of bad apples. The remark of one perceptive eighteenth-century observer indicates precisely this. As he put it, "great robbers as they are to all besides, [pirates] are precisely just among themselves; without which they could no more Subsist than a Structure without a Foundation" (Slush 1709: viii).[40]

"[K]ings were not needed to invent the pirate system of governance" (Rogozinski 2000: 184). And, as the next essay discusses, they aren't needed to invent systems of self-governance in other outlaw societies either. Captain Charles Johnson (1726–1728: 114) described pirates' criminal organization as "that abominable Society." However abominable, because of pirates' self-governing system, it was a society nonetheless.

---

[39] Quoted in Rediker (2006: 260).
[40] Quoted in Rediker (2006: 287).

7

Criminal Constitutions*

Caribbean pirates aren't the only society of bad apples that relied on constitutions to produce successful self-governance. Many outlaw societies do so. Twenty-two of the thirty-seven street gangs Jankowski (1991: 78–82) studied have written constitutions. Sicilian Mafiosi follow a largely unwritten code of rules, and recently police found a written set of "ten commandments" outlining the Mafia's core laws (Gambetta 1993; Lubrano 2007). Kaminski (2004) identifies extensive (yet unwritten) rules dictating nearly every aspect of incarcerated Polish prisoners' lives, from what words are acceptable to use in greeting a stranger to how and when to use the bathroom. And the National Gang Crime Research Center considers constitutions so central to criminal societies that the use of a constitution is one of the defining characteristics it uses when classifying gangs (Knox 2006: 22–25).

This essay develops a framework for thinking about the prevalence of constitutional self-governance in criminal societies rooted in the idea of profit-maximizing outlaws.[1] Unlike most legitimate societies, criminal ones, such as pirates', are also *organizations* – groups of people who come together seeking cooperation for a narrow purpose. Firms are organizations that have profit as that purpose and, ultimately, criminal organizations have this as their purpose too. In contrast to legitimate firms, however, criminal

---

* This chapter is based on and uses material from Leeson, Peter T., and David B. Skarbek. 2010. "Criminal Constitutions." *Global Crime* 11(3): 279–298 [© 2010 Taylor & Francis].

[1] The organizational issues confronting criminals are part of a larger literature on the economics of crime that examines the determinants of crime (Levitt 2004; Glaeser, Sacerdote, and Scheinkman 1996), its social costs (Anderson 1999), optimal deterrence theories, (Levitt 1998), and policy implications (DiIulio 1996; Miron and Zwiebel 1995). This literature was pioneered by Becker (1968). See also Anderson (1979); Reuter (1985); Jennings (1984); Arlacchi (1988); Dick (1995); Konrad and Skaperdas (1998); Garoupa (2000); Chang et al. (2005).

ones must produce *social order* to maximize profit. Hewlett-Packard doesn't need a constitutional rule that prohibits murder, nor does the Kiwanis Club. Instead, these organizations' members rely on the government's rules that prohibit murder. In contrast, criminals have *no* rules of social order unless their organizations create them. It's in this sense that criminal organizations are more than ordinary firms and, in fact, more than ordinary organizations more generally: they're also societies. The key to understanding how criminal organizations use constitutions to maximize profit therefore lies in understanding how they use constitutions to produce organizational cooperation in this broad and most basic sense.[2] To illustrate how they do so, I examine the constitutional self-governance of a contemporary Californian prison gang: La Nuestra Familia.

A FRAMEWORK FOR UNDERSTANDING CRIMINAL CONSTITUTIONS

Constitutions perform three functions that help criminal organizations create cooperation. First, they create consensus by generating common knowledge about the organization's rules. If the criminals who compose an organization have different ideas and expectations about what members' rights and duties consist of, how the organization does or should work, or what the organization's goals are, conflict is likely and criminals will often work at cross-purposes. In contrast, common knowledge exists when all members of an organization know the rules, everyone knows that everyone knows the rules, and everyone knows that everyone knows that everyone knows the rules, ad infinitum.

Constitutions create common knowledge by making the organization's rules explicit. They enumerate the most critical expectations of members' behavior, such as how members join, the rules of organizational decision making, the rules of commitment, the rights of membership, and restrictions on members' behavior.[3] Common knowledge about the organization's

---

[2] The difficulties of criminal enterprise extend beyond cooperation within the organization and to strategic cooperative and noncooperative games with victims, other criminals, and the police. See, for example, Konrad and Skaperdas (1997, 1998), Gambetta (1994), and Smith and Varese (2001).

[3] Successful criminal cooperation within the organization is necessary but not sufficient for the organization to succeed. Characteristics of life outside of the criminal organization, such as the local economy, also affect their ability to thrive. For example, examining the 'Ndrangheta in Northern Italy, Varese (2006a) argues that construction companies' reliance on illegal workers provided an important opportunity for the 'Ndrangheta to establish itself. These two spheres – one within the organization and the other being the

rules creates common expectations among the organization's members. Whether they're written or unwritten, because they're *constitutional* rules, the organization requires that all members be introduced to these rules and familiar with their essential components. The organization introduces potential members to constitutional rules so that potential members have an understanding of what the rules entail when making their decision about joining. Common expectations promote intraorganizational consensus by putting all of the organization's members "on the same page" with respect to duties, privileges, and obligations of their and others' membership. In achieving this, constitutions greatly reduce the potential for intraorganizational conflicts and facilitate the enforcement of constitutional provisions.

Criminal constitutions also promote consensus by creating entrance requirements for would-be members. If each would-be member must acknowledge and agree to the organization's constitutional rules before they can join, every other member of the organization can have greater confidence that the would-be member's intentions comport with their own. Requiring ex ante agreement to constitutional rules serves to sort would-be organization members into those who agree to be bound by the organization's constitutional rules, and thus are permitted membership, and those who refuse to be bound by these rules, and thus are denied membership. The organization therefore consists only of criminals who agree to be bound by the same set of rules that other members have agreed to be bound by.

Having all of a criminal organization's members' expectations aligned is particularly important for outlaws precisely because they're outlaws. The possibility of a disgruntled organization member providing law enforcement with sensitive information poses a serious threat to the organization's existence and profitability. In contrast, legitimate organizations don't typically fear a dismissed employee, even when disgruntled, because they're not engaged in illegal activity. Furthermore, state-enforced contracts, such as nondisclosure agreements, effectively protect legitimate organizations' sensitive information. Thus, while having the same high level of constitutional commitment across members is critically important for criminal organizations, it's less important for legitimate ones.

Second, criminal constitutions regulate individual behaviors that are privately beneficial but harmful to the organization. In legitimate organizations individuals have opportunities to engage in behaviors that improve their

environment in which the organization acts – can affect each other too. For example, the reciprocal influence between the Yakuza and Japanese films on organized crime led to the latter's decline and reduced the former's reputational capital (Varese 2006b).

own situation but adversely affect others in the organization. This is also true in criminal organizations. For instance, the leaders of a criminal organization may use their positions of authority to prey on lower-ranking members. If lower-ranking members must devote resources to avoiding their superiors' predation, organizational productivity declines. Unless the organization's leader is the sole residual claimant on the organization's profits (in which case he fully capitalizes the productivity losses of his predation), he may have an incentive to engage in predation.

Alternatively, lower-ranking organization members may be tempted to engage in activities that undermine their colleagues' welfare. For example, a drug-selling gang may have an agreement with a neighboring gang not to sell drugs in the latter's territory. This agreement is beneficial for both gangs as a whole because it prevents a costly war. However, an individual gang member of the former group can benefit by "chiseling" and selling drugs in the other gang's territory against the agreement. If his chiseling goes undetected, this gang member will enjoy profits that his fellow gang members (and the members of the other gang) don't. But if the other gang detects him, the chiseler's behavior may lead to a war against his gang, which will harm the chiseler, but only by a fraction of the total harm his gang incurs.

Other behaviors in which members of criminal organizations may engage can also generate significant negative spillovers for their colleagues. Consider, for example, "communication cheating." Because they wish to avoid arrest and incarceration, criminal organizations often create rules restricting the manner and timing of intraorganizational communication. For example, prison gang members develop elaborate codes and ciphers, learn obscure languages, such as the Aztec language Nahuatl, hide messages in artwork, and even write letters in urine, which correctional officers are less likely to see, but which can be revealed by a knowing recipient.[4]

Communication restrictions are very important for the overall criminal organization but are costly for individual organization members to follow. It's difficult and unpleasant to write and decode secret messages written in urine. An individual gang member may desire to avoid these costly communication techniques but, by doing so, risks providing evidence that can incriminate members of the entire organization. This is especially so in the United States where the Pinkerton Doctrine makes each co-conspirator in a criminal enterprise responsible for reasonably foreseeable crimes

---

[4] For a discussion of the rules governing inter-criminal communication, see Gambetta (2009).

committed by all other members of the organization (*Pinkerton v. United States* 328 U.S. 640 1946). Each member's ability to commit crimes covertly therefore significantly affects others' livelihoods. Constitutional rules that deter such behaviors prevent privately beneficial but organizationally costly behaviors that threaten to undermine organization members' ability to cooperate. In this way constitutions help criminals cope with divergences between intraorganizational private and social costs that would otherwise threaten criminals' ability to work together for profit.

Third, criminal constitutions generate information about member misconduct and coordinate the enforcement of the organization's rules. In the absence of explicit rules defining acceptable behavior, it can be hard for members to know whether one of their colleagues' questionable behaviors is legitimate or not. Further, if one member observes misconduct, he may be unlikely to intercede to stop it. If he alone challenges his comrade's behavior, he may be subject to reprisals. Even if an organization member is willing to risk challenging and attempting to discipline another member, he may find it hard to do so successfully if effective discipline, such as multilateral punishment, must be jointly produced.

Criminal constitutions help overcome these obstacles to rule enforcement. Because constitutions explicitly define acceptable behavior and stipulate penalties for violating such behavior, they make rule violations easier to detect and coordinate members' response to these violations. Constitutions clarify ambiguities about when misconduct has occurred and about how members are supposed to react to such behavior. Additionally, by creating common expectations among all organization members about how to handle misconduct, constitutions assist the enforcement of their terms by improving the probability that multiple members will challenge prohibited behavior by another member. In this way constitutions also make jointly produced punishments possible.

Criminal constitutions vary considerably in their length, level of detail, and focus. Some organizations emphasize one of the three functions discussed earlier, while other organizations emphasize others. These differences reflect particular criminal organizations' specific needs. For example, given the different criminal activities in which Caribbean pirates and California prison gangs are engaged, and the different contexts in which they operate, these criminal organizations have rather different criminal constitutions. Despite these variations in emphasis, both organizations' constitutions perform all three functions I have described.

Chapter 7 considered the constitutions of Caribbean pirates. Here I consider the constitution of a Californian prison gang. However, in doing so, it's useful to recall the features of pirates' constitutions. To facilitate a comparison of the similarities and differences between the particular ways in which each criminal organization's constitution performs the functions discussed above, the appendix to this essay contains each organization's constitution in full. In that appendix I code each element of both criminal organizations' constitutions comprehensively to correspond to the three functions of criminal constitutions elaborated earlier.

A CONSTITUTION FOR CONVICTS

La Nuestra Familia (Spanish for "Our Family") prison gang controls Northern California prison cellblocks and neighborhoods. In addition to narcotics distribution, it earns profits through robbery, murder for hire, and various other criminal exploits (Federal Bureau of Investigation 2008; California Department of Justice 2003).

Hispanic inmates established the gang in the 1960s. To do so the gang's founders wrote "The Supreme Power Structure of La Nuestra Familia," a lengthy constitution that details the structure and operational protocols of La Nuestra Familia's criminal organization.[5] The nuestro general, to whom the constitution granted "absolute authority," initially led the organization. He supervised ten captains, each of whom resided in a different correctional facility. Each of these captains in turn directed regiments consisting of lieutenants and soldiers.

La Nuestra Familia (NF) confronts substantial organizational difficulties. Law enforcement officials estimate its membership between 400 and 600 incarcerated members. Additionally, though not official NF members, approximately 1,000 "associates" regularly work for the gang (Lewis 1980: 133; Fuentes 2006: 297). Unlike the members of a Caribbean pirate outfit, who sailed together in one crew, the NF's members are scattered throughout the California prison system and Northern California neighborhoods. Running the equivalent of a large business without government, under the constraints of incarceration, and with members dispersed across a large geographic area seems virtually impossible. Yet the NF's constitution successfully facilitates this criminal organization's operations by creating consensus, constraining organizationally harmful behavior, and generating information about misconduct.

---

[5] The NF constitution has changed over the years. I focus on the constitution as it was originally written. It's taken from a recent history of the Nuestra Familia (Fuentes 2006) and reproduced in the appendix at the end of the chapter.

The NF constitution creates consensus by clarifying members' expectations through making organizational duties explicit. According to the constitution, "It is the sacred duty of a familianos *guerrero* [warrior] to do battle for La Nuestra Familia, and no soldado should feel that because he fought for his O that he is entitled to special privileges. All that matters is that you as a *guerrero* of La Nuestra Familia are living up to your responsibilities." The constitution also requires that "No member of this O shall put material things, whether it be drugs, money, women, or punks (as related to the *pinta*) before the best interest of La Nuestra Familia or a familianos," and that "[n]o familiano shall lie about his position in La Nuestra Familia nor when discussing familianos business to a superior or a brother member" (Fuentes 2006: 10). Further, the NF constitution requires all gang members to swear to work "for the betterment of its members and the building up of this O on the outside into a strong and self-supporting familia" and to "work solely for this objective and will put all personal goals and feelings aside" (Fuentes 2006: 5).

Like Caribbean pirates who used agreement to their constitutions to filter organizational membership by requiring all members to explicitly agree to the organization's rules ex ante, the NF constitution creates consensus by ensuring that every person who joins the NF explicitly acknowledges familiarity with the constitution and agrees to its provisions. According to the NF constitution, "All present familianos in said O La Nuestra Familia acknowledges said constitution upon reading it and will be held accountable for his actions if said constitution is not followed" (Fuentes 2006: 6). Notably, all organization members swear allegiance to the constitution rather than to a particular gang leader.

The NF constitution also creates consensus by enshrining the organization's policy of "blood in, blood out," which requires that "[a] Familiano will remain a member until death or otherwise discharged from the O" (Fuentes 2006: 5). Because of this provision, gang members know that to exit the organization they must pay the ultimate price. This rule gives gang members a strong incentive to create consensus and cooperation within the organization. Mandatory lifetime membership also lowers the uncertainty associated with frequently changing organization members. Given the high constitutionally created barriers to entering and exiting the organization, radical changes in its composition, which might disturb organizational consensus, are less likely.

The NF constitution prevents organization members from engaging in privately beneficial but organizationally harmful activities by creating rules that prohibit them. In the NF the most important such behavior that must be prevented is gang leader self-dealing. The NF's hierarchical structure permits the organization to reduce decision-making costs for many issues that would be very costly or in some cases impossible to decide if the entire organization had to consult. However, a hierarchical structure also empowers leaders with authority they may be tempted to abuse for personal benefit.

For example, because exit is very costly, the general may have an incentive to abuse his power and mistreat his underlings. To prevent this, the NF constitution gives captains the right to impeach the general for misconduct. According to the constitution, the "NG may be impeached from office where it is the opinion of all commanders holding office at that time that he isn't working in the best interest of the organization" (Fuentes 2006: 5). In 1978 NF members learned the then-general was embezzling tens of thousands of dollars from the organization's treasury. According to a former high-ranking member, the general denied "any wrong doing and refused to relinquish any financial records. Believing that something should be done, NF members charged [the general] with misappropriating NF funds and impeached him." When the general refused to relinquish his post and return the funds, the organization invoked the constitutionally prescribed punishment for such a crime: death (Fuentes 2006: 28).

Surprisingly, the general lived through the organization's attack on his life. But the NF expelled him from the gang and he remained on the organization's hit list.[6] Because the general was embezzling resources to which the captains had a partial claim, it was in their interest to initiate the constitutionally specified process of enforcement to put a stop to it. However, if each individual captain had been unsure about the rules or his authority to censure a higher-ranking member, this predatory behavior may have continued. Constitutional rules provided common knowledge about what constituted a violation, so members were able to coordinate enforcement through constitutionally established mechanisms.

NF captains, who control their own regiments, may be similarly tempted to abuse their authority for personal gain at the organization's expense. The variety of potential abuses is large and ranges from stealing from underlings to shirking organizational duties. To prevent such behavior, the NF constitution empowers the general "to discharge any commander that is negligent in the functions of his position" (Fuentes 2006: 4). Because the general is a partial residual claimant on the revenues created by the NF's activities, it's

---

[6] Former law enforcement members have identified other situations in which organization members impeached a leader for violating the NF's rules. See, for instance, Morales (2008).

in his interest to enforce such punishments providing that doing so is not prohibitively costly. By clarifying his demotion of the negligent captain as a legitimate act of rule enforcement, as opposed to an abuse of his authority, to the gang's other members and coordinating these members' support of this act, the NF constitution reduces the general's cost of enforcing such punishments to make this possible. For instance, the NF leadership demoted one captain outside of prison for being lax in his operations and failing to properly enforce the NF's order within his regiment in favor of a captain who would do so (Reynolds 2008).

The NF constitution creates information about when organizational misconduct occurs and coordinates organization members' response to such behavior by creating an official complaint process that members may use to inform the organization about colleagues' misconduct. Such misconduct includes mistreatment and mismanagement by their superiors who are, for example, running their regiment inefficiently. According to the NF constitution, "if a familianos soldado feels that the power or powers of the structure in his regiment is misusing their appointed authority against him due to conflicting personalities, he has the right as an honorable member of this O to appeal to the supreme commander" (Fuentes 2006: 8). During times of peace, soldiers may complain to captains or the general if lieutenants violate constitutional rules or unfairly demote members. Lieutenants may appeal to the general if they have grievances against the captain of their regiment or if he is derelict in his duties. Given that soldiers suffer directly if their lieutenants mistreat them, and lieutenants suffer directly if their captains mistreat them, both groups have an incentive to appeal to such mechanisms to enforce the organization's rules against misbehaving superiors and the constitution's coordinating effect makes doing so sufficiently inexpensive.

When organization members file grievances, the constitution requires that "upon receiving a complaint from one of his soldados ... [the Nuestro General] will appoint a committee of no less than three soldados from that particular clan to investigate said charges, and each is to report to the NG" (Fuentes 2006: 4).[7] This information-generating process is important for

---

[7] Other gangs also use official complaint processes to coordinate the enforcement of rules. Evidence about the Melanic Islamic Palace of the Rising Sun prison gang, for example, sheds light on what happened when a member filed a complaint accusing another member of being a law enforcement informant in a past court case. The leader recorded the accusation, requested evidence on the person's guilt, and shared this information with other members who reached the conclusion that the individual was guilty. The gang leaders conveyed their judgment, writing "That Melid #2 [the criminal organization's name] have competently

three reasons. First, it provides an orderly and peaceable mechanism for investigating and resolving disagreements between organization members. Second, by involving multiple members of the organization, this process helps generate common knowledge about suspected rule violations and, if these suspicions turn out to be supported, helps generate common knowledge that a rule violation has occurred and requires punishment, facilitating the enforcement of constitutionally specified rules.[8] Finally, by making the procedure for addressing potential rule violations explicit, the NF constitution coordinates organization members on how to respond to rule violations and ensures that there will in fact be a response. Potential rule violations in such a large organization are liable to slip through the cracks, especially if members who observe them are unsure about if or how to address them. The NF's constitution attenuates this problem by creating an explicit means of addressing potential rule violations, which creates information about such violations and helps ensure that members follow the rules.

It would be a mistake to think that criminals always strictly follow their organizations' constitutions. Like legitimate political officers operating under legitimate constitutions, criminals may violate or ignore their constitutions. Similarly, like those officers, criminals may come to interpret their constitutions in ways that are at odds with their "original intent." Even when they're followed, criminal constitutions' helpfulness in promoting social order and cooperation within criminal organizations is imperfect. Criminal constitutions weren't able to eliminate all conflict among Caribbean pirate crews, and neither are they able to do so in the NF. Still, as I discuss later, existing evidence on which criminal organizations use constitutions supports the idea that criminal constitutions are effective much of the time, which explains why many outlaw organizations use them.

In light of the benefits my discussion suggests constitutions create for criminal organizations, why doesn't *every* criminal organization rely on a constitution? My framework for understanding criminal constitutions' prevalence suggests that criminal organizations adopt constitutions because

witnessed by personally reading the [court] transcripts that the information contained therein displays a true violation of Sup. Const., Art. V, Cl.5" (Knox 2004).

[8] Gang members who aren't directly harmed by a rule violator's behavior are willing to aid gang members who are directly harmed because at some point the former expect to seek the punishment assistance of the latter when a rule violator does directly harm them. Gang members who refuse to help their colleagues now will be refused help by their colleagues in the future. Gang members are therefore led through repeated interaction to find it in their interest to assist others in enforcing constitutional rules even when they don't immediately or directly benefit by doing so. This, of course, is an application of the discipline of continuous dealings.

they produce social order by promoting organizational consensus, regulating externality generating behaviors, and helping enforce organizational rules, which in turn enhances profits. But constitutions aren't the only way to achieve these goals.

For example, families often secure a high degree of internal consensus, restrict privately beneficial activities that could be destructive to the whole, and enforce rules without the aid of written constitutions. They rely on their members' extremely small numbers, close proximity, and social closeness to facilitate these ends instead. Even if families didn't benefit from the broad social order that government provides, these features would largely preclude the kind of social dilemma that persons face when they're part of larger populations, located more remotely from one another, and aren't closely related by blood or otherwise, and thus preclude the kind of problem situation in which constitutions might provide significant benefits.

Criminal organizations that share family-type features can also achieve these ends without constitutions. Those that are small, have highly homogeneous membership, and reside in close proximity to one another will benefit less from creating constitutions. Because of their particular features, such organizations enjoy "natural" consensus, find it cheaper to identify organizationally harmful behavior, and find it easier to coordinate an effective response to such behavior.

Because, like creating any contract, creating a constitution is costly, the lower benefit of constitutions to small, homogeneous criminal organizations makes such organizations less likely to adopt constitutions than large criminal organizations whose members are scattered and don't have strong extra-organizational ties. This suggests that some criminal organizations with these characteristics will find creating a constitution unprofitable and so won't have one. And the evidence is consistent with this suggestion. Knox (2006: 22–25), for example, notes that the use of criminal constitutions is associated with larger group size and more complicated operations. Similarly, Jankowski (1991: 82) finds that smaller street gangs that engage in simple criminal activities are less likely to rely on constitutions than larger, more sophisticated gangs are.

In supporting the idea that criminal organizations only adopt constitutions when they anticipate net benefits from doing so, this evidence also supports the idea that criminal constitutions are often effective. If they weren't, constitutions would typically pose net costs to criminal organizations that adopted them, making it puzzling why *any* criminal organization would choose to adopt them, let alone why many criminal organizations choose to.

Just as some criminal organizations don't find it profitable to create constitutions at all, my discussion highlights that among the criminal organizations that do find it profitable to create constitutions, points of constitutional emphasis will differ across those organizations. This reflects different criminal organizations' specific contexts and thus needs. For example, compared to the NF, eighteenth-century Caribbean pirates found it easier to detect rule violations because their organizations were much smaller and their organizations' members were in much closer proximity to one another.[9] Pirates could obtain information about rule infractions more easily than NF members can. The need to create information about rule violations through constitutions in pirates' organization was therefore less urgent than in the NF. Consequently, pirate constitutions emphasized consensus building and the coordination of diverse individuals more than they emphasized generating information about misconduct. In contrast, NF members are almost all Californian Hispanics. Because of this, consensus is easier to attain in this criminal organization than it was among pirates. However, because the NF is very large and its membership is dispersed, it faces significantly higher costs of generating information about rule violations. The NF's constitution therefore focuses more on mechanisms that facilitate the discovery of misconduct.

Despite these important differences in constitutional specifics, all criminal organizations that use constitutions do so for the same basic purpose: to facilitate social cooperation in the face of information costs, coordination problems, and externalities that threaten such cooperation without government and thus criminals' ability to maximize profit. Through those constitutions, criminal organizations are able to secure successful self-governance despite the fact that the societies they reflect are populated exclusively by bad apples.

APPENDIX

This appendix reproduces the constitutions of Captain Bartholomew Robert's pirate crew and La Nuestra Familia prison gang. The former is contained in the eighteenth-century pirate chronicler Captain Charles Johnson's

---

[9] Monitoring production activities, however, was probably more difficult in pirate organizations than it was in the NF despite pirate organizations' smaller size and more physically concentrated membership. As Leeson and Rogers (2012) point out, piracy's production activities were necessarily jointly produced and therefore harder to monitor. In contrast, many of the production activities of the NF are individually produced and thus easier to monitor.

(1726–1728) book, *A General History of the Pyrates.* The latter is contained in Nina Fuentes's (2006) *The Rise and Fall of the Nuestra Familia.*

I have coded each component of these constitutions (in parenthesis) to identify its function in terms of the theory of criminal constitutions presented earlier. Code (1) indicates that a provision relates to the common knowledge function of criminal constitutions. Code (2) indicates that a provision limits behavior within organizations that may be individually beneficial but harmful to the organization. Code (3) indicates that a provision provides information about misconduct and/or mechanisms for enforcement. A constitutional provision can perform multiple purposes, so many of the provisions have been coded for multiple functions.

The Constitution of Captain Bartholomew Roberts's Pirate Crew

   I Every Man has a Vote in the Affairs of Moment; has equal Title to the fresh Provisions, or strong Liquors, at any Time seized, and may use them at Pleasure, unless a Scarcity make it necessary, for the Good of all, to vote a Retrenchment. (1, 3)

  II Every Man to be called fairly in Turn, by List, on board of Prizes, because, (over and above their proper Share) they were on these Occasions allowed a Shift of Cloaths: But if they defrauded the Company to the Value of a Dollar, in Plate, Jewels, or Money, Marooning was their Punishment. If the Robbery was only betwixt one another, they contented themselves with slitting the Ears and Nose of him that was Guilty, and set him on Shore, not in an uninhabited Place, but somewhere, where he was sure to encounter Hardships. (1, 3)

 III No person to Game at Cards or Dice for Money. (2)

  IV The Lights and Candles to be put out at eight a-Clock at Night: If any of the Crew, after that Hour, still remained enclined for Drinking, they were to do it on the open Deck. (2)

   V To keep their Piece, Pistols, and Cutlash clean, and fit for Service. (2)

  VI No Boy or Woman to be allowed amongst them. If any Man were found seducing any of the latter Sex, and carry'd her to Sea, disguised, he was to suffer Death. (2)

 VII To Desert the Ship, or their Quarters in Battle, was punished with Death or Marooning. (3)

VIII No striking one another on board, but every Man's Quarrels to be ended on Shore, at Sword and Pistol. (2)

   IX No Man to talk of breaking up their Way of Living, till each shared a 1000 l. If in order to this, any Man should lose a Limb, or become a Cripple in their Service, he was to have 800 Dollars, out of the public Stock, and for lesser Hurts, proportionately. (2)

   X The Captain and Quarter-Master to receive two Shares of a Prize; the Master, Boatswain, and Gunner, one Share and a half, and other Officers one and a Quarter. (1)

   XI The Musicians to have Rest on the Sabbath Day, but the other six Days and Nights, none without special Favour. (3)

The Supreme Power Structure of Nuestra Familia

Article 1: Supreme Commander

Section I. The Nuestro General (NG) is the supreme power in the organization known as La Nuestra Familia. His power shall have no limit (within Art. I, II, III). Solely he can declare war for the entire O and once in a state of war, peace shall not prevail until the announcement from the NG. (1, 3)

Section II. NG will be automatically released from any duties and responsibilities upon receiving a date of one year or less. (1)

Section III. NG will be a seasoned experienced warrior. This qualification is mandatory in order to hold this high office. When the time comes for the NG to pick a successor, he will do so from the ranks of commanders at his disposal. (1, 3)

Section III (a). In case of emergency and the NG is downed, the captain at the *pinta* will take over and automatically declare war until the first captain can automatically assume the rank of NG. In this emergency, the home captain will have no power to appoint or replace any or all positions in the high command of La Nuestra Familia. (1, 3)

Section IV. NG has the power, in the state of war conditions (as regards to structure), to appoint captains. In peace time, he will retain the power to discharge any commander that is negligent in the functions of his position; however, he will relinquish his power to appoint captains if the *familia* where the captain has been discharged has no reserve captain to take command. The *familia* body of said disposed captain will elect a successor. (3)

Section IV (a). A discharged commander will lose his rank of captain and said authority of that rank. (1, 3)

Section V. Only applies in time of peace [sic]. (1)

Section V (a). NG, upon receiving a complaint from one of his *soldados* that the authority of which he is under is unjustly using their power over him due to personal conflict, he (NG) will appoint a committee of no less than three *soldados* from that particular clan to investigate said charges, and each is to report to the NG. (3)

Section VI. NG will always keep in touch with all *familianos* leaving to the streets, until a branch in union of La Nuestra Familia is established. (2)

Section VII. NG can have as many as ten (10) active commanders at one time. He will grade them as 1st, 2nd, 3rd, and so on according to their leadership abilities and their overall foresight. (1)

Section VIII. NG will appoint a first captain or commander who will be his successor, and if the NG becomes incommunicado, the first captain of the Nuestra Familia will have the responsibility to see that every captain of said O works and governs within this constitution. (1, 3)

Section IX. The successor only applies as far as the first captain is concerned. The NG has the right to select the first captain. (1, 3)

Article I (a). Discharge of All Duties from NG

Section I. NG may be impeached from office where it is the opinion of all commanders holding office at that time that he isn't working in the best interest of the organization. This can be derived from a petition or document with signatures in each captain's own writing. (3)

Section II. Upon receiving the document, the NG will automatically lose all power, but he may challenge the legality of the signatures, in which case a *soldado* will be appointed by the body to write to the captains and verify their votes. (3)

Section III. Upon confirmation of a discharge of the NG, he will lose all rank, power, and the successor will move into that position. (3)

Article II. Objectives and Bylaws of Nuestra Familia

Section I. The primary purpose and goals of this O is for the betterment of its members and the building up of this O on the outside into a strong and self-supporting *familia*. (1)

Section II. All members will work solely for this objective and will put all personal goals and feelings aside until said fulfillment is accomplished. (1)

Section III. A *familianos* will not be released from his obligation towards the O because he is released from prison, but will work twice as hard to see that a *familia* is established and works in hand with the O already established behind the walls (*pinta*). (1)

Section IV. A *familianos* will remain a member until death or otherwise discharged from the O. He will always be subject to put the best interest of the O first and always above everything else, in prison or out. (1, 3)

Section V. An automatic death sentence will be put on a *familianos* that turns coward, traitor or deserter. Under no other circumstances will a brother *familiano* be responsible for spilling the blood of another *familiano*. To do so will be considered an act of treason. (1, 3)

Section VI. In order for (Art. II, Sec. V) to be invoked, the regimental governing body will hold a vote amongst themselves and pass sentence. Majority rules. In the case of a tie vote, the decision will lie with the captain, and his decision shall be final. (3)

Section VII. All present familianos in said O La Nuestra Familia acknowledge said constitution upon reading it and will be held accountable for his actions if said constitution is not followed. (1)

Article III. Regimental Captains

Section I. A captain is the regimental commander of La Nuestra Familia and holds the rank just below el NG. Their responsibilities are to lead and direct La Familia regiments under his care to successfully accomplish the goals set forth in (Art. I, Sec. V). (1, 3)

Section II. For this purpose, he (captain) shall have the choice of selecting his own lieutenants (*tenientes*) and shall have the power to dismiss the lieutenant if he (captain) feels that they are not accepting or handling their responsibilities of leadership. In times of peace, a dismissed lieutenant has the option to invoke (Art. I, Sec. V). (1, 3)

Section III. Due to circumstances beyond our control, it may be that there will be more than one captain in a regiment at the same time. If a captain is transferred from a *familia* regiment to another where there is already a captain, the captain with the highest rank will take command, and the others will be in reserve according to their ranks. (1, 2, 3)

Section IV (a). A captain will have a grade rating of 1st, 2nd, 3rd and so forth, as (Art. III, Sec. III) can be invoked. Also, the lower the numbered rating, the greater their authority. No captain can override or contradict the orders of a higher-ranking commander without direction of Nuestra Familia's NG. (1, 3)

Section IV (b). All other captains in a regiment other than the governing captain will be classified as reserves and will act as advisors, although they will not have any powers as to the running of the regiment. (1, 3)

Section V. There shall never be more than ten (10) captains in the O at any time. This includes reserves. If there are already ten captains in the O and a regiment is without a captain or commander due to (Art. III, Sec. III), the 1st lieutenant will run the *familia* (regiment) temporarily until a commander arrives or there is an opening in the ranks of captain. (1, 3)

Section VI. The reserve captains will only take power if the governing one is downed or discharged by the NG. It will be the duty of the governing commander to take and show him the internal functions of the regiment in order that the reserve captain will be qualified to govern the regiment if need arrives. (1, 3)

Section VII. All captains will hold equal rank and therefore one cannot order the other, except under (Art. III, Sec. III), or where the reserve captain is hindering the rules and orders that the governing captain has set forth efficiently running the *familia* (regiment). In that case, the reserve captain will cease to interfere or he will be brought before the NG. (1, 2, 3)

Section VIII. The reserve captain only has as much power as the governing commander wants bestowed on him and not more. The *familia* body, should at all times know the structure of the reserve captain. (1, 3)

Section IX. In time of war, the captain is only answerable to the NG, and no *soldado* shall question the orders set forth by him personally or one of his *tenientes*. To question said orders could be a treasonable act, as outlined in (Art. I, II, Sec. V), depending on the seriousness of the offense, which will lie with the captain to determine. (1, 2, 3)

Section X. In time of peace, as in time of war, a captain is answerable to the NG; however, in time of peace, if a *familianos soldado* feels that the power or powers of the structure in the regiment is misusing their appointed authority against him due to conflicting personalities, he has a right as an honorable member of this O to appeal to the supreme commander NG, as per (Art. I, Sec. V). (3)

Section XI. The commander shall be responsible for the welfare and lives of the *soldados* under his command at all times, and there shall be no suicidal missions ordered by a commander. A suicidal mission shall be translated as an act where the *soldado* has no chance of survival. (3)

Section XII. Home captain where NG has his headquarters shall be held responsible if anything should happen to the NG. It will be the duty of the captain to personally see that two of his best warriors be with the NG whenever possible. If the NG is downed, the captain will be stripped of all rank after the state of war is over (Art. I, Sec. III a). (3)

Article IV. Functions and Qualities of a Lieutenant

Section I. A lieutenant is third in the power ladder of La Nuestra Familia, he is under the captain. He's the representative of La Nuestra Familia, as he will be in contact with *familianos* at all times and, therefore, he should at all times set a good example for the *soldados* to follow. (1)

Section II (a). While in a state of war, and the arms quota drops below the specified requirement, it shall be first priority of the lieu-tenant to restore to restore to par as outlined in (Art. V, Sec. II) [sic]. (1, 2, 3)

Section III. Each lieutenant shall have a certain number of *soldados* assigned to him. He shall be responsible for their schooling and basic needs and conduct. (1, 3)

Section III (a). Whenever one or all of his *soldados* goes into combat with any of the enemies of La Nuestra Familia, he (lieutenant) shall present the captain with a full report of what occurred. (1, 3)

Section IV. The lieutenants shall have ratings of 1st, 2nd, 3rd. This rating shall be given to them by the captain according to their experience and leadership abilities. (1, 3)

Section V. It shall be the duties of the lieutenants to keep a record of all known names and numbers of La Nuestra Familia. Each day, he shall check all new arrivals who entered his territory against his record book and make a report to his captain. (1)

Section V (a). All lieutenants shall question all new *familianos* assigned to him for information as to unknown enemies of La Nuestra Familia. New information shall go into the record book and whenever one of his *soldados* is transferred to another *pinta*, a copy of the record book shall be sent with the *soldado*. (1)

Section V (b). It shall be the responsibility of the lieutenant to inform the captain of the departure of his *soldados* in order that the *familia* of the other regiment can be informed. (1, 2)

Article V. *Familiano* Soldado

Section I. All requests for membership into this O shall be made to the captain. Any member can make such a request for any individual providing such requesting *familiano* is will to accept full responsibility for said individual. (1, 2)

Section II. Final decision for membership shall not be made until 30 days have elapsed from such a request, and the governing body of the regiment must approve the request for any new membership. (1, 2)

Section III. No applicant will be considered for membership if he (applicant) misrepresents his qualifications. Also, once a member and *soldado* misrepresents his actions in battle for the benefit of making his actions seem more valorous, he will be subject to be disqualified under (Art. II, Sec. V b), a minor offense, or (Art. I, Sec. V), expelled from the O, depending upon the circumstances and seriousness of the lie. (1, 2)

Section IV. Membership of this O shall be restricted only to those of Latin extraction. No maximum or minimum shall be invoked by this constitution in so far as membership in this O is concerned; however, such limitations may be established by NG as to be necessary to maintain proper control, although others of other extractions (races) will be considered with the consent of both the captain and the NG. (1, 2)

Article VI. Discipline and Conduct

Section I. The regimental captains shall pass sentence for all minor infractions of conduct. In time of war, there will be no appeal to NG. (1, 3)

Section II. Punishment shall be administered by the regimental lieutenant (Art. IV, Sec. III) or by the regiment as a whole, when ordered by the *familia* commander. (1, 3)

Section III. All *familianos* shall be subject to disciplinary action or immediate expulsion from this O (Art. II, Sec. V). In the case of misconduct or behavior unbecoming of a member, said conditions shall prevail with regards to the individual towards another member, the O as a whole, or his superiors. (1, 2, 3)

Section IV. Under no conditions will there be fighting between *familianos*. To do so will bring on disciplinary action and if blood is spilled, it will result in the expulsion of one or all parties involved (Art II, Sec V). (1, 2)

Section V. No member of this O shall put material things, whether it be drugs, money, women, or punks (as related to the *pinta*) before the best interest of La Nuestra Familia or a familianos. (1, 2)

Section V (a). No *familiano* shall lie about his position in La Nuestra Familia nor when discussing *familianos* business to a superior or a brother member. There shall be no lying or giving false impressions. (1, 2)

Section VI. It is the sacred duty of a *familianos guerrero* to do battle for La Nuestra Familia, and no *soldado* should feel that because he fought for his O that he is entitled to special privileges. All that matters is that you as a *guerrero* of La Nuestra Familia are living up to your responsibilities. Remember that a true *guerrero* does not need to boast of his accomplishments. (1, 2)

Section VII. Under no circumstances is any of this constitution to be altered without notification of el NG and one third of his captain's staff, nor shall a *familiano* or *familianos* regiment put their own interpretations upon said constitution. It is to be read in its entirety. All sections that relate to one concept are to be read as such. (1, 2)

PART IV

SELF-GOVERNANCE AS SUPERIOR
TO THE STATE

8

Efficient Anarchy[*]

Can anarchy be efficient? Conventional wisdom unequivocally answers no.[1] By providing monopolized social-rule creation and enforcement, government enables individuals to realize gains from cooperation they couldn't capture without it. Given the choice, welfare-maximizing persons therefore choose to form government. As Nobel Prize–winning economist Douglass North (1981: 24) puts it: "Throughout history, individuals given a choice between a state – no matter how exploitative it might be – and anarchy, have decided for the former."

The ubiquity of government today makes it easy to forget that numerous societies were stateless for most of their histories and that some remained so well into the twentieth century. Several of these societies encompassed many people. Consider, for instance, African groups such as the Tiv, which included more than one million individuals, the Nuer whose population has been estimated at 400,000, or the Lugbara with more than 300,000 members. More striking yet is the fact that, globally, the world has always been, and continues to be, in international anarchy.

The observed absence of government in these environments requires explanation. If conventional wisdom is correct, anarchy is inefficient and government should have quickly replaced vacuums of centralized authority. Why then did statelessness among numerous societies last so long? For that matter, what accounts for anarchy's continued presence internationally? In short, how do we explain the persistence of significant arenas of anarchy over time?[2]

---

[*] This chapter is based on and uses material from Leeson, Peter T. 2007. "Efficient Anarchy." *Public Choice* 130(1–2): 41–53 [© 2007 Springer Science + Business Media B.V.].

[1] David Friedman (1973), Murray Rothbard (1977), Bruce Benson (1999), and Randy Holcombe (2004) are rare exceptions in this regard.

[2] While no one has addressed this question, a growing literature deals broadly with the economics of anarchy. See, for instance, Dixit (2003, 2004) Hirshleifer (1994), and Bates

North (1990) suggests that inefficient forms of social organization may persist because of path dependence. Path dependence offers one potential explanation for anarchy's persistence, which explains that persistence despite anarchy's inefficiency. In contrast, this essay explores why in some cases welfare-maximizing individuals would rationally choose *not* to form any government at all. It offers a potential explanation for anarchy's persistence, which explains that persistence as resulting from anarchy's efficiency.

I examine self-governance's superiority to government when government is ideal. An ideal government works in precisely the way society's inhabitants desire it to. It faithfully uses its coercive monopoly to protect citizens' property rights and promote exchange, and suffers no problems of corruption, rent seeking, or related issues that principal-agent problems create. No such government actually exists, nor is one possible. Nevertheless, I use ideal government in this essay's comparison because it offers the strongest justification for the state and thus allows me to demonstrate that, *even in this case*, there are important conditions under which anarchy is the socially efficient governance arrangement and thus the one that welfare-maximizing individuals would choose if they confronted such a choice.[3] Comparing ideal government to anarchy is also useful because such government is the kind most persons are wont to imagine when they mentally compare how anarchy might fare relative to government, or indeed imagine government as the solution to any problem people face. Chapter 9 illustrates why such imaginations are just that and, indeed, why they can be downright dangerous.[4] Here, however, to make my point as strongly as possible, I use ideal government as the relevant alternative to anarchy.

---

et al. (2002). Dixit's (2003) analysis is probably the most closely related to mine in that it considers the limits of self-governance and when government becomes efficient.

[3] This essay also considers the choice between anarchy and (ideal) government as considered by a population of persons interested in maximizing social welfare. In fact, individuals are interested in maximizing their own personal welfare, not that of society as a whole. My justification for this analytical departure from reality is that it provides the perspective required to evaluate the comparative efficiency of anarchy versus government. Such a comparison requires a "social planner's perspective," which I generally abhor, but which imagining the population's members as welfare maximizers achieves. Of course, I could adopt this perspective without introducing the fiction whereby a population's members also deliberately choose their governance arrangement. But given that my purpose is to explain why, from the perspective of those such as North, who describes the popularity of government as a social choice reflecting a concern for efficiency, anarchy's observed persistence in certain arenas can be understood in similar terms, I also present my discussion in terms of populations choosing on the basis of what maximizes social welfare.

[4] It bears emphasis, then, that this essay considers only *some* of the conditions under which anarchy is efficient. As the next chapter explores, anarchy may also be efficient under

WHEN IS ANARCHY EFFICIENT?

The discipline of continuous dealings by itself is capable of supporting some level of cooperation under anarchy, albeit, for reasons described already, a limited one. The previous essays in this book suggest that a variety of other mechanisms of self-governance are capable of raising that level. Still, these mechanisms are highly imperfect. They undoubtedly leave some of the gains available from cooperation on the table.

As the traditional rationale for government suggests, by strengthening individuals' security in their property still further, an ideal government can improve social wealth compared to that under anarchy by permitting individuals to realize some portion of the gains from trade that go uncaptured when self-governing mechanisms are exclusively relied on for that purpose. Instead of arguing that ideal governments don't exist (they don't) or that self-governance can secure the same level of property protection that government can (which it sometimes can), this essay accepts the claim that government is capable of enabling a higher degree of social cooperation than anarchy is capable of enabling.

For some population of individuals, let H be the sum of the payoffs to individuals of trade when government is present and let L be the sum of their payoffs of the relatively lower level of trade they enjoy when government is absent, where $H > L > 0$. Individuals may choose the high-trade equilibrium by introducing government or the low-trade equilibrium by interacting under anarchy.

For government to be efficient and thus for welfare-maximizing persons to rationally choose its presence, the cost of government, G, must be smaller than the benefits it provides. The benefit of government is the difference between social wealth in the two states of the world just described – that in which government exists and individuals are in the higher-trade equilibrium, and that in which it doesn't exist and individuals are in the lower-trade equilibrium. Government is therefore an efficient solution to the social dilemma only if $G < H - L$. In contrast, where $G > H - L$, anarchy is efficient. Whether G is actually greater than $H - L$ depends on two things: (1) the size of G and (2) the size of the gap between social wealth

other conditions, in particular when government is far from ideal. Further, this chapter compares "total anarchy" – that is, the absence of government for any functions – to (ideal) government. If one instead considered cases in which we have "pockets of anarchy" – that is, government existed and protected property in certain kinds of interactions, but for other kinds government was effectively absent (for example, in black markets) – one would be able to add further to the conditions under which anarchy is efficient.

when individuals are in the higher-trade equilibrium versus when they're in the lower-trade one.

The Cost of Government

The cost of an ideal government can be broken into three primary components. The first is the simple organizational cost of creating a state – the cost of organizing collective action. Concretely, the organizational costs of government include (1) the decision-making costs of arriving at the specific set of rules the state is to enforce and (2) the external costs of collective decision making, which result from the fact that the group will sometimes make choices that are privately costly to the individual (Buchanan and Tullock 1962). The organizational cost of government thus depends on, in addition to other possible factors, the form of government or decision-making process that's followed in determining what set of rules the state is to enforce.

The second cost of government is the cost of enforcing decided-on rules. These costs are expenditures associated with creating and maintaining police and military forces and a court system. Enforcement costs increase as the population size increases; it's more expensive to police 1,000 people, for instance, than it is to police 10. The enforcement costs of government also increase as population heterogeneity increases. Ethnically, religiously, linguistically, and otherwise fractionalized populations are more prone to disagreement, mistrust, and violent conflict than those that are less fractionalized (see, for instance, Alesina et al. 2003; Alesina and Spolaore 2003; Alesina and La Ferrara 2002). Thus the state's enforcement entities – for instance, the police and courts – are deployed more frequently for the purposes of preventing and settling disputes among socially disparate populations than among more homogeneous ones. The form of government influences enforcement costs as well.

The third cost of government is the cost of providing public goods other than those necessary to enforce decided-on rules (such as the cost of police and courts, which falls under the enforcement costs of government), but which contribute to individuals' ability to engage in higher levels of trade.[5]

---

[5] These goods need not be non-excludable and non-rivalrous, per the classic definition of public goods. Roads, for example, are both excludable and rivalrous, and yet government is traditionally viewed as the appropriate provider of transportation systems. Many, if not most, of the "public goods" traditionally thought of as within the purview of state provision (including roads) can be provided for privately and have been historically.

Roads, which permit interactions between larger numbers of individuals, are an example of this. The public goods cost of government is largely determined by the same factors as government's enforcement costs are. Public goods costs increase as the size of the population increases, because it's more expensive to supply, for instance, an adequate system of transportation for a large population than a small one. Similarly, ceteris paribus, public goods costs will be higher among heterogeneous populations than among more homogeneous ones (Alesina, Baqir, and Easterly 1999). Where persons have more diverse characteristics, they have more diverse needs, requiring multiple forms of the same public goods (for instance, roadways coming from, and going to, different places), which raises the cost of providing such services.

The Benefit of Government

The factors presented in the preceding section determine G's size. Anarchy's efficiency, however, depends on the cost of government *relative* to the benefit government provides by moving society to the higher-trade equilibrium. What, then, affects the size of $H - L$?

The difference between social wealth when individuals engage in higher trade versus when they engage in lower trade is determined by the potential for gains from exchange. The size of these gains is in turn a function of the range of exchange opportunities that are available to them. Five main factors affect this range:

1. Individuals' endowments: ceteris paribus, where individuals begin with more disparate endowments, the gains from trading will be larger and vice versa.
2. The size of the potential trading population: a larger population of potential exchange partners means a larger number of opportunities to gain from trading. A smaller population means fewer potential gains from exchange.
3. Individuals' productive abilities: ceteris paribus, where individuals' productive abilities are more disparate, there are larger gains from them exchanging. Where productive abilities are more similar, the opposite is true.

See, for instance, Beito et al. (2002). Here, however, I take the traditional view, which assumes that government will provide these goods.

4. Individuals' preferences: ceteris paribus, more diverse persons' preferences create more opportunities for exchange. Less diverse preferences mean fewer opportunities from exchange.

5. The presence or absence of mechanisms of self-governance that facilitate exchange: where private institutions, such as arbitration, reputation mechanisms, or other private institutions that promote cooperation are present, such as those considered in the previous chapters of this book, individuals are able to realize additional gains from exchange without government. Thus social wealth in the lower-trade equilibrium will be higher than it would have been without these institutions (albeit, because of the limitations assumed earlier, still lower than if government existed). The presence of mechanisms of self-governance facilitating exchange thus shrinks the gap between social wealth in the higher- and lower-trade equilibrium. The absence of such mechanisms increases this gap.

These five factors together determine the thickness of the market. Thick markets have many (i.e., widespread) opportunities for exchange and thus generate high gains from trade. In contrast, thin markets have very few opportunities for exchange and thus generate minimal gains from trade.

When markets are sufficiently thin, the relative difference in social wealth between a situation in which individuals engage in higher trade and a situation in which they engage in lower trade is negligible. This corresponds to the case when $H - L$ is very small. Alternatively, when markets are very thick, this difference is large.

Having established what affects the cost of government and what affects the benefits government provides by moving society from a lower-trade equilibrium to a higher-trade one, it's possible to distinguish two types of efficient anarchy: "small $H - L$ anarchy," in which, even though government may be inexpensive to create, the difference between social wealth in the higher- and lower-trade equilibrium is so small as to make the state inefficient on cost-benefit grounds, and "big G anarchy," in which, despite the presence of a substantial gap between social wealth in the higher- and lower-trade equilibrium, government is too costly to justify its emergence. At least theoretically these are situations in which statelessness is socially optimal, even compared to an ideal government. A population of welfare-maximizing persons operating in either environment would thus choose anarchy over government.

This framework predicts anarchy in two distinct sets of circumstances: one in which the absence of trading opportunities makes the benefit of introducing the state prohibitively small (small $H - L$ anarchy) and one in which the costliness of the state prevents government from emerging (big G anarchy). I explore evidence for these predictions in the next section.

TWO ARCHETYPES OF ACTUAL ANARCHY

Small $H - L$ Anarchy

The first archetype of statelessness – small $H - L$ anarchy – is character-istic of statelessness observed in small, primitive societies.[6] The historical presence of long-standing, anarchic societies of this variety spans the globe. Consider, for example, societies such as the Eskimo tribes of the North American Arctic (Hoebel 1954), Pygmies in Zaire (Turnbull 1961), Native American tribes like the Yoruk (Benson 1989a), the Ifugao of the Philippines (Barton 1967), the Massims of East Paupo-Melanesia (Landa 1994), South American native tribes like the Kuikuru (Dole 1966), the Kabyle Berbers of Algeria, the Land Dyaks of Sarawak, and the tribal Santals of India (Barclay 1990), none of which had governments. In some cases primitive anarchic societies remained anarchic well into the twentieth century. The Kapauku society of West New Guinea, for instance, was stateless until about 1960 (Pospisil 1963).

In his classic anthropological work, E. E. Evans-Pritchard (1940) des-cribed the Nuer society of the southern Sudan circa the 1930s. The Nuer people were far from alone in precolonial Africa in eschewing government. The Barabaig, Dinka, Jie, Karamojong, Turkana, Tiv, Lugbara, Konkomba, Plateau Tonga, and others long stood as stateless or near-anarchic societies too.[7] The Nuer, however, is among the best studied of these groups, and in many ways typifies the features found among other primitive stateless societies. For this reason I consider the Nuer exclusively, although it should be kept in mind that the lessons of this analysis apply to other primitive anarchic societies with similar characteristics.

Primitive societies like the Nuer reflect instances in which rational, welfare-maximizing individuals would choose anarchy over government because the difference between social wealth in the higher-trade and

---

[6] This isn't to say, however, that anarchy is only efficient and thus only arises in situations where H and L are themselves small. $H - L$ can also be small when H and L are both large. For instance, as discussed later, modern international trade has a large L because of highly effective private institutions. Thus, adding government may not add substantially to trade, making $H - L$ small despite the fact that H and L are themselves large.

[7] For reference to these and other stateless societies in Africa, see Bohannan (1968) and Barclay (1990).

lower-trade equilibrium is extremely small. Because the formation of even the leanest government involves some fixed cost, and this cost isn't insignificant, a very small $H - L$ is enough to make anarchy the efficient pattern of social organization.

The small gap between payoffs from higher and lower trade in primitive societies is a function of five main factors, which tend to make potential markets inside them extremely thin:

1. These societies are often small, meaning there are relatively few opportunities for exchange even if government is introduced. This tends to make lower levels of trade enabled by private institutional arrangements not much less profitable than higher levels of trade that would be possible if government were established.[8]

The size of the relevant trading population is largely determined by the size of the population over which government is introduced. Thus, to understand why the relevant potential trading population for the Nuer was very small, we first need to understand why government among the Nuer, if it had been introduced, would have been introduced at a low level – that is, over a small population.

The Nuer are among the largest primitive stateless societies.[9] The most liberal estimate of the Nuer population is around 400,000 individuals (Barclay 1990). However, Evans-Pritchard, who studied the Nuer most closely, estimated the Nuer population at only half that size. This figure is inclusive of all Nuer group members. This inclusive population was divided into eleven tribes: the Bul, Leek, western Jikany, Nyuong, Dok, Jagei, Gaawar, Thiang, Lak, Lou, and eastern Jikany. Each tribe was in turn subdivided into numerous sections based on lineage, and these sections were further subdivided into numerous village communities. Nuer communities tended to be extremely close-knit, as they were composed of individuals connected by lineage.

The largest Nuer organizational unit in which private rules and arbitration procedures were respected by other individuals was the tribe. Beyond

---

[8] I say presumably here because it's not at all clear that government would actually enable a higher level of trade in these societies. There are tribal societies that have had governments imposed on them by colonizers and then, following the withdrawal of the colonial government, have economically crashed. In some of these societies, at least, trade was more expansive under statelessness than it was following the imposition of government. Leeson (2005) examines such cases in precolonial/postcolonial Africa.

[9] To my knowledge, only the Tiv and the Lugbara were larger.

the bounds of each tribe there was no recognition of such rules or procedures. The largest conceivable level at which government might have been introduced among the Nuer would therefore have been the tribal level, and even this is questionable. Evans-Pritchard, for instance, indicates that in many cases the largest effective organizational unit of the Nuer was actually much smaller, perhaps somewhere between the village and tribal levels. This suggests that, were government introduced, it would have been over an even smaller population than that of the tribe. The presence of self-governing mechanisms, such as the "leopard-skin chief" who arbitrated disagreements among tribe members, enabled some exchange between individuals at this level. While introducing government at the tribal level might increase this exchange somewhat, the small population involved, coupled with private institutions like the leopard-skin chief, suggests that this increase would have been minimal.

2. Individuals in primitive societies typically have very similar productive abilities. Most are either pastoral or horticultural.

The Nuer, who were of the pastoral variety, were overwhelmingly a cattle-herding people. Although they were sometimes forced to raise crops (for instance, when rinderpest destroyed their livestock), a combination of the natural environment in which they found themselves and Nuer culture created a situation in which there was very little differentiation in individuals' productive capacities. Evans-Pritchard (1940: 55) described the fundamental environmental features of Nuerland as follows: "(1) It is dead flat. (2) It has clay soils. (3) It is very thinly and sporadically wooded. (4) It is covered with high grasses in the rains. (5) It is subject to heavy rainfall. (6) It is traversed by large rivers that flood annually. (7) When the rains cease and the rivers fall it is subject to severe draught." While these conditions allowed for occasional horticulture, hunting, and fishing, they overwhelmingly dictated the productive activity of cattle herding of which the Nuer were so fond. Production was thus almost exclusively directed at raising cattle for meat and milk.

From top to bottom, Nuer culture was organized around the importance of cattle, which reinforced herding as the virtually exclusive productive activity of the Nuer people. As Evans-Pritchard (1940: 18) put it, nearly all of Nuer "social behavior directly concerns their cattle." This fact was manifested in practices and institutions among the Nuer, from the giving of names (which were based on the names of family cattle), to their networks of kinship ties (which were based on cattle ownership), to rituals and religious activities. This intensely focused interest on cattle that was fundamental to

Nuer culture strengthened the singularly directed aims of Nuer productive activities in herding.[10] Neither this feature of Nuer life nor the fact that the Nuer environment wasn't suitable for much other than cattle herding is to deny that innately occurring comparative advantage among individuals in, say, the production of milk versus the production of meat allowed for some specialization. However, for reasons discussed earlier, the degree of this specialization was limited. This in turn limited the gains that could be had from higher levels of exchange, which introducing government might bring.

3. Often (but not always) the individuals who populate primitive societies have homogeneous preferences.

As previously mentioned, in the case of the Nuer this preference was nearly unidimensional and aimed at the ownership of cattle. This lack of diversity tended to diminish the increase in exchange opportunities that introducing government might bring. As Evans-Pritchard (1940: 88) observed, the "Nuer have nothing to trade except their cattle and have no inclination to dispose of these; all they greatly desire are more cattle.... This narrow focus of interest causes them to be inattentive to the products of other people, for which, indeed, they feel no need and often enough show contempt."[11]

4. Individuals in primitive societies often have very similar endowments. Because they're frequently egalitarian, these societies create a situation in which, across current members and even generations, individuals have similar levels and forms of wealth.

For the Nuer, while disparities in wealth levels were permitted, the form of individual endowments was nearly identical for all individuals in that wealth was construed almost exclusively in the form of cattle, which was singularly desired.

---

[10] The Nuer focus on cattle was both a cause and consequence of the cultural characteristics described.

[11] To satisfy basic dietary requirements to sustain life, the Nuer were forced to spend some time in agricultural activity directed at producing carbohydrate-rich foods. In their case this was grain. However, as discussed earlier, for reasons of climate and preferences, the time they spent on agricultural activities was minimal. Evans-Pritchard (1940: 81) described the situation as follows: "(1) that Nuer cultivate only enough grain for it to be one element in their food-supply and not enough to live on it alone; (2) that with their present climate and technology considerable increase in horticulture would be unprofitable; and (3) that the dominance of the pastoral value over horticultural interests is in accord with oecological relations which favour cattle husbandry at the expense of horticulture."

5. Because of their small, close-knit nature, primitive societies often find is easy to use even very crude self-governing mechanisms effectively to facilitate considerable cooperation.

Within the same communities, for instance, the Nuer shared common norms regarding the settlement of disputes, which typically involved cattle. Disagreeing members would see the leopard-skin chief who, sometimes in conjunction with community elders, would recommend how the dispute should be settled. This form of private arbitration enabled community interaction despite the absence of government. Similarly, within the same tribe, the institution of the feud, which involved specific steps for dealing with more serious transgressions, was respected by the Nuer and provided a strong incentive for individuals to refrain from theft and violence.[12] The strong presence of these mechanisms of self-governance raised the relative payoff to individuals in the lower-trade equilibrium, which served to shrink the gap between social wealth in this and the higher-trade equilibrium and, with it, the benefit of introducing a state.

Big G Anarchy

Anarchy is also efficient if the cost of government is very large. In this case even a substantial gap between social wealth in the higher- and lower-trade equilibrium may not be large enough to make the state efficient from a cost-benefit perspective. In this environment rational, welfare-maximizing persons confronted with the choice will again be led to choose anarchy over government. Thus big G anarchy is the second archetype of statelessness I consider.

Instances of big G anarchy are less prevalent than instances of small $H - L$ anarchy simply because the cases in which G is likely to be massive are also the cases in which government is being extended over a massive population, which means that the potential increase in gains from trading are also massive. It's therefore harder for the cost of government to be larger than the difference between social wealth in the lower- versus higher-trade equilibrium.

Nevertheless, one particular instance of big G anarchy is hard to miss: international anarchy. The second half of the twentieth century in particular saw the growth of supranational organizations aimed at increasing the

---

[12] For an analysis of the feud and leopard-skin chief as institutions of self-enforcement, see Bates (1983).

degree of centralized enforcement in the international sphere, such as the World Court and the United Nations. However, these organizations haven't fundamentally affected the anarchic nature of the international sphere in that none of them give final, ultimate authority to the governing body to offer binding decisions on the parties involved. They don't override national sovereignty but instead rely fundamentally on the willingness and voluntary consent of the various sovereigns involved. If a sovereign chooses not to appear before such a court or doesn't abide by the court's decision, no centralized authority exists to compel it to do otherwise. Likewise, no formal supranational authority exists to adjudicate and enforce commercial contracts between private international traders who, because of their differing nationalities, frequently find it impossible or prohibitively costly to use their nations' domestic state courts to adjudicate and enforce such contracts.

It might be presumed that the difference between social wealth in the higher- and lower-trade equilibrium in the international sphere would be very substantial given the considerable population of the world. Even if this is the case, however, the organizational and enforcement costs of a global government extending over 6.5 billion people are prohibitively expensive. Consider, for instance, the substantial increase in organizational costs that would result from most voters (assuming a democratic government) being far removed from their public representatives (at least at the highest level).

Organizational costs would also rise considerably because of the vast increase in the heterogeneity of the relevant population. If it's difficult to arrive at a decision regarding where a new police station is to be located within a community of 20,000 suburbanites, imagine the difficulty of coming to a much larger decision when more than a billion people are involved from Beirut to Mexico City. Increased heterogeneity among the relevant population will lead to substantial increases in enforcement and public goods costs, for similar reasons. Indeed, as Alesina and Spolaore (2003) show, the attendant increase in such costs associated with extending government over larger and more socially diverse populations is a primary constraint on the effective size of nations. At the size necessary to govern the entire globe effectively, any economies of scale in having a centralized governance arrangement that might normally exist on the national level are overwhelmed by diseconomies that exist on the global level.

Although it relates to the difference between $H - L$ instead of the size of G, the strong presence of mechanisms of self-governance that facilitate exchange in the international arena also contributes to anarchy's efficiency in this sphere. Modern-day international trade is based largely on the set of private institutions that governed such exchange when it first emerged on a significant scale in medieval Europe. I briefly considered the medieval incarnation of this set of institutions, called the *lex mercatoria*, or law merchant, in Chapter 2.[13]

The medieval law merchant, recall, was a polycentric system of customary law that arose from the desire of traders in the late eleventh century to engage in cross-cultural exchange. My discussion of the medieval law merchant emphasized traders' use of social-distance-reducing signals to facilitate intergroup exchange without government. One way traders did so was by submitting voluntarily to the decisions of private merchant courts, or so-called dusty feet courts because of the dust merchants' feet collected as they busily traveled between commercial fairs across Europe. These private courts adjudicated disagreements between medieval traders in light of the law merchant's customary law.

Contemporary international traders continue to make wide use of private courts as a means of settling disputes in the form of international commercial arbitration. Today at least 90 percent of all international trade contracts contain arbitration clauses (Casella 1996). Among the most notable arbitration organizations that exist for this purpose are the International Chamber of Commerce (ICC), the London Court of International Arbitration (LCIA), the Arbitration Association of the Stockholm Chamber of Commerce, and the American Arbitration Association's International Center for Dispute Resolution (ICDR). In 2001 nearly 1,500 parties from more than 115 nations across the globe utilized the services of the ICC alone (ICC 2001). The amounts in dispute varied from $50,000 to more than $1 billion, with more than 60 percent of all disputes involving sums of money between $1 million and $1 billion (ICC 2002). Similarly, the ICDR arbitrated a caseload in 2001 worth more than $10 billion involving parties from sixty-three countries across the globe (ICDR 2002).

These arbitration associations often rely on evolved customary law that dictates how exchange disagreements are to be settled, and "arbitral awards are most generally promptly and willingly executed by business people" (David 1985: 357). Indeed, virtually "[e]very research into the practice of international arbitration shows that by far the great majority of arbitration awards is fulfilled without the need for enforcement" (Böckstiegal 1984: 49). In a study published in 1981, for instance, a survey of international oil traders indicated that more than 88 percent of all contracts entered were carried out without dispute. Of the remaining 12 percent,

---

[13] For discussions of the law merchant, modern and medieval, see, for instance, Mattli (2001), Casella (1996), and Benson (1989b).

respondents indicated that 76 percent of disputes were arbitrated successfully by private adjudication (Trakman 1983: 53). The world's largest international arbitration association, the ICC, estimates that 90 percent of all its
arbitral decisions are complied with voluntarily (Craig et al. 2000: 404). This
high degree of compliance is attributable in large part to traders' reliance
on social-distance-reducing signaling and the discipline of continuous
dealings.

The presence of private institutional arrangements in the international
sphere, such as private arbitration and reliance on customary law, enables
a substantial amount of trade despite the absence of global government.
Consider the staggering level of international trade. In 2003 world exports
of merchandise and commercial services alone exceeded $9 trillion – nearly
a quarter of world GDP (World Trade Organization 2004). Although without centralized enforcement international traders may be situated in the
low-trade equilibrium, this level of trade isn't very low at all and quite
possibly not significantly lower than it would be if an agency of centralized
enforcement were introduced.[14] In conjunction with the fact that the cost
of such an agency would be extremely high, this suggests that anarchy is the
most efficient way of organizing the international arena. Thus, while some
attempts have been made to introduce bodies of centralized enforcement on
the global level, it isn't surprising that global anarchy continues to persist.

Anarchy's probable efficiency in some primitive stateless societies and on
the international level doesn't mean statelessness is always or must remain
efficient in these areas. For example, if members of primitive societies, such
as the Nuer, had decided to widen their preferences, diversify their productive activities further, be more inclusive of other groups, or, what's equivalent, take an interest in interacting with a wider, more diverse population, as
this book's first essay suggested some precolonial African communities did,
the thickness of potential markets would grow and, with it, so too would the
gap between social wealth in the higher- and lower-trade equilibrium. If this
gap grows large enough, the introduction of a state may become efficient.

Clearly, a significant factor contributing to this process – enlarging the
number and range of individuals who might interact – is partially endogenous to government's presence. The establishment of a state may make
individuals feel more secure in interacting with outsiders and thus increase

---

[14] On the relative unimportance of international treaties that attempt to provide for the formal enforcement of private international arbitration decisions through countries' domestic
state courts for this trade, see Leeson (2008). The "shadow of the state" explanation of
large and growing international trade is therefore not a convincing argument.

market thickness, which increases the benefit of having a state in the first place. However, it doesn't follow that introducing government in small $H - L$ anarchies would necessarily make government efficient. In addition to the other factors affecting the distance between social wealth in the higher- and lower-trade equilibrium that aren't endogenous to government, individuals would need to desire to interact with those outside their relatively small communities.[15] In the case of the Nuer, for instance, it doesn't seem that this was so.

More critically, it's important to recognize that the circumstances under which my discussion here suggests that anarchy is efficient aren't the only ones under which this may be true. Neither are they the most important ones. This essay compared anarchy to an ideal government – one that doesn't suffer from "public choice problems" – which, in fact, all real-world governments do. Those problems can add substantially to the cost of government, making anarchy efficient in a much large number of situations. Indeed, as the next essay considers, in practice such costs of government are often the ones that matter most.

---

[15] In addition to this, if the benefits that introducing government creates are not immediate (or at least not completely so), agents will need to be sufficiently forward looking for the state to be profitable to adopt. If agents are sufficiently impatient, or if a significant portion of the benefits from introducing government will only come near the end of (or only after the end of) current inhabitants' lives, government will remain prohibitively costly to merit its introduction. In societies where life spans are not very long, this may present a problem. Short-lived persons will find government too costly to adopt and their resulting failure to adopt government will in turn contribute to the short life span of the next generation, which will confront the same dilemma.

9

Better Off Stateless*

In the developed world the relationship between state and society is fairly straightforward. Although rent seeking, public corruption, and government abuse exist, to a large extent developed economies have developed precisely because they have succeeded in overcoming these problems. While far from perfect in this respect, government in the United States, for example, does a good job of protecting citizens' property rights and uses its monopoly on coercion to provide public goods that, at least in principle, stand to make society more productive.

In the developing world, however, the relationship between government and citizens is often very different. Here many political rulers routinely use government to benefit themselves and their supporters at citizens' expense. Rather than using state power to protect citizens' property rights, these governments use that power to prey on society. In the extreme they devolve into little more than glorified thuggery, seizing every opportunity to extort their citizens. Ultra-dysfunctional states not only fail to provide public goods and protect citizens' property. They're the primary threat to their citizens' property rights and security.

It's common to think that most governments in world are the well-functioning variety and that the minority are dysfunctional. But this thinking has it backward. Well-functioning, highly constrained governments that protect property rights and supply welfare-enhancing public goods are the exception, not the rule. According to the 2007 Failed States Index, nearly 16 percent of the world's countries (thirty-two) have "failing states" (Foreign Policy/Fund for Peace 2007). In them, governments are often

---

* This chapter is based on and uses material from Leeson, Peter T. 2007. "Better off Stateless: Somalia Before and After Government Collapse." *Journal of Comparative Economics* 35(4): 698–710 [© 2007 Association for Comparative Economic Studies. Published by Elsevier Inc.].

ultra-predatory and dysfunctional. According to this index, another 49 percent of the world's countries (ninety-seven) are in "warning" mode. Although they have not yet reached the deterioration of countries in "alert" mode, they are approaching it. If these measures are correct, in more than half the world, states are either critically or dangerously dysfunctional. The world's "experiment" with government, then, has produced far more mixed results than most people think. Indeed, if we're to grade this experiment as a solution to the social dilemma by the share of the world's countries in which that solution has clearly succeeded, we must grade government a failure.

Dysfunctional and predatory governments are disproportionately located in the poorest countries, which raises an important question about the link between state and economic development in the developing world. Is it possible that some least-developed countries could actually perform better without any government at all?

This essay makes a simple point: although a properly constrained government may be superior to statelessness, it doesn't follow that *any* government is superior to no government all. If a state is highly predatory and its behavior goes unchecked, government may not only fail to add to social welfare; it may reduce welfare below its level under anarchy.[1] As John Stuart Mill (1848: 882–883) put it:

[O]ppression by the government... has so much more baneful an effect on the springs of national prosperity, than almost any degree of lawlessness and turbulence under free institutions. Nations have acquired some wealth, and made some progress in improvement in states of social union so imperfect as to border on anarchy: but no countries in which the people were exposed without limit to arbitrary exactions from the officers of government ever yet continued to have industry and wealth.

To investigate anarchy's welfare implications compared to government when government is dysfunctional, I examine the case of Somalia. In several respects Somalia is typical of many least-developed countries (LDCs). Like most other LDCs, Somalia is located in Sub-Saharan Africa. Similar to other countries in this region, Somalia was a former European colony, achieved independence, and subsequently came under the rule of a brutal and highly predatory political regime. Somalia is different from other LDCs in one important respect, however: it has no government.

In 1991 Somalia's state collapsed, creating anarchy in its wake. Although there have been several attempts to resurrect central government in

---

[1] Moselle and Polak (2001) provide a theoretical model demonstrating when this is the case.

Somalia – including an ongoing one – none has yet succeeded, leaving the country effectively stateless. Somalia therefore provides an interesting natural experiment to explore the idea that if government is predatory enough, anarchy may actually prove superior in terms of economic development.

There has been much hand-wringing over what to do about the situation of anarchy that has characterized Somalia since 1991. Reports from international organizations commonly express fear about the "chaos" of Somalia without a state. According to the World Security Network, for example, under anarchy Somalia has had "no functioning economy." Instead, "clan-based warfare and anarchy have dominated" it (Wolfe 2005). Shortly after Somalia's government collapsed, the United Nations was similarly "*gravely alarmed* at the rapid deterioration" of Somalia and expressed serious "concern with the situation prevailing in that country" (UN Resolution 751 1992: 55). The popular press has tended to go even further in its condemnation of the "internal anarchy . . . [that] has consumed Somalia" (Gettleman and Mazzetti 2006). The view commonly presented by these observers is that Somalia has "been mired in chaos since 1991" when statelessness emerged (Hassan 2007).

To be sure, this concern isn't without cause. In the year following the state's collapse, civil war, exacerbated by severe drought, devastated the Sub-Saharan territory, killing 300,000 Somalis (Prendergast 1997). For a time it seemed that Somali statelessness would mean endless bloody conflict, starvation, and an eventual descent into total annihilation of the Somali people. Thus conventional wisdom sees Somalia as a land of chaos, deterioration, and war, and is certain that statelessness has been detrimental to Somali development.

The reason for this belief is twofold. On the one hand, conventional wisdom sees government as unexceptionally superior to anarchy. Government is considered necessary to prevent violent conflicts like those that erupted when Somalia's state first crumbled, which disrupt economic activity. Government is also considered critical to supplying public goods such as roads, schools, and law and order, which are important to the process of development. From this perspective, it's easy to conclude that Somalia, which has no central government, must have been better off when it had one.

Second, there's a tendency, upon observing problems in distressed regions of the world, to concentrate only on the "failure" of the current situation, ignoring the quite possibly even worse state of affairs that preceded it (or could follow it).[2] This is especially easy to do for Somalia, which by

---

[2] This remains a common problem in evaluations of Russia as well. As with Somalia, the tendency here has been to focus on the significant defects that remain without an

international standards is far behind indeed. Educational enrollment is abysmally low – as of 2001, a mere 7 percent for combined primary, secondary, and tertiary schooling. Average annual income is less than $1,000 (PPP), and preventable diseases like malaria are a genuine threat to Somalia's inhabitants. These facts, however, say nothing about the status of Somalia before its state collapsed. Forgetting Somalia's experience under government, it's easy to imagine that nothing could be more damaging to Somali development than anarchy.

To investigate statelessness' impact on Somali development, I compare the state of eighteen key development indicators in Somalia before and after its government collapsed. These indicators are comprehensive in covering all angles of development for which data were available pre- and post-statelessness as of 2007. While it's important to avoid romanticizing Somalia, the data suggest that statelessness has *improved* Somali development substantially. On nearly all indicators Somalia performs significantly better under anarchy than it did under government. This improvement has been made possible by renewed vibrancy in key sectors of the economy and public goods following the collapse of government and of government predation along with it.

My analysis of Somali data stops in 2005. Thus, although my description of Somalia under anarchy uses the present tense, unless otherwise noted it describes Somalia circa 2000–2005. Since then the situation in Somalia has changed somewhat. For example, in late 2006 Somali conflict renewed when the international community–backed Transitional Federal Government (TFG) attempted to oust the Supreme Council of Islamic Courts (SCIC), which controlled the southern Somali city of Mogadishu. This conflict disrupted the relatively long-lasting period of peace that preceded it, resurrecting the violence Somalia had largely under control leading up to this. As I discuss in greater detail later in this chapter, in early 2007 the TFG succeeded in taking control of Mogadishu. However, like previous attempts to reinstate government in Somalia, the TFG's authority proved extremely weak and didn't succeed in establishing a new central government in Somalia.

In August 2012 the expiration of the TFG's tenure led to the establishment of the Federal Government of Somalia (FGS), which, unlike its predecessors, is supposed to be permanent. Although in some respects the FGS has a stronger claim to statehood than previous efforts to recreate central

---

appreciation of the fact that, however severe these troubles are, they pale in comparison to the troubles of Russia under communist rule. Russia is undoubtedly better off today than it was under socialism. See Shleifer and Treisman (2004).

government in Somalia, it would be premature in the extreme to declare this most recent effort to reestablish government the end of Somali anarchy. Indeed, as the United Nations Security Council (2013: 12) reported in July 2013: "At present, Al-Shabaab" – an offshoot faction of the SCIC – "remains in control of most of southern and central Somalia."

It thus remains to be seen whether present efforts by and on behalf of the FGS will succeed in establishing what might meaningfully be called a government, or whether, like previous attempts to recreate a Somalia state, this one, too, will fail. Until the FGS has proved durable and wields substantially more authority in Somalia than it does currently, it's appropriate and accurate to continue to characterize the country as anarchic, as I do in this and the next chapter.

THE GRABBING HAND: SOMALIA UNDER GOVERNMENT

In 1960 British Somaliland and Italian Somalia gained independence from their colonizers and joined together to form the Republic of Somalia. A bloodless coup in 1969 led by Major-General Mohamed Siad Barre overthrew the democratic government that ruled Somalia since independence. Barre went on to take power and established an oppressive military dictatorship.[3] He reigned for twenty-one years until 1991, when Somalia's government collapsed and statelessness ensued.

Under the influence of the Soviet Union, in 1970 Barre transformed his military dictatorship into a socialist one. Full-scale central planning pursued under the government's policy of "scientific socialism" brutalized the Somali people. The government slaughtered civilians who posed threats to the government's plans or political power, used coercive intimidation to create artificial support for its activities, and forcibly relocated others to further the political or economic ends of Barre and his cronies. "Both the urban population and nomads living in the countryside [were] subjected to summary killings, arbitrary arrest, detention in squalid conditions, torture, rape, crippling constraints on freedom of movement and expression and a pattern of psychological intimidation" (Africa Watch Committee 1990: 9).

The state ruthlessly suppressed free speech and controlled all forms of information reaching Somalis. Newspapers (only one was officially

---

[3] As is often the case in dictatorships, technically, the Somali "constitution" of 1979 guaranteed democratic elections for its "president." In practice, however, this guarantee was worthless. The first "election" for Barre was in 1986 in which he received 99.9 percent of the votes (U.S. Library of Congress 2006).

permitted by the government), radio, and television were fully censored and dissent in any form squelched with force. Under Somalia's National Security Law No. 54, "gossip" became a capital offense. Twenty other basic civil freedoms involving speech, association, and organization also carried the death penalty.

The state invested aggressively in building its military. Besides weapons and troops for foreign defense, massive resources were devoted to military structures of domestic repression. Government created a secret police squad called the National Security Service and paramilitary unit called the Victory Pioneers for spying on and eliminating dissenters. Both had legal discretion to detain, invade, kill, and torture at the state's behest (Africa Watch Committee 1990).

This state of affairs had a twofold dire effect on development in Somalia. On the one hand, it left few resources for investment in welfare-enhancing public goods such as education, health, or transportation infrastructure. This was especially so in pastoral areas where most Somalis lived (Little 2003: 15). On the other hand, Barre's military dictatorship eliminated any vestiges of restraint on the government's predatory power. Law No. 1 repealed the constitution and all democratic checks. There were no elections for any political positions: Barre appointed them all. Military suppression prevented popular uprising. Even dissent through free expression was eliminated. Government was let loose to plunder and abuse citizens for political rulers' ends.

The Somali state was notoriously corrupt and violent. Political actors and bureaucrats embezzled state funds, extorted and murdered weak portions of the population, and engaged in aggressive asset stripping of state-owned firms. As the UN Development Program characterized it, "The 21-year regime of Siyad Barre had one of the worst human rights records in Africa" (UNDP 2001: 42). This is no small feat considering that during this period Africa was home to some of history's most savage dictatorships, including the Democratic Republic of Congo's Mobutu.

In 1975 all land was nationalized along with nearly all major industries and the financial sector. This facilitated government's ability to expropriate citizens' property for state projects, like massive state-operated farms, and for politicos' personal use. Unpopular minority groups, such as the Gosha, were particularly easy prey. In the 1970s and 1980s Barre expropriated Gosha-occupied land to create state-owned irrigation schemes that benefited his allies. In other cases his minions expropriated land for their private use, turning Gosha into serfs on their own property (Menkhaus and Craven 1996).

State control of industry in Somalia created inefficiencies similar to those experienced in the Soviet Union. Between 1984 and 1988, for instance, the government-owned Kismayo Meat Factory was open only three months per year. Government also owned tanneries. The "Hides and Skins Agency" paid herders less than half the market value of hides to process in these factories. These firms also utilized only a tiny fraction of their capacity. All told, capacity utilization of Somalia's state manufacturing firms was less than 20 percent (Mubarak 1997: 2028).

Incentives to be productive, keep costs down, or cater to consumer demands were virtually absent. Factory managers cared only about meeting quotas. This led them to pursue wasteful activities, such as purchasing inputs worth more as raw materials than the output they produced (Little 2003: 39). Some state-owned enterprises were developed purely to benefit political rulers and their friends. For instance, government created the Water Development Program to subsidize private watering holes for the livestock of Barre's allies.

In the late 1970s Barre abandoned full-blown socialism to attract foreign aid from the IMF. However, government continued to rely on central planning. "Parastatal companies continued to receive subsidies, foreign aid was channeled through state institutions and the state remained sole arbiter in the allocation of profitable contracts. Private sector autonomy was further curtailed by political patronage, which was the easiest way to access resources controlled by the state" (UNDP 2001: 140). In the 1980s there was only one bank in Somalia, state owned and operated. Government used it to keep afloat failing public firms and to reward political supporters. Only state enterprises or politically well-connected Somalis were able to obtain loans (Mubarak 1997).

Government also remained involved in most other important economic sectors. Livestock and pastoral-product exports have long been critical to Somalia's economy. In the 1970s Barre nationalized most of this trade and continued to control it throughout the 1980s. Government restricted imports and exports and introduced a bewildering array of regulations. Foreign exchange controls were also strict. They required exporters to exchange at least half their foreign-exchange earnings at the state-set rate, which in 1988 overvalued the Somali shilling to the U.S. dollar by more than 120 percent (Little 2003). This benefited wealthy political patrons who consumed imports, but it decimated Somalia's export industry.

In the 1980s Somalia's government turned to inflation to finance its corrupt and bankrupt projects. Between 1983 and 1990 average annual depreciation of the Somali shilling against the U.S. dollar was more than

100 percent. In some years depreciation exceeded 300 percent (Little 2003). Hyperinflation destroyed the savings of Somalis who managed to accrue modest sums over time. It also incapacitated the monetary unit as a means of economic calculation.

Government's willful mismanagement of public resources prevented the state from being self-supporting. Eager to woo Somalia from the influences of Eastern Europe, international development agencies filled the shortfall with massive inflows of foreign aid. By the mid-1980s 100 percent of Somalia's development budget and 50 percent of its recurrent budget was funded by foreign aid (UNDP 2001: 118). In 1987 more than 70 percent of the state's total operating budget was financed this way (Mubarak 1996).

The early 1980s saw a temporary spike in government expenditures on items such as education. But by the late 1980s the weight of nearly twenty years of rampant predation, repression, and state control had reduced Somali welfare to horrifically low levels. Well prior to the government's collapse the agricultural economy was in shambles, and malnutrition and starvation were commonplace (Samatar 1987). In the 1980s Somalia had one of the lowest per capita caloric intakes in the world (UNDP 2004). At the end of the decade government spent less than 1 percent of GDP on economic and social services, while military and administration consumed 90 percent of the state's total recurrent expenditure (Mubarak 1997).

Government consistently used state resources to privilege members of Barre's clan at others' expense. "The Barre regime awarded certain client groups preferential access to arable land and water. . . . Indeed, the Somalia case is a good example of ethnic (and clan) favoritism where private land-grabbing in the Jubba and Shebelle Valleys favored the late president's clan, the Marehan, while alienating other groups" (Little 2003: 36). For example, in 1988 Barre supported Marehan herders' unlawful appropriation of Ogaden water points in Southern Somalia.

Barre's "ethnic favoritism" created tension between Somali clans. In the late 1980s exploited clans reacted by forming faction groups like the Somali Patriotic Movement (comprised largely of Ogaden), the Somali National Movement (comprised largely of Isaaq), and the United Somali Congress (comprised largely of Hawiye). United against government's predation on non-Marehans, they joined forces to oust Barre. Unfortunately, the interclan tensions Barre created didn't immediately disappear with him. The seeds of clan conflict sewn by twenty years of divide-and-rule policy erupted into violence when government crumbled.[4]

---

[4] The application of this terminology to Barre's regime is from Little (2003).

THE HIDDEN HAND: SOMALIA UNDER ANARCHY

In 1988 civil war broke out in the northern part of the country (Somaliland), setting in motion the beginning of the end of government in Somalia. In January 1991 a coup d'etat toppled Barre's regime, creating statelessness in its wake.[5] Tellingly, the same year anarchy replaced government, 400,000 Somali refugees in Ethiopia returned to their homes in Somalia (UNDP 2001: 59). For the next two years, rival factions fought to establish power. These were the days when Somali "warlords," such as General Hussein Aideed of Mogadishu and Ali Mohamed Mahdi, battled to solidify their bases of strength. At the same time severe drought struck the country, creating famine in its aftermath. In 1992 the UN sent troops to Somalia to quell the conflict and ease suffering, but failed to establish authority, stability, or peace in the region.[6]

Some fighting continued into the mid-1990s, but died down considerably since 1991. By the late 1990s peace prevailed over most of Somalia. Until 2006, when the attempted reestablishment of central government sparked new violence, conflict was isolated and sporadic, confined when it did occur to pockets of small-scale rivalry in a few areas (Menkhaus 1998, 2004; Nenova 2004). Important to this expanding peace was expanding commerce, discussed later in this chapter (Menkhaus 2004; Nenova 2004).

Most depictions of Somalia leading up to the 2006 period grossly exaggerate the extent of Somali violence. In reality fewer people died from armed conflict in some parts of Somalia than did in neighboring countries that have governments. In these areas security was better than it was under government (UNDP 2001). About the same number of annual deaths in Somalia during this period – roughly 4 percent of the total – were a result of complications at childbirth as were attributable to war (UNDP/World

---

[5] When Somalia's government first collapsed, clans in the northwestern part of Somalia declared this territory an independent sovereignty called the Republic of Somaliland. Somaliland continues to exist, though unrecognized by the global community. In 1998 a number of clans in neighboring eastern portions of northern Somalia also declared themselves autonomous, forming Puntland. Unlike Somaliland, Puntland does not aim at independence from Somalia, but instead sees itself as an independent territory within Somalia. Although Puntland and Somaliland (to a lesser extent) both have "governments," and thus more formal structure than does the southern part of Somalia, these "states" remain weak at best. Neither "government," for instance, has exhibited the ability to raise significant revenue through taxation. Somaliland and Puntland also dispute territory along their border, creating confusion about which entity governs what and contributing to the stateless or quasi-stateless atmosphere in both.

[6] After the UN evacuated the country in 1995, rather than deteriorate, the Somali economy actually improved (Little 2003: xvii).

Bank 2003: 16). And these war-related deaths were combatants, not civilians. Indeed, "[a]trocities against civilians... [were] almost of unheard of" (Menkhaus 2004: 30). This is still too high, but far from cataclysmic. In fact, it's not far from the percentage of homicide deaths in middle-income countries such as Mexico, which in 2001 was 3.6 (WHO 2006).

In 2006 "a loose coalition of clerics, business leaders, and Islamic court militias known as the Supreme Council of Islamic Courts (SCIC)" gained increasing dominance over key areas of Somalia, including the capital, Mogadishu (CIA World Factbook 2007). In response the international community–backed Transitional Federal Government (TFG) attacked the SCIC, leading to a battle for power. In the short run, at least, this conflict reversed the strides toward more peaceful anarchy that Somalia had largely succeeded in creating prior to the TFG-SCIC clash. The TFG's victory over the SCIC set the stage in 2012 for the establishment of the FGS, which succeeded the TFG following the expiration of the latter's interim mandate and is intended to be the new permanent central government of Somalia.

Improved Overall Human Development

There's no statistical office in Somalia to collect economic, demographic, or other types of data that could be used for regression analyses.[7] Even before 1991 government collected almost no such information. However, the UNDP, World Bank, CIA, and World Health Organization have collected sufficient data to conduct a study that allows us to compare Somali development before and after statelessness emerged. To do this I examine all development indicators in Somalia for which data were available pre- and post-statelessness as of 2007, using figures for the most recent year that was available in each case. Eighteen key development indicators allow for comparison. I consider the last five years of government preceding the emergence of statelessness (1985–1990) and the most recent five years of Somali anarchy (2000–2005) for which data were available as of 2007.

Before considering the results of this analysis, it's important to underscore several features of the comparison. First, because my data stop in 2005, my comparison doesn't capture any change in Somali performance on these indicators since that time. Second, this analysis compares Somalia under government to Somalia under anarchy circa 2000–2005, not to Somalia anarchy in the period of intense civil war immediately following

---

[7] The "governments" in Somaliland and Puntland have been able to collect some statistics, but nothing substantial or that covers Somalia as a whole.

Table 9.1. *Key development indicators before and after statelessness*

	1985–1990[a]	2000–2005	Welfare change
GDP per capita (PPP constant $)	836[b]	600[c,e]	?
Life expectancy (years)	46.0[b]	48.47[c,g]	Improved
One-year-olds fully immunized against measles (%)	30	40[h]	Improved
One-year-olds fully immunized against TB (%)	31	50[h]	Improved
Physicians (per 100,000)	3.4	4[h]	Improved
Infants with low birth weight (%)	16	0.3[l]	Improved
Infant mortality rate (per 1,000)	152	114.89[c,g]	Improved
Maternal mortality rate (per 100,000)	1,600	1,100[i]	Improved
Population with access to water (%)	29	29[h]	Same
Population with access to sanitation (%)	18	26[h]	Improved
Population with access to at least one health facility (%)	28	54.8[k]	Improved
Extreme poverty (% < $1 per day)	60	43.2[k]	Improved
Radios (per 1,000)	4.0	98.5[k]	Improved
Telephones (per 1,000)	1.92[d]	14.9[k]	Improved
TVs (per 1,000)	1.2	3.7[k]	Improved
Fatality from measles	8,000	5,598[j,m]	Improved
Adult literacy rate (%)	24[b]	19.2[j]	Worse
Combined[n] school enrollment (%)	12.9[b]	7.5[a,f]	Worse

Notes: [a]UNDP (2001); [b]1989–1990; [c]CIA World Factbook (2006); [d]1987–1990, World Bank/UNDP (2003); [e]2005; [f]2001; [g]2006; [h]2004, UNDP (2006); [i]2000, UNDP (2006); [j]2002, WHO (2004); [k]2002, World Bank/UNDP (2003); [l]1999, UNDP (2001); [m]2003; [n]refers to primary, secondary, and tertiary gross enrollment.

government's collapse circa 1991–1992. Of course, when state collapse coincides with high levels of armed conflict, economic development isn't possible. Third, while highly suggestive, these data must be interpreted with caution. The correlation presented here cannot establish causation. In addition to the possibility that state collapse is the reason for the improvements we observe in Somali development over this period, it's possible that other factors may have contributed to this improvement. I discuss what these factors may be and their plausibility relative to the government-collapse hypothesis later.

Data for the pre-1991 period come from the United Nations Development Program's (UNDP) *Human Development Report-Somalia 2001* and the World Bank/UNDP's (2003) *Socio-Economic Survey in Somalia*. Data for the post-stateless period are from the *CIA World Factbook* (2006), UNDP's (2001, 2006) *Human Development Report*, the World Health Organization's *WHO Somalia Annual Report 2003* (2004), and the World Bank/UNDP (2003) *Socio-Economic Survey in Somalia*. Table 9.1 contains all eighteen indicators and the results of the pre- and post-statelessness comparison.

The data depict a country with severe problems, but one that's clearly doing better under statelessness than it was under government. Of the eighteen development indicators, fourteen show unambiguous improvement under anarchy. Life expectancy is higher under anarchy than it was in the last years of government's existence; infant mortality has decreased 24 percent; maternal mortality has fallen more than 30 percent; the number of infants with low birth weight has fallen more than 15 percentage points; access to health facilities has increased more than 25 percentage points; access to sanitation has risen 8 percentage points; extreme poverty has plummeted nearly 20 percentage points; the number of one-year-olds fully immunized against tuberculosis has grown nearly 20 percentage points, and for measles that number has increased 10 percentage points; fatalities from measles have dropped 30 percent; and the prevalence of TVs, radios, and telephones has jumped between three and twenty-five times.

Per capita GDP (PPP) is lower than its 1989–1990 level, but the data overstate the size of average income in the pre-1991 period, which was likely lower than it is under anarchy. Three sources of bias inflate pre-1991 per capita GDP as a measurement of well-being. First, firm managers in planned economies have strong incentives to overreport output to meet quotas or obtain rewards (Shleifer and Treisman 2004). Although Somalia officially abandoned socialism by 1980, the state continued to play a significant role in production until its collapse. In this environment firm managers likely inflated reported output, leading to artificially high GDP figures. Second, under government a great deal of Somali production was military hardware that citizens didn't consume. In fact, to the extent that this hardware was used to suppress the Somali population, this sizeable portion of pre-1991 GDP was actually negative value added from the perspective of citizens' welfare. Finally, in the pre-stateless period Somalia was one of the largest per capita foreign aid recipients in the world (UNDP 2001). In fact, "[p]re-war Somalia was considered a classic case of an aid-dependent state" (UNDP 2001: 118). By the mid-1980s foreign aid was 58 percent of Somali GNP (UNDP 1998: 57), compared to only 9 percent as of 2001 (UNDP 2001). In 1987 more than 70 percent of the state's operating budget was financed by foreign aid (Mubarak 1996). And before government collapsed, nearly 100 percent of Somali education was financed by foreign aid (UNDP 2001: 120). This discrepancy inflates pre-1991 GDP per capita compared to per capita income under statelessness.

If it were possible, accounting for fictitious production under government, the negative value added of military expenditures, and the foreign-aid gap would likely reduce Somalia's pre-1991 average income level below its post-1991 level.[8] The dramatic increase in post-1991 Somali consumption depicted in the data corroborates this fact. A substantial observed rise in consumption without an attendant rise in per capita GDP suggests an unmeasured increase in per capita income between the pre- and post-anarchy periods not reflected in the data.

Only two of the eighteen development indicators in Table 9.1 show a clear welfare decline under statelessness: adult literacy and combined gross school enrollment. Given that foreign aid was completely financing education in Somalia pre-1991, it's unsurprising that there has been some fall in school enrollment and literacy. This is less a statement about the Somali government's willingness to generate welfare-enhancing outcomes for its citizens than it is a reflection of foreign aid poured into Somali education by the international development community before government collapsed.[9]

Importantly, the indicators in Table 9.1 also don't measure the substantial increase in personal freedoms and civil liberties enjoyed by Somalis under anarchy. The Somali government ruthlessly suppressed free speech, censoring newspapers, radio, and television. Most forms of free expression were punishable by death, and foreign travel was severely restricted. Under statelessness, in contrast, Somalis are free to travel as they please (restricted only by governments of other nations) and enjoy greater freedom of expression, both privately and publicly. Twenty private newspapers, twelve radio and television stations, and several Internet sites provide information to the Somali public (Reporters Sans Frontieres 2003). Satellite-based televisions enable the transmission of international news services, including CNN (Little 2003: 170–171). Authorities in Somaliland and Puntland have attempted to interfere with media providers in their territories, but freedom of expression remains improved compared to its status under government. This constitutes an additional important, albeit unmeasured, increase in Somali welfare under anarchy.

As a point of comparison, it's useful to consider Somalia's development improvements from the 1985–1990 period to the 2000–2005 period relative to movements in the same development indicators in its neighboring countries, Djibouti, Ethiopia, and Kenya. Looking at these countries helps

---

[8] The census information used to calculate pre-1991 per capita GDP in Somalia is also controversial (UNDP 2001: 57) and, if understated, would further overstate per capita GDP under government compared to statelessness.

[9] Furthermore, according to one source at least, overall enrollment in Somalia may actually be higher than its peak in the 1980s (Nenova 2004).

Table 9.2. *Somalia and its neighbors*

% Improvement or decline in development indicators between 1990 and 2005				
	Djibouti	Ethiopia	Kenya	Somalia[d]
GDP per capita (PPP)[a]	–	+15.5	−4.1	+?
Life expectancy (years)[b]	−15.4	+9	−15.6	+5.4
Adult literacy (%)[c]	–	–	+3.7	−20
Infant mortality rate (per 1,000)[a]	+16	+28.5	+7.4	+24.4
Population with access to improved water (%)[c]	+1.4	−4.3	+35.6	0
Population with access to improved sanitation (%)[c]	+3.8	+333.3	+7.5	+44.4
Telephone mainlines (per 1,000)[c]	+40	–	+28.6	+1,150

Notes: Except for Somalia: [a]1990–2005, WDI (2005) and CIA World Factbook (2006); [b]1990–2006, WDI (2005) and CIA World Factbook (2006); [c]1990–2004, WDI (2005) and UNDP (2006); [d]For sources and years, see notes in Table 9.1.

interpret the findings in Table 9.1. In particular, it helps establish if Somalia's development improvements were the result of its predatory government's collapse and substitution with anarchy, or if Somalia would have experienced the same improvements even if it had remained under government simply because "it was time" for Somalia to improve. Similarly, this comparison helps establish if, for instance, the rise of new information technology in this part of Africa is responsible for Somali improvement and would have occurred with or without government collapse, or rather if there's something unique about Somalia – namely the collapse of its predatory state – that accounts for Somalia' progress.

In Table 9.2 I perform this comparison for all development indicators that data permit. I calculate the percent improvement (+) or decline (−) for each indicator in each of Somalia's neighbors between the 1985–1990 period and the 2000–2005 period. The comparisons are unavoidably rough in the sense that they don't compare the precise years from Table 9.1 in all cases. Further, they fail to capture the fact that Somalia's government was more predatory than the governments of Djibouti, Kenya, or Ethiopia. Thus the experiences of these countries provide imperfect points of comparison that tend to understate the difference between Somalia's strides under anarchy and the strides it would likely have made under Barre. Nevertheless, they're sufficient to address the general question I'm interested in.

The data reject the hypothesis that Somalia would have improved equally whether it remained under government or not. Consistent with Table 9.1,

Somalia performs worse on adult literacy compared to its neighbors between the periods. Still, on the majority of the indicators considered here Somalia improved more than its neighbors over the same period, suggesting that the collapse of government resulted in greater development improvements than would have occurred in its absence. In several cases Somalia has been improving while its neighbors have been declining.

Although this analysis helps exclude some alternative factors that might be driving Somali improvement apart from state collapse, only a tentative conclusion can be drawn on the basis of the available data. Further, the comparison in Table 9.2 doesn't help exclude other possible sources of Somalia's improvement unrelated to anarchy. For example, the period of Somalia's state collapse coincides with the rise of a large Somali diaspora, which supports an enormous remittance economy that has undoubtedly been important to Somalia's improvement. Similarly, in 1993–1994 UNOSOM intervened in Somalia and provided large quantities of humanitarian and other aid to Somali citizens, which might also have contributed to Somalia's improvement without government.

While the importance of these factors can't be definitively decided, there's strong reason to be skeptical that they, rather than state collapse, are responsible for the improvements in Somali welfare depicted in Table 9.1. For example, rather than an independent cause of Somali improvement under statelessness, the rise of Somali remittances after government's collapse is likely a result of government's collapse. In stateless Somalia remittances are handled through the *hawilaad* system, discussed later in this chapter, a private and self-governing financial system for transferring remittances sent to Somalia from abroad. Under Barre's government, however, the *hawilaad* system's predecessor, the *franco valuta* system, which served a similar purpose, was eventually criminalized, making it more difficult to remit finances to Somalia. When the government collapsed, this barrier was removed, leading to the growth of Somali remittances under anarchy.

Similarly, although UNOSOM's intervention provided critical humanitarian aid to many Somalis, its effect on the situation in Somalia wasn't exclusively positive. UNOSOM's presence led to surges in Somali violence, both against UNOSOM and between competing factions, which feared a shift in the balance of power that UNOSOM's presence threatened to create. Thus in addition to providing resources, which likely helped Somali development, UNOSOM also spurred additional violence, which likely inhibited Somali development.

Another factor that complicates my analysis is Somaliland and Puntland, the two northern regions of Somalia, both of which, nominally at least, have

Table 9.3. *Somalia disaggregated*

	GDP per capita ($US)	Infant mortality rate (per 1,000 live births)	Maternal mortality rate (per 100,000)	Population with access to water (%)	Population with access to sanitation (%)
Somalia[a]	226	114.89	1,100	29	26
Somaliland[b]	250	113	1,600	45	47
Puntland[c]	–	133	–	25.9	41.5

Notes: [a]See Table 9.1; [b]UN (2006 III); [c]UN (2006 IV).

some kind of government. Somaliland declared itself a fully independent sovereignty in 1991. Puntland, in contrast, identified itself as an independent territory within Somalia in 1998. Although Puntland and Somaliland both have "governments," and thus more formal structure than the southern part of Somalia in the period my data consider, these "states" are weak at best. Neither is recognized as a state by the international community. Further, neither exhibits some of even the most basic characteristics we associate with governments. For example, the "governments" in Puntland and Somaliland don't have a monopoly on the law or its enforcement. Although some public laws and courts exist, in both regions the legal system functions primarily on the basis of private, customary law and mechanisms of enforcement – the same self-governing legal institutions that govern the southern portion of Somalia – which I discuss later (Notten 2005).

Similarly, neither Somaliland nor Puntland has proved very successful in extracting taxes from their citizens. In Puntland, government's "[r]evenue capacity is very limited" (UN 2006 III: 6). Likewise, Somaliland suffers from "weak revenue collection capacity" (UN 2006 IV: 3). In addition to this, similar to southern Somalia, in both Puntland and Somaliland the private sector delivers many, if not most, public goods (UN 2006 III, IV). Calling Puntland or Somaliland "governments," then, is misleading. It's more appropriate to think of these as ultra-minimal states, if it's appropriate to think about them as states at all.

Unfortunately there are little data that would allow for a disaggregated examination of Somali improvement in the post–state collapse period. Nevertheless, in Table 9.3 I present all of the disaggregated data I could find as of 2007 that allow for a comparison of Puntland and Somaliland development to Somalia's development overall to try to get some sense of how these different regions might be influencing the overall figures presented in Table 9.1.

Only five indicators allow at least partial comparison. What they suggest is mixed. Somaliland has substantially better access to water and sanitation than Somalia does overall. On the other hand, Somaliland fares worse on maternal mortality than Somalia does overall and has about the same GDP per capita and infant mortality rate. Puntland also has significantly better access to sanitation, but does worse than Somalia overall on access to water and infant mortality. Although disaggregated data that would allow for a thorough comparison are lacking, these figures suggest that while Puntland and Somaliland may be "pulling up" Somalia overall on certain indicators, they may be "pulling down" or not really influencing Somalia overall on several others. The UNDP (2001) reports that Puntland and Somaliland are doing better than southern Somalia, which may well be the case. However, it doesn't seem that these regions are the exclusive locations of post-Barre progress in the country. Still, the absence of additional data renders any judgments along these lines very tentative. It's therefore important to keep in mind that the indicators reported in Table 9.1 don't disaggregate the regions of Somalia, and thus reflect overall conditions that include both citizens in Puntland and Somaliland, as well as citizens in the southern portion of Somalia.

THE SOURCES OF SOMALIA'S PROGRESS

Economic Advance

Much of the credit for Somalia's improved development under anarchy belongs to its economy, which has been allowed to grow in the absence of government predation. Although economic advance has been uneven, "in some areas, the local economy is thriving and is experiencing an unparalleled economic boom" (Mubarak 1997: 2027). Somalia's cross-border cattle trade with Kenya is particularly instructive of this progress. Livestock is the most important sector of the Somali economy. It constitutes an estimated 40 percent of Somalia's GDP and 65 percent of its exports (CIA World Factbook 2006). Examining changes in the cross-border cattle trade before and after statelessness is therefore a useful way of establishing changes in Somalia's economy under anarchy.

According to data from the Kenyan Ministry of Agriculture and Livestock Development collected by Peter Little (2003), Somalia's export of cattle to Kenya more than doubled between 1991 and 2000. Figure 9.1 provides an event study investigating the effect of statelessness on Somalia's cross-border cattle trade.

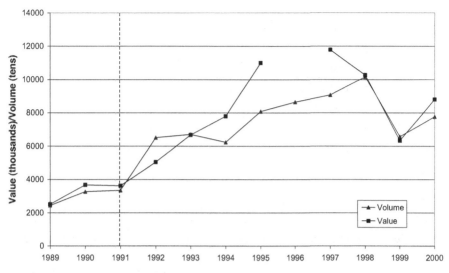

Figure 9.1. Cross-Border Cattle Trade

This figure examines changes in the Somali-Kenya cross-border cattle trade between 1989 and 2000. These data draw on the cattle trade at Garissa, the main Kenyan border district and a major livestock trading market in the Kenya-Somali borderlands. The dashed vertical line at 1991 demarcates the emergence of anarchy. Between 1991 and 2000 the value of the cattle trade increased 143 percent and its volume increased 132 percent. Between 1989 and 2000 the value and volume of the cattle trade increased 250 and 218 percent, respectively. Even during the most intense period of civil war between 1991 and 1992 the cattle trade grew substantially.

This growth tends to understate the true increase in cross-border cattle trade since the onset of statelessness. In 2000 severe drought struck Somalia, and Kenya closed its border to Somali livestock for fear of importing animals infected with Rift Valley Fever.[10] This depressed livestock trade in the final year for which I have data, shrinking its growth for the 1991–2000 period. Between 1991 and 1998, for instance, the value of cattle traded at Garissa grew 400 percent, and between 1989 and 1998 this trade grew 600 percent. In terms of volume, annual sales grew from less than 25,000 cattle in 1989 to more than 100,000 by 1998.

Further, these data reflect only official cross-border cattle exports from Somalia to Kenya. They don't include the substantial cattle trade that occurs

---

[10] Saudi Arabia also banned livestock exports from Somalia during this period owing to the Rift Valley Fever.

Table 9.4. *The growth of large-scale livestock traders*

Annual sales	% of traders		
	1987–1988	1996	1998
1–300	50	17	34
301–600	30	18	26
601–900	–	20	5
901–1,200	5	28	22
1,200	15	17	13

Notes: Data from Little (2003).

without the Kenyan government's approval. In 1998 unofficial exports entering Kenya from the Lower Jubba region alone add an estimated 70,000 cattle to these data (Little 2003: 38).

The frequency of larger-scale livestock traders has also grown under statelessness. In 1987–1988, 80 percent of livestock traders had annual sales between 1 and 600 (small scale). Only 20 percent had annual sales above this level (large scale). By 1998 the percentage of large-scale traders had doubled (see Table 9.4).

Information about crime in stateless Somalia can also be gleaned from this sector. The cross-border livestock trade is facilitated by brokers (*dilaal*) who certify for buyers and sellers that traded livestock aren't stolen. *Dilaal* incur liability if livestock they certify is illegitimate. In this capacity they act as insurance for cross-border traders. Data on brokers' fees pre- and post-anarchy suggest that fees haven't risen under statelessness. Between 1988 and 1998 *dilaal* fees remained the same (Little 2003: 109). If theft increased between 1988 and 1998, we would expect *dilaal* fees to have risen. The fact that they didn't suggests that, at least in the sizeable livestock sector, theft didn't increase under anarchy. In fact, *dilaal* fees are lower on the Somali side of the cross-border trade than they are on the Kenyan side, suggesting that theft may be more problematic in Kenya, which has a government, than in Somalia.

The livestock sector's expansion under anarchy isn't limited to cross-border trade with Kenya. During the 1990s Somalia accounted for more than 60 percent of all livestock exports in East Africa. In the northern part of Somalia (Somaliland and Puntland) production and annual exports of sheep and goats from the major ports of Berbera and Bossaso have surpassed their pre-1991 levels (Little 2003: 37–38). In 1999 these two ports alone were responsible for 95 percent of goat and 52 percent of sheep exports for all of eastern Africa (Little 2001: 194).

Nor is Somalia's economic improvement under statelessness limited to its largest economic activity. Other sectors that have grown under anarchy include service and hospitality. A large part of this progress has been in telecommunications. Local providers have joined forces with multinationals like Sprint, ITT, and Telenor to provide cheap, high-quality, and extensive service (UNDP 2001: 107; *The Economist* 2005). Transportation is also a growing service industry in Somalia. In addition to local transportation services, Somali-owned airlines provide international service for Somalis. By 1997 fourteen firms operating sixty-two aircraft were up and running, an improvement over this industry's status under government (Nenova 2004). In the hospitality sector, "unprecedented" construction has taken place in Mogadishu and other major urban centers (UNDP 2001: 203), facilitating the growth of new restaurants and hotels. "In Hargeisa, Mogadishu, and Bosasso, investments in light manufacturing have expanded, indicating local investor confidence in the economy and local security" (UNDP 2001: 39).

An improved monetary climate has also contributed to Somalia's stateless economy. Inflation was a significant problem pre-1991, when government turned to the printing presses to fund its corrupt activities. Skyrocketing inflation made it increasingly difficult to purchase consumables. It also created business uncertainty and distorted monetary calculations of economic participants. Although the monetary situation in Somalia remains problematic, under anarchy the Somali shilling (SoSh) has been more stable.

The SoSh was the official currency of pre-1991 Somalia. Post-1991 there was no government to mandate its usage. Still, the SoSh continued to trade on the world market. Under anarchy the SoSh, along with the U.S. dollar, is the basis of Somalia's private monetary system.[11] In the absence of a central bank or treasury, both of which nominally surfaced only in 2009, this means that primarily old notes circulate. However, in some cases discussed later, private parties have printed new currency, adding to the SoSh supply. Figure 9.2 examines the SoSh/U.S. dollar exchange rate between 1986 and March 2000.

The first dashed line in 1991 indicates the emergence of anarchy. Under Barre's predatory regime the exchange rate soared. Steep depreciation drove

[11] Somaliland also has its own currency, the Somaliland shilling.

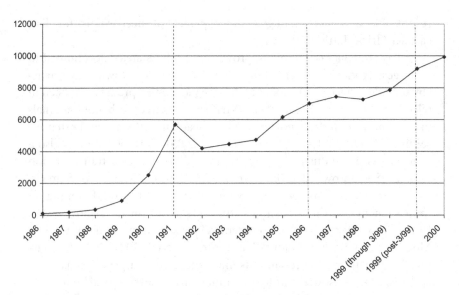

Figure 9.2. SoSh/U.S. Dollar Exchange Rate

the SoSh from SoSh 110 per $1 in 1986 to SoSh 5,700 per $1 by 1991. Following the coup, the exchange rate fell precipitously to SoSh 4,200 per $1, despite the fact that Somalia was in the throes of civil war. Under statelessness the SoSh has shown significantly greater stability. It lost significant value against the dollar twice during this period – first around 1996, and then after March 1999. These dates, indicated by the second and third dashed lines, mark two monetary increases. The first was instigated by the Mogadishu-based warlord, Hussein Aideed, who imported new shillings he had printed abroad to fund his faction's activities. The second was instigated by the fledgling Transitional National Government (TNG) in the spring of 1999. In an attempt to establish the TNG as a formal authority, its supporters imported SoSh 30 billion they had printed in Canada.

Following 2000, TNG supporters added further to Somalia's money supply, leading to additional depreciation against the dollar. Nevertheless, the average annual rate of depreciation under anarchy is still only a fraction of its size under government. In just the last four years under government (1986–1990) average annual depreciation of the SoSh was nearly 120 percent. In the first nine years of statelessness (1991–2000) average annual depreciation of the SoSh was just slightly higher than 6 percent. The 2000 monetary injection of TNG supporters boosted the 1991–2001 average to around 14.7 percent, and subsequent injections depreciated the currency further.[12] Still, money appears to be more stable under Somali anarchy that it was under the last years of government.

The SoSh's improved stability is also reflected by the fact that, at least until the early 2000s, in parts of neighboring Ethiopia the SoSh was used more extensively than Ethiopia's own currency (Little 2003: 144). In fact, prior to the large monetary injections in Somalia in March 1999 and then in 2000, the SoSh showed greater stability than did the national currencies of both Ethiopia and Kenya. From 1996 to February 1999 the SoSh depreciated only 12.14 percent against the U.S. dollar. Between 1996 and 1999 the Kenyan shilling lost 32.55 percent against the U.S. dollar and the Ethiopian birr depreciated 26.58 percent against the U.S. dollar.[13]

Somalia's financial market has also improved under statelessness. Numerous remittance firms mentioned earlier, called *hawilaad*, handle an estimated $500 million to $1 billion sent by members of the Somali diaspora to their friends and family in Somalia each year (UNDP 2001). *Hawilaad* are instrumental in connecting Somalis with the resources they need to survive and expand their enterprises. At least one of the Mogadishu-based firms is multinational, with branches in countries throughout the world (Little 2003; UNDP 2001). Remittance businesses are also morphing into private depository/lending institutions and may contribute to the development of a Somali banking sector. Some offer travelers checks and non-interest-bearing deposits, make small loans, and perform other bank-related services (Nenova 2004). Although still in its nascent stages, Somalia's financial sector affords greater access to most Somalis under statelessness than it did under government when financial services (especially loans) went exclusively to public enterprises and political allies (Mubarak 1997). As a result, under anarchy "Somalis lend and borrow and extraordinary amount of money to one another" (Menkhaus 2004: 34).

The financial sector hasn't been alone to attract attention from multinational businesses. Others have also found stateless Somalia an attractive place to invest. Dole Fruit, for instance, has invested in Somalia. General Motors' Kenya subsidiary has as well. Coca-Cola Company operates in Somaliland, and the BBC has forged a formal affiliation with one of Somalia's emergent media companies. Several international companies have expressed interest in investing in Somalia's energy industry, and numerous fishing fleets from Europe and Asia have reached agreements for commercial fishing in

---

[12] Calculated using data from Little (2003) and UNDP (2001).
[13] Calculated using data from (IMF 2006) and Little (2003).

Puntland (Little 2003: 166–167). The Somali economy has a long way to go, but in many ways it has progressed since statelessness emerged.

Improvement in Public Goods

Supporting the growth of the Somali economy is an improved public goods sector. Welfare-enhancing public goods provision remains extremely low, especially in Somalia's rural areas. However, like Somalia's economy, they show progress under anarchy. While factions are able to "tax" Somalis traveling on roadways they control, taxes and restrictions on Somalis' movement and trading activities are substantially lower under statelessness than they were under government. "Taxes, payable to a tentative local authority or strongman, are seldom more than 5%, security is another 5% (more in Mogadishu), and customs duties are next to nothing. There is no need to pay for licenses, or to pay to put up masts" (*The Economist* 2005). Further, it doesn't seem that Somalis are any less likely to enjoy the benefits of fees paid to militia leaders than they were when they paid considerably higher taxes to government (Little 2003: 7–9).

Public goods come from a variety of sources in stateless Somalia, including the "taxes" charged by militia. Clan militias provide security to citizens in their territories, and militiamen for hire protect businesses, seaports, large markets, and trade convoys. In other cases *shari'a*, a form of religious law/courts discussed later, provide security by including guards in their court militia in return for payment from businessmen (UNDP 2001: 109–110). Clan leaders also work together to provide needed public goods in areas outside of Somalia's big cities where few exist.

Law and order is provided privately by *xeer*, Somali customary law, which establishes rules regarding marriage, war, resource use, and social contracts between clans. It's also supported by *diya*, which defines rules regarding the punishment of misconduct, such as murder or theft. Although some secular courts exist, *shari'a* courts perform an instrumental function in creating legal order. Private courts are funded by the donations of successful businessmen who benefit from the presence of this public good in urban centers. Under anarchy dispute resolution is free and speedy by international standards (Nenova 2004; Nenova and Harford 2004). This constitutes an important improvement in the provision of law and order compared to before 1991. Under government the legal system was often used as a tool for preying on Somali citizens and punishing the opposition (Africa Watch Committee 1990; Menkhaus 2004). "[H]arassment, arbitrary arrest and imprisonment, denial of a fair public trial, and invasion of the home were common features of the life of the Somali citizen" (Hashim 1997: 90). Rampant corruption and political pressures rendered the police and judiciary useless for most Somalis.

Because of the state's collapse, private providers of law and order have been freed to step in. Somalia's stateless legal system is far from perfect. The justice system is still subject to abuse, and the climate in a number of areas remained insecure even before the renewed conflict of late 2006. Nevertheless, there has been improvement compared to the situation under government. "[I]n some parts of Somalia, local communities enjoy more responsive and participatory governance, and a more predictable, profitable, and safer commercial climate, than at any time in recent decades" (Menkhaus 1998: 220).

Education has also benefited in important ways under anarchy. There are more primary schools in stateless Somalia than there were in the late 1980s under government (UNDP 2001: 84), and their number is growing. The number of formal schools has increased from 600 in 1990 to 1,172 under statelessness (UNICEF 2005b). There are many Koranic schools as well. These focus mostly on the Koran, but students also learn Arabic. Higher education has benefited similarly by statelessness. There was only one university in Somalia prior to the emergence of anarchy. Under statelessness universities have emerged in Borama, Hargeisa, Bossaso, and Mogadishu. These universities offer subjects from computer skills to accounting. According to UNICEF, although the state of education in Somalia remains poor, there's evidence of "gaining momentum in the education sector" (UNICEF 2005a: 2) and improving children's literacy and numeracy.

Somalia's "private sector has [also] proved to be a relatively effective provider of key social services, such as water or transport" (UNDP 2001: 42). Transportation for freight and people connects even small villages in Somalia to major urban centers and is relatively inexpensive (Nenova 2004). A state-owned electricity provider opened in Hargeisa in 2003. However, most Somali electricity is provided privately. Water needs are also supplied by private firms. Private social insurance provides a safety net financed through remittances from abroad. These remittances average $4,170 annually per household (Ahmed 2000: 384). Expansive, domestic clan-based social networks also provide social insurance. In hard times private welfare can contribute as much as 25–60 percent of household income (UNDP 2001: 68). Private health care is also available. Although the state of medicine in Somalia remains extremely low, medical consultations are affordable ($0.50/visit) (UNDP 2001: 108). Further, the percentage of Somalis with access to a medical facility has nearly doubled since 1989–1990 before

statelessness emerged. Privately provided public goods like "education and
health care services... and utility companies such as electricity and water,
are also providing new income generating and employment opportunities" (UNDP 2001: 39) that have further contributed to Somalia's economic
improvement.

Recognition of Somalia's improved performance under anarchy compared to under government isn't to deny that Somalia could be doing much
better. It clearly could. Nor is this to say that Somalia is better off stateless
than it would be under *any* government. A constitutionally constrained
state with limited powers to do harm but strong enough to support the
private sector may very well do more for Somalia than statelessness can.
Further, Somalia's improvement under anarchy doesn't tell us whether continual improvement is possible if Somalia remains stateless. It's possible
that, past some point, to enjoy further development, Somalia might require
a central government capable of providing more widespread security and
public goods. De Long and Shleifer (1993), for example, show that while
preindustrial European countries under "feudal anarchy" performed better
in some ways than did those under absolutist autocracies, countries under
limited government performed better than did both. While it's important
to keep this is mind, it's equally important to keep in mind that this wasn't
the type of government that collapsed in Somalia twenty-two years ago.

The relevant question for Somalia's future is whether a government, were
a stable one to reemerge, would be more like the constrained variety we
observe in the West or more like the predatory variety that systematically
exploited Somalis between 1969 and the emergence of anarchy in 1991. In the
latter case, even if Somalia's ability to improve is constrained by statelessness,
Somali development may still be better served under anarchy than it would
be under government. For reasons I elaborate in the next chapter, if "good
government" isn't one of the options in Somalia's governance opportunity
set, anarchy may be a constrained optimum. Among the governance options
that are available in countries with histories similar to Somalia's – ultra-
predatory government or statelessness – statelessness could be superior.

In August 2000 select Somali clan leaders gathered in Djibouti at the
urging of the international community. At this meeting they established
the TNG in an attempt to reestablish formal government in Somalia. The
TNG, while remaining in name for three years, failed to establish authority.
It was crippled by a lack of popular support and an inability to raise tax
revenues. The terms of the TNG expired in 2003. This gave rise in 2004
to the TFG, led by Abdullahi Yusuf Ahmed. The plan was for the TFG to
go to Mogadishu and set up the new central government. However, strong

divisions among the members of the TFG initially prevented this. Instead of creating a new government, the TFG effectively fractured into two new rival faction groups that didn't fundamentally differ from the "warlord"-led factions they sought to replace.

In May 2006 the TFG and the SCIC, which provided the basis of Somalia's private legal system, entered into a conflict over control of Mogadishu and other key areas in Somalia. With Ethiopia's assistance, in early 2007 the TFG succeeded in taking control of the capital city. The renewed violence that this attempt to reestablish government in Somalia created upset the relative peace and stability that preceded it in the earlier period of Somali anarchy. Perhaps surprisingly, however, Somalia's private sector didn't totally collapse in the face of the new violence. As one Mogadishu-based electronics store owner commented, for example, even "[a]fter the fighting between the Islamists [the SCIC-backed militia] and the warlords [the TFG-backed militias], people are still buying computers. The security [situation] is very, very good" (Tek 2006: 31).

Further, while it's certain that this conflict was harmful to the progress Somalia achieved leading up to it, what little data we have on Somalia shortly following that conflict suggests that it didn't totally reverse the strides toward improvement that were made since 1991. As of 2007, the only two development indicators from Table 9.1 available for that year, infant mortality and life expectancy, both showed improvement not only over their levels under Somali government, but also over their levels in 2006. The improvement was minimal in only one year, but is present nevertheless. Infant mortality fell from 114.89 to 113.08 per 1,000 and life expectancy rose from 48.47 to 48.84 years (CIA World Factbook 2007).

The TFG-SCIC struggle wasn't the last conflict created by the attempted reestablishment of government in Somalia, however. Like the TFG and the TNG before it, the FGS lacks the domestic support needed to establish authority. The result is a continued, violent struggle for power, each new instance of which again threatens the progress Somalia has achieved under anarchy. "In 2012 in Mogadishu," for instance, "some 6,680 civilian casualties suffered weapons-related injuries, many of them from improvised explosive devices deployed by Al-Shabaab. Data collected by human rights and humanitarian agencies demonstrate that pro-Government forces have also caused civilian casualties as a result of aerial attacks and naval and ground engagement" (United Nations Security Council 2013: 9).

Leading up to the establishment of the FGS, three of the greatest disruptions of relative stability and renewed social conflict in stateless Somalia occurred precisely in the three instances that a formal government was most forcefully attempted: first with the TNG, later with the TFG, and finally when the TFG mobilized violently to oust the SCIC. In each case the specter of government disturbed the delicate equilibrium of power that exists between competing factions and led to increased violence and deaths from armed conflict (Menkhaus 2004). These experiences suggest that by upsetting this delicate balance of power again, current efforts to reestablish government in Somalia may similarly lead to more, rather than less, conflict and to new obstacles to progress.

10

An Argument for Anarchy in LDCs*

Somalia's experience highlights the importance of comparing really existing anarchy to the really existing government that might replace it. For the rest of the least-developed world, where governments exist, Somalia's experience highlights the importance of comparing really existing governments to the really existing anarchies that might replace them.

Anarchies and governments come in a range of qualities, from very-high-quality (or close to ideal) anarchies and governments, which are highly functional, to very-low-quality anarchies and governments, which are highly dysfunctional. Without explicitly acknowledging as much, the approach most commentators take when comparing anarchy and government is to compare high-quality government with low-quality anarchy. Somalia, considered in the previous chapter, is a case in point. Most everyone who sees central government as a solution to the current "chaos" created by anarchy imagines replacing that anarchy with a Western-style government – a government that looks and operates similar to the highly functioning ones that exist in the countries from which such persons typically hail, rather than a least-developed country (LDC)-style government, such as the brutal and predatory one that actually dominated Somalia's reality under Mohamed Siad Barre. This is problematic: comparing high-quality government to low-quality anarchy is sensible only if the anarchy one expects would prevail in a particular circumstance is of the most dysfunctional kind and the government one expects would prevail in that same circumstance is of the most functional kind.

* This essay is based on and uses material from Leeson, Peter T., and Claudia R. Williamson. 2009. "Anarchy and Development: An Application of the Theory of Second Best." *Law and Development Review* 2(1): 77–96 [© 2009 Law and Development Review].

In the least-developed world in particular, such an expectation seems very much unwarranted. I doubt anyone believes that, say, American-quality government is part of Somalia's current "governance opportunity set." But for those who might, I encourage looking at Somalia's present attempt at statehood: the FGS. This attempt is but a year old. Yet, before even becoming what we might meaningfully call a government, it's already pre-symptomatic of very-low-quality government. For example, according to the United Nations Security Council (2013: 23), "Despite the change in leadership in Mogadishu . . . the misappropriation of public resources continues according to past practices and patterns." The FGS, it seems, is simply "recycling many of the patterns of corruption of the past." This is hardly surprising given that "widespread manipulation, financial bribes and threats occurring before and during the September 2012 Parliamentarian and Presidential elections" characterized the process of establishing the FGS (UN Security Council 2013: 154; 144).

To take one example of recurring predation, "the CBS [Central Bank of Somalia] has effectively functioned as a 'slush fund' for" private patronage "rather than as a financing mechanism for Government expenditures" (UN Security Council 2013: 155). Indeed, an estimated 80 percent of funds withdrawn from the central bank have been for private purposes rather than the public purposes for which the funds are intended. Another familiar pattern is the use of official armed forces to plunder Somali citizens. "Government forces and affiliated militias have committed a range of abuses against civilians, including looting in civilian areas, as well as arbitrary arrests and detentions, often for purposes of extortion" (United Nations Security Council 2013: 34).

The reason high-quality government isn't part of Somalia's current governance opportunity set is that, as in all countries, in Somalia too, exogenous factors, such as the country's "history," shape and constrain what quality governance arrangement of *any* kind it has among its feasible governance alternatives. For example, "following the collapse of the Government, Somalis did not consider looting national assets in customary law terms as stealing. Such attitudes became institutionalised as a sense of entitlement in successive transitional authorities with public and private officials seeking personal profit from public resources." Because of this history, "the systematic misappropriation, embezzlement and outright theft of public resources have essentially become a system of governance" in Somalia (United Nations Security Council 2013: 154).

The idea that "history matters" in this way is no more than a recognition that creating the possibility for moving from a governance system of lower quality to one of significantly higher quality requires time, sometimes significant time, as the experiences of several struggling post-socialist transition countries attest. Although an extremely low-quality government similar to the one that governed Somalia before its state collapsed is certainly within Somalia's current governance opportunity set, Western-quality government almost certainly isn't.

It's possible in some cases that historically created constraints on a country's governance opportunity set might operate asymmetrically on the quality of anarchy that would prevail if that country eschewed government relative to how such constraints might operate on the quality of government that would prevail if that country relied on this governance arrangement instead. For example, a country whose culture strongly emphasizes tribal cleavages may permit a disproportionately better-functioning anarchy than government, owing to its ability to better leverage the discipline of continuous dealings within small in-groups. In this case the same set of governance constraints (a culture that emphasizes tribal cleavages) would present anarchy of some quality x, but only government of quality $x - y$, as feasible governance alternatives.

On the other hand, a country whose culture emphasizes cosmopolitanism may permit a disproportionately better-functioning government than anarchy, because anarchy in such an environment would have a harder time leveraging the discipline of continuous dealings effectively, whereas government wouldn't confront such a problem. In such a case the same set of governance constraints (a culture of cosmopolitanism) would present government of some quality f, but only anarchy of quality $f - g$, as feasible governance alternatives.

While such asymmetries are possible, in general it seems that a given array of constraints on a country's governance opportunity set will present governance options – anarchies or governments – of roughly the same quality. The governance opportunity set a particular country confronts will tend to consist of high-quality governments and high-quality anarchies, or low-quality governments and low-quality anarchies, making these the relevant comparisons, rather than comparisons between high-quality government and low-quality anarchy. Because of its far less constrained governance opportunity set, the United States, for instance, has among its governance alternatives both high-quality government and, I suspect, high-quality anarchy. In contrast, because of its far more constrained governance opportunity set, the Democratic Republic of Congo, for example, faces a more sobering choice: one between very low-quality government or very-low-quality anarchy.

The comparison between nearly ideal government and nearly ideal anarchy is interesting to consider. But it's also relatively unimportant. In countries with very-high-quality governments, welfare is already very high and, even in the best case for anarchy, little is likely to be gained by a major departure from the existing governance arrangement. Further, as the previous chapter pointed out, the majority of the world's governments are much closer to the extremely-low-quality end of the spectrum than they are to extremely-high-quality end. More than half of those governments, recall, are on or near the cusp of failure. In terms of potentially improving the plight of suffering populations, then, the important comparison to consider is between low-quality government and low-quality anarchy, not their high-quality counterparts. No matter your evaluation of anarchy versus government for the developed world, your evaluation of anarchy versus government for the poorest part of the *developing* world should, I think, be substantially more disposed to anarchy as a realistically superior governance arrangement. Building on the previous chapter's discussion, I explain why in the section that follows.

CONDITIONS FOR FIRST-BEST GOVERNANCE

To achieve high-quality government, a country's political institutions must satisfy four conditions:

1. Binding constraints on political rulers: to protect individuals' private property rights, political actors require power. However, to ensure political actors don't abuse this power for personal gain, using their authority to violate citizens' property rights rather than protecting them, binding constraints on rulers are necessary. Failure to satisfy this institutional condition means the absence of effective institutional constraints on government's behavior or, what's equivalent, a political environment in which political actors are able to wield political authority for private benefit at their discretion. In such an environment the state is a vehicle of corruption and expropriation rather than a means of private property protection.

2. A government-supplied legal system: to protect individuals' private property rights, government must have the power to create rules that clearly define citizens' property claims and provide mechanisms, such as courts, to resolve property-related disputes.

3. A government-supplied police system: to protect individuals' private property rights, government must have the power to enforce legal rules protecting their property claims.

4. Government-supplied public goods: to protect individuals' property rights, at a minimum, government must have the power to provide courts and police needed to satisfy institutional conditions (2) and (3). Additionally, the power to provide critical infrastructure, such as that which connects individuals in different parts of the country, and goods, such as basic education and health, may also be required to support individuals' ability to realize the opportunities for social cooperation that government-supplied property protection creates.

The alternative, and necessarily lower-quality, governance opportunities available to a country that doesn't satisfy one or more of the foregoing conditions depend on which of these conditions it doesn't satisfy. Stated somewhat differently, a country's lower-quality governance alternatives depend on the particular reason why it has failed to secure high-quality government. For example, the governance options available to a country that has effective constraints on political actors and the power to provide police and courts, but whose government has difficulty producing other public goods, are different from those available to a country that fails to supply binding constraints on political actors.

For reasons described earlier, this chapter is concerned with LDCs, which are characterized by a failure to achieve high-quality government because of a failure to satisfy institutional condition (1): constraints on political actors. In what follows I therefore consider the case in which a country that doesn't achieve high-quality political governance doesn't to do so because it doesn't satisfy this condition. Legal and police institutions in LDCs also tend to be administered poorly and ineffectively from the perspective of their ostensible purpose, which is to facilitate social cooperation. Similarly, public goods are poorly provided in such countries. However, these deficiencies shouldn't be confused with a dearth of power to supply legal or police institutions, or public goods, or such institutions'/goods' total absence, nor should they be confused with those institutions'/goods' ineffectiveness in achieving the *actual* ends to which political actors in such countries apply them. As I discuss later, these institutions/public goods are the primary tools political actors use to achieve their predatory purposes where government is unconstrained. Their ineffectiveness from the standpoint of improving social welfare is a by-product of the absence of binding constraints on political actors, not a result of political actors' powerlessness to provide them, their absence, or their ineffectiveness in securing the goals political actors seek through them.

ANARCHY AS A GOVERNANCE SECOND BEST IN LDCs

Multiple aspects of LDCs' "histories" can preclude high-quality governments from appearing among their current governance opportunity sets.
They do so by preventing the satisfaction of institutional condition (1):
constraints on political rulers. Such aspects include, for example, ethnic
conflict, the presence of abundant natural resources and subsequent long-
lasting fights over their control, and substantial experiences with socialism.

Histories of ethnic conflict have a close relationship with unconstrained,
predatory government (see, for instance, Easterly 2001; Easterly and Levine
1997). In many LDCs, members of one ethnic group had power and, absent
constraints on their behavior, preyed on rival ethnic groups to benefit
members of their own group. Later, one of these rival groups secured enough
strength to overthrow those in power, asserting itself as government. In this
capacity the ill-will shown toward its group's members was repaid in its
turn at the helm, and government's ability to arbitrarily wield power, which
facilitated such behavior, remained intact to permit this – and so on in a
vicious cycle. The result is a history of unconstrained and highly predatory
government that perpetually uses its authority to extort citizens for the
benefit of political rulers and those they favor.

A similar situation has often prevailed in the case of natural resource
abundance. Free to exploit this low-hanging fruit, some resource-rich countries never developed effective institutional constraints on the state, such as
safeguards against arbitrary government takings and other violations of citizens' private property rights. In some cases governmental constraints were
deliberately eschewed to facilitate the exploitation of rich resources. As a
result, a history of unconstrained government began and, alongside it, a history of struggle to gain political power so as to have greater control over the
chief source of economic opportunity in the country (see, for instance, Auty
2001; Baland and Francois 2000; Wick and Bulte 2006; Mehlum, Moene,
and Torvik 2006; Robinson, Torvik, and Verdier 2006; Torvik 2002).

The same is true of many LDCs' experiences with socialism. In the 1960s
and 1970s, for example, when many countries in Sub-Saharan Africa were
gaining independence from their European colonizers, under the influence
of the Soviet Union or of their own accord, many turned to economic
central planning. As Hayek (1944) points out, central planning as a form
of economic organization requires government to have the authority and
discretion needed to direct national economic activity, and requires political actors to have autonomy from citizens' desires that might conflict with

their plan.[1] If government doesn't have ultimate authority to direct economic resources, or citizens' competing ideas about how resources should be used are allowed to interfere with the central plan, the plan's coherence is undermined and government's ability to centrally direct the economy breaks down. Because of this dynamic, constrained politics is incompatible with central planning. Thus the selection of this mode of economic organization in some LDCs at their time of independence, or shortly after, facilitated unconstrained government, which created an institutional precedent that persisted long after these countries abandoned full-blown central planning.

These constraints on the governance opportunity sets confronted in LDCs do more than simply exclude high-quality government from those sets. Because they tend to preclude the satisfaction of institutional condition (1) – constraints on political rulers – as opposed to one of the other conditions, they tend to restrict political governance alternatives to the *lowest-quality* sort, or what I call predatory government.

Predatory government is characterized by political actors who, because they're unconstrained, systematically abuse political authority for personal benefit. Such abuse can take many forms, from expropriation, to preferential treatment for a small, politically connected minority, to the persecution, arbitrary arrest, incarceration, and even execution of political enemies or other pockets of the population politicos may target. This includes both explicitly corrupt (i.e., officially criminal) acts and legalized forms of related behavior, such as the confiscation of property and participation in rent-seeking activities. Classic examples of predatory governments include some of the governments one finds in Sub-Saharan Africa, such as Somalia's government before it collapsed in 1991 and the government of Sierra Leone, which I consider later.

A useful way of thinking about how the exclusion of high-quality government from some LDCs' governance opportunity sets because of a failure to satisfy institutional condition (1) affects which of the governance opportunities that remain in those sets is superior is in terms of what Lipsey and Lancaster (1956–1957: 11) called "The General Theory of Second Best." As they developed that theory:

[T]he general theorem for the second best optimum states that if there is introduced into a general equilibrium system a constraint which prevents the attainment of one of the Paretian conditions, the other Paretian conditions, although still attainable, are, in general, no longer desirable. In other words, given that one of the Paretian

---

[1]　See also Mises (1949) and Boettke (1990).

optimum conditions cannot be fulfilled, than an optimum situation can be achieved only by departing from all other Paretian conditions. The optimum situation finally achieved may be termed a second best optimum because it is achieved subject to a constraint which, by definition, prevents the attainment of a Paretian optimum.

We can apply this kind of thinking to governance opportunities in LDCs. If institutional condition (1) required for ideal political governance – binding constraints on political actors – isn't satisfied, as it tends not to be in the poorest parts of the developing world, the second-best governance arrangement can be achieved only by departing from institutional requirements (2)–(4): government power to provide law, enforcement, and public goods. That is, conditional on government being unconstrained if it exists, welfare may be maximized if doesn't.

The reasoning here is straightforward. If government is unconstrained, fulfilling conditions (2)–(4) *enables* predatory government – it creates the very means of such predation. For example, an unconstrained government may use state-supplied law to arbitrarily punish political enemies and reward friends; it may use the state-supplied police to enforce its arbitrary will on citizens and suppress dissenting members of the population; and it may use its power to produce and allocate public goods to further expand its authority, centralize control, and privilege a small minority at the expense of the majority. The previous chapter illustrated how, when government predation is severe enough, it can depress a country's welfare below that obtainable without any government at all. Thus, where first-best governance – high-quality government – can't be achieved, low-quality anarchy, which can be achieved, may constitute the second-best governance alternative.

This book has highlighted how when government is absent and thus fails to provide the institutional means of social order, individuals develop private institutions for that purpose instead. This suggests that citizens who suffer under predatory government can at least partly overcome what such governance arrangements *don't* provide. What the foregoing discussion suggests individuals cannot so easily overcome is that which such governance arrangements *do* provide: state-sponsored predation. Anarchy, in contrast, leverages what citizens can cope with – the absence of politically supplied social order – and avoids what they largely cannot cope with: political predation.

SOMALIA AND ITS COHORT

My preceding remarks embellish the basic point from the previous chapter: low-quality anarchy can outperform predatory government, which in the poorest parts of the world are often the only two styles of governance available in countries' governance opportunity sets. The question for the least-developed world, where predatory governments flourish, is whether, following this logic and the evidence adduced for Somalia, they might also benefit from exchanging predatory government for anarchy. Here I explore that question empirically. No direct or conclusive evidence of how LDCs in general might fare under anarchy relative to their current, predatory governments is possible. But some indirect and suggestive evidence of how they might fare is. That evidence is found in comparing Somali welfare under anarchy to welfare in other Sub-Saharan African countries, several of which are governed by predatory governments.

Before proceeding I should make explicit a point that I presume you have already gleaned: owing to the governance constraints discussed earlier, I take Somali anarchy to be an instance of low-quality anarchy rather than high-quality anarchy. If this is correct, according to the standards of appropriate comparison discussed earlier, comparing development under Somali anarchy to development under other LDCs' predatory, and thus low-quality, government is reasonable. If I'm wrong, and Somali anarchy is in fact of the high-quality variety – for instance, the type of anarchy one could reasonable expect to prevail in a country such as the United States – then my comparison isn't reasonable. I believe that common sense, and the broad similarity of Somalia's history to that of other LDCs, supports my judgment about the quality of anarchy we observe in Somalia. But if your judgment differs substantially, the implications of the subsequent analysis will of course differ.

I begin by comparing the state of development in anarchic Somalia with one of the LDCs currently closest to state collapse: Sierra Leone. I consider Sierra Leone because in this country little would be needed to permit anarchy to emerge. Indeed, if the international community simply ceased its efforts to prevent anarchy from emerging, this would probably be enough for it to do so.

Consider Table 10.1, which presents data for twenty-eight key development indicators that permit comparison between Somalia and Sierra Leone. In bold are the indicators on which Somalia outperforms Sierra Leone.[2]

On sixteen of the twenty-eight indicators, anarchic Somalia has higher development than Sierra Leone under predatory government. This includes life expectancy, number of physicians, infants with low birth weight, infant

---

[2] In comparing current Somalia and current Sierra Leone, I draw on the most recent data available for each indicator at the time data were collected.

Table 10.1. *Somalia and Sierra Leone: Key development indicators*

	Somalia 1985–1990[a]	Somalia 2000–2005	Sierra Leone 1990	Sierra Leone 2000–2005
GDP (PPP constant $)	836[b]	600[c,e]	903[o]	800[c,e]
Life expectancy (years)	46.0[b]	48.47[c,g]	39[o]	40.22[c,g]
One-year-olds fully immunized against measles (%)	30	40[h]		64[h]
One-year-olds fully immunized against TB (%)	31	50[h]		83[h]
Physicians (per 100,000)	3.4	4[h]		3[h,r]
Infants with low birth weight (%)	16	0.3[l]	11[v]	23[h,s]
Infant mortality rate (per 1,000)	152	114.89[c,g]	175[o]	160.39[c,g]
Maternal mortality rate (per 100,000)	1,600	1,100[i]	1,800[u]	2000[i]
Population with access to water (%)	29	29[h]		57[h]
Population with access to sanitation (%)	18	26[h]		39[h]
Adult literacy rate (%)	24[b]	19.2[j]		35.1[h]
Combined[n] school enrollment (%)	12.9[b]	7.5[a,f]		65[h]
Telephones (per 1,000)	1.92[d]	14.9[k]		4.8[q,p]
TVs (per 1,000)	1.2	3.7[k]		13.2[q,f]
Extreme poverty (<$1 per day)	60	43.2[k]		57[t]
Births attended by a skilled health professional (%)		25[w]		42[w]
Children underweight for their age (% under age 5)		26[w]		24[w]
Children under height for their age (% under age 5)		23[w]		34[w]
Children under 5 using insecticide-treated bednets (%)		0[x]		2[x]
Children under 5 treated with antimalarial drugs (%)		19[x]		61[x]
TB cases (per 100,000)		673[h]		847[h]
TB cases cured under DOTS (%)		90[m]		83[m]
Under-5 mortality rate (per 1,000)		225[h]		283[h]
Probability at birth of surviving to 65, male (% of cohort)		36.5[y]		30.7[y]
Probability at birth of surviving to 65, female (% of cohort)		41.3[y]		36.2[y]
Telephone mainlines (per 1,000)	2[z]	25[h]	3[z]	5[h]
Cellular subscribers (per 1,000)	0[z]	63[h]	0[z]	22[h]
Internet users (per 1,000)	0[z]	25[m]	0[z]	2[m]

Notes: [a]UNDP (2001); [b]1989–1990; [c]CIA World Factbook (2006); [d]1987–1990, World Bank/UNDP (2003); [e]2005; [f]2001; [g]2006; [h]2004, UNDP (2006); [i]2000, UNDP (2006); [j]2002, WHO (2004); [k]2002, World Bank/UNDP (2003); [l]1999, UNDP (2001); [m]2003, UNDP (2006); [n]refers to primary, secondary, and tertiary gross enrollment; [o]1990, WDI (2005); [p]2002; [q]WDI (2005); [r]1990–2004; [s]1996–2004; [t]1990–2003, UNDP (2005); [u]1990, UNDP (1999); [v]1990–1997, UNDP (1999); [w]1996–2004, UNDP (2006); [x]1999–2004, UNDP (2006); [y]2000–2005, UNDP (2006); [z]1990, UNDP (2006).

mortality, maternal mortality, telephones, and extreme poverty. Anarchic Somalia outperforms Sierra Leone on 57 percent of the available indicators despite the fact that Sierra Leone receives nearly five times the amount of foreign aid that Somalia does and has a smaller population (CIA World Factbook 2006).

Equally important, on fourteen of the eighteen development indicators that allow for comparison within country over time, Somalia has improved. Although data limitations only allow a similar across-time comparison for Sierra Leone on eight indicators, more than a third of that country's indicators show a decline since the previous period, and the others show only minimal progress compared to Somalia. These data are only suggestive, of course. But they suggest that, like Somalia, Sierra Leone might benefit from "going stateless."

Next, using data from Powell, Ford, and Nowrasteh (2008) that cover thirteen development indicators, I compare anarchic Somalia to forty-one other Sub-Saharan African countries, all of which have governments, and many, though not all, of which are predatory. Consider Table 10.2, which ranks Somalia on each indicator among its regional cohort.

On five of the thirteen development indicators that allow comparison, Somalia ranks in the top half of Sub-Saharan African countries, and on two of these Somalia ranks in the top third. On three other indicators Somalia is in the top two-thirds of its cohort. On the remaining five – immunizations (DPT and measles), tuberculosis, infant mortality, and access to improved water sources – Somalia falls close to or at the very bottom. It's a checkered record, to be sure. But it suggests that anarchic Somalia may be outperforming at least some countries in Sub-Saharan Africa governed by predatory governments.

More important, Somalia improved relative to a number of countries in Sub-Saharan Africa since its government collapsed in 1991. Between 1990 – Somalia's last year under government – and 2005, Somalia improved its ranking relative to the other Sub-Saharan African countries considered in Table 10.2 on four of seven indicators that allow for comparison across time. These data must again be interpreted with caution. But they, too, suggest that at least some LDCs in Sub-Saharan Africa currently under predatory government may be able to profit from going stateless as Somalia did.

Would embracing anarchy be a welfare-enhancing move for LDCs on the brink of government collapse? Because of the international community's efforts aimed at preventing these governments from doing so, we have only one country that, despite such efforts, has operated under statelessness for

Table 10.2. *Somalia and its Sub-Saharan African cohort*

	Rank among 42 Sub-Saharan African Countries		
	2005	1990	1985
Death Rate (per 1,000)	17	37	30
Infant Mortality (per 1,000)	38	32^b	31
Life Expectancy (years)	*18*	*37*	*34*
Child Malnutrition (% of children underweight)	20^a		
Telephone–Main Lines (per 1,000)	8	29^d	33^b
Mobile Cellular Phones (per 1,000)	*16*		
Internet Users (per 1,000)	*11*		
Households with TV (% households)	27^c		
Immunization, DPT (% children 12–23 months)	41	38^d	21^c
Immunization, Measles (% children 12–23 months)	42	38^d	19^f
Improved Sanitation Facilities (% of population with access)	24		
Improved Water Source (% of population with access)	41		
Tuberculosis (per 100,000)	31	40	

Source: Powell, Ford, and Nowrasteh (2008). Data from closest year preceding listed date were used when data were unavailable. The 42 countries included in the full ranking are: Angola, Benin, Botswana, Burkina Faso, Burundi, Cameroon, Central African Rep., Chad, Congo, Dem. Rep. of, Congo, Rep. of, Cote d'Ivoire, Djibouti, Equatorial Guinea, Eritrea, Ethiopia, Gabon, Gambia, Ghana, Guinea-Bissau, Kenya Liberia Madagascar, Malawi, Mali, Mauritania, Mozambique, Namibia, Niger, Nigeria, Rwanda, Senegal Sierra Leone, Somalia, South Africa, Sudan, Swaziland, Tanzania, Togo, Uganda, Zambia, and Zimbabwe. Italics indicate a tie for the rank given with at least one other country. [a]ranking out of 36; [b]ranking out of 41; [c]ranking out of 40; [d]ranking out of 30; [e]ranking out of 37; [f]ranking out of 36.

any significant period of time. Still, at a minimum, the data presented earlier suggest that arguments *for* permitting state collapse and permitting anarchy to emerge in the least-developed world deserve more than the usual chuckle or sneer.

Harold Demsetz (1969) famously cautioned social scientists to avoid committing the "nirvana fallacy," which compares an imperfect reality with a hypothetical ideal state. Instead, he pointed out, we should compare the situation we confront with the relevant alternatives actually available to us. The plans for a path from here to there must be grounded in an assessment of how things were, how they are, and how they realistically could be. His caution is especially useful when considering reforms in the developing world and, as Coyne (2006) points out, for Somalia in particular.

Policy makers shouldn't allow the best to be the enemy of the good – or, in the case of LDCs that confront highly constrained governance opportunity sets, even the not so good. In Somalia, for example, a consideration of the relevant governance alternatives based on realistically assessing the country's past and present suggests that, in the near future at least, it's unlikely that a new central government, should the most recent attempt to reintroduce one prove successful, would resemble anything like a constrained, supportive state. The history of Somalia's experience under government, as well as the ongoing experiences of its regional cohort, implies less optimism than is often projected by the advocates of recreating government in that country. Factional disagreements similar to those that led to civil war in the few years after government's collapse remain strong. Any ruler who established encompassing power from one of these groups would likely turn the state's power against its rivals rather than to the good of the country, much as Barre's regime did before it ended. The FGS, which, as the previous chapter noted, has limited domestic support, may lack more inclusive support precisely because of this and because faction leaders recognize the strong possibility that any one faction gaining too much power could mean the virtual annihilation of the others.

The theory of second best as applied to governance alternatives in the least-developed world suggests that if high-quality political governance is unattainable because of constraints that prevent rule-bound, non-predatory government, deviating from the other conditions required for high-quality government – namely state power to provide law, enforcement, and public goods – may be required to achieve the second-best outcome, which is anarchy. This line of reasoning does *not* suggest that *any* degree of political predation (i.e., the absence of perfectly effective constraints on government) requires the abandonment of government. Not even the most successful developed countries, such as those in North America and Western Europe, satisfy this impossible benchmark. My discussion has focused on the total absence of constraints on government and thus unchecked political predation, which we observe in the poorest parts of the world. When this is the case, government may generate more costs than benefits for its citizens, and the potential for anarchy's relative superiority reemerges. The task then becomes identifying for which specific countries this potential is a reality.

At least for the poorest of the LDCs, where government often hangs on only by an externally funded thread, it seems that such a reality is plausible.

For these countries, it may make more sense to welcome anarchy than to fear it. If, as my discussion suggests, predatory government is the worst-possible governance arrangement, the poorest of the LDCs are already at the bottom of the governance barrel. Under anarchy, there's nowhere for welfare to go but up.

11

A Future for Thinking about Self-Governance*

In the course of arguing that anarchy works better than you think, this book has elaborated two basic themes. First, individuals who are unable or unwilling to rely on government to facilitate social cooperation find their own, often surprising ways to do so, even in situations where we might expect it least, such as where the discipline of continuous dealings alone is insufficient to produce cooperation (Parts I–III). Second, in some cases at least, the mechanisms of self-governance those individuals develop for this purpose may be capable of producing more social cooperation, and thus a superior level of welfare, than their realistic government alternative could produce if it were relied on instead (Part IV). Together these themes suggest that significantly more optimism about anarchy, and significantly more pessimism about government, as governance alternatives is in order.

In this concluding chapter I hope to underscore these themes by considering two examples of a class of self-governing mechanisms I have until now neglected: self-governing mechanisms rooted in superstition – that is, objectively false beliefs. Superstition-based mechanisms of self-governance are especially useful for emphasizing the dual themes pointed to earlier, for two reasons. First, their "exoticness" highlights the incredible ingenuity of persons in anarchy to develop self-governing solutions to the problems of social cooperation they confront, and the incredible variety of self-governing manifestations that ingenuity can take, in particular when the discipline of

* This chapter is based on and uses material from Leeson, Peter T. 2014. "God Damn: The Law and Economics of Monastic Malediction." *Journal of Law, Economics, and Organization*, XXXX [© 2014 Oxford University Press] and Leeson, Peter T., and Christopher J. Coyne. 2012. "Sassywood." *Journal of Comparative Economics*, 40(4): 608–620 [© 2012 Association for Comparative Economic Studies. Published by Elsevier Inc.].

continuous dealings by itself is of little or no avail.[1] Second, while previous chapters discussed how self-governance can in some cases outperform its relevant government alternative, it should be especially surprising to most readers to find *superstition-based* self-governance doing so precisely because this self-governance is grounded in what would appear to be the flimsiest of foundations: objectively false thinking. Suggesting, as I intend to do, that even superstition-based self-governance can outperform its relevant government alternative should therefore supply particularly powerful evidence of self-governance's potential to produce better outcomes than the state.

GOD DAMN

Self-governing mechanisms rooted in superstition often appear senseless and socially chaotic, just as the anarchic environments they govern appear to be. In actuality, however, these mechanisms are often sensible and conducive to promoting social order, just as their anarchic environments often are. Consider the practice of cursing.

A curse is an appeal to a supernatural power to physically, emotionally, spiritually, or otherwise bring harm to another person. By imposing expected costs on social rule breakers in the absence of government or traditional self-governing mechanisms that could do the same, curses can incentivize would-be rule breakers to respect social rules. As long as individuals repose some positive level of belief in a curse's legitimacy, the threat of being cursed can influence their behavior in desirable ways, just as the threat of being incarcerated, ostracized, or executed under government or traditional mechanism of self-governance can.

For centuries communities of monks in medieval West Francia – the territory encompassing most of modern-day France – leveraged this cursing logic to protect their property rights against violent theft. Monks called their curses maledictions.[2] "Maledictions were part of the stock-in-trade of monastic defense programs" (Rosenwein, Head, and Farmer 1991: 771).

---

[1] For additional examples of superstition-based mechanisms of self-governance besides those considered here, see Leeson (2012b, 2013).

[2] This chapter abuses the term "malediction" in the sense that it considers various forms of clerical cursing under this title. In fact, as I discuss later in the chapter, "malediction" technically refers to a specific kind of clerical curse, the liturgical *malediction*, rather than to the variety of clerical curse-type forms I consider. Because my analysis deals with clerical curses, I use the term "malediction" to encompass all these forms and to distinguish them from other kinds of curses one can envisage, which aren't the province of ecclesiastics.

Indeed, it wasn't only monastic communities that used maledictions to defend property. Other communities of clerics, such as canons, did too.[3]

Contrary to contemporary images of monks and canons, which see these churchmen as paupers, medieval communities of monks and canons in West Francia were wealthy (see, for instance, Geary 1991: 20). Their most valuable possessions were their vast land holdings and the appurtenances that came with them. In much of West Francia, communities of clerics were the largest landowners in the kingdom (see, for instance, Little 1993: 208).

Between the tenth and twelfth centuries these communities' significant wealth confronted great insecurity. Under the Carolingian dynasty, a system of royal justice – king-appointed counts and, failing them, the king himself – protected monks' and canons' property rights.[4] But beginning with the reign of the last Carolingian king, Louis the Pious, that system began to degrade.

Aided by the Viking incursions in the ninth century, which did much to disrupt the previous pattern of governance, in the tenth century the Carolingian system of royal justice broke down. First, comital authority became hereditary instead of dependent on royal discretion. This rendered counts largely independent of the central government's control. Not long after, counts lost their public authority too. Local strongmen fortified in castles, or "castellans," replaced independent counts as the basic unit of governance. The result was a system of petty fiefdoms headed by strongmen accountable to no one but strongmen stronger than themselves.[5]

---

[3] Maledictions weren't the only method to which communities of monks and canons resorted to improve their property protection. But they were a major one. For a discussion of some of their other methods, see Rosenwein, Head, and Farmer (1991).

[4] This wasn't from benevolence. The Church provided important benefits to royal government. The Church could curse or otherwise use its relationship to the divine to delegitimize secular rulers. Conversely, it could bless or otherwise lend divine legitimacy to secular rulers. In return for the Church's support, secular rulers supported Church property rights.

[5] The degraded state of public law and order in the equivalent of modern-day France in the tenth through twelfth centuries has been discussed at length by historians of the Middle Ages. See, for instance, Duby (1977), Dunbabin (1985), Bisson (1994), and Geary (1995). However, the breakdown of public law and order should not be taken to imply that no courts at all functioned, for example. At the level of individual landholders, private courts with some semblance of authority often did exist. The problem was that courts with the formal authority to adjudicate and enforce decisions regarding disputes between persons from different lords did not. The years following Carolingian justice's breakdown were not anarchic in the sense of lacking all governance. Indeed, as the case of cursing this chapter considers suggests, private governance did exist. Rather, these years were anarchic in the sense that widespread public justice was lacking. During these years malediction was an important source of Church property protection.

This situation might not have been dire for clerical communities if they had the physical strength – the military means – of self-protection. But most didn't. A "monastery did not directly command the physical or military means to defend its own properties" (Little 1993: 53). Monks and canons surrendered arms, horses, and other means of self-protection when they gave up their lives as laypersons and took up the cloth.[6] Their communities' extensive properties were like sitting ducks for unscrupulous secular strongmen who, as a group, enjoyed a monopoly on the means of physical coercion.

This situation has been dubbed feudal anarchy. Many medieval scholars now eschew this term. But it provides a good sense of the decrepit state that public institutions of property protection were in between the tenth and twelfth centuries in the equivalent of modern-day France.

It was in this context that clerical communities began to rely on maledictions – divine curses – to improve their property protection. Monks and canons used several kinds of maledictions to deal with persons who threatened their property rights. Historian Lester Little (1993) has translated and compiled many of these curses. In what follows I draw from his work to illustrate their forms.

The first kind of malediction monks and canons used to improve their property protection against castellan plunder was the liturgical *maledictio*. Liturgical benedictions are divine blessings following prescribed forms that clerics bestow on persons they want to venerate at times of community worship, such as mass.[7] Benedictionals are the books containing clerical formulas for these blessings.

Medieval clerics had no "maledictionals." But they did have liturgical maledictions: divine curses following prescribed forms that they leveled at persons they wanted to *damn* at times of community worship. Consider the following malediction formula from the Abbey of Féfchamp circa the late tenth century (Little 1993: 9):

[W]e curse them and we separate them from the company of the holy mother church and of all faithful Christians, unless they change their ways and give back what they

---

[6] This was in keeping with the monastic principle of the "renunciation of . . . the means and symbols of earthly power" (Little 1993: 51). When public institutions were well functioning, monks' and canons' expectation was that government would protect them. When those institutions eroded, their expectation was to rely on alternative mechanisms for this purpose, such as the ones this essay describes.

[7] Ecclesiastics used negative and positive spiritual incentives to secure their ends. Just as persons who trammeled Church property could be cursed, persons who contributed to Church property could be blessed.

unjustly took away.... May they be cursed in the head and the brain. May they be cursed in their eyes and their foreheads. May they be cursed in their ears and their noses. May they be cursed in fields and in pastures.... May they be cursed when sleeping and when awake, when going out and returning, when eating and drinking, when speaking and being silent. May they be cursed in all places at all times.

The second kind of malediction clerics used to improve their property protection was called a clamor. Clamors weren't technically curses. But clerics could use them to invoke curse-like effects and sometimes did so in tandem with proper maledictions.

To clamor is to make a vigorous appeal. That's precisely what monks and canons did when they used clamors to curse. Clamoring clerics appealed to God and other holy figures, such as apostles, confessors, and, most frequently, saints.

Clerical communities were officially the property of the saints in whose name they were established. According to popular belief, it was those saints' duty to protect their communities. Thus, when monks' or canons' property rights came under attack, it was only natural for them to clamor their patron saints to thwart their oppressors.[8]

Sometimes clamors were simply public supplications to saints or other holy figures for this purpose. Other times they were more severe. In these cases clerics didn't just supplicate their supernatural overseers. They publicly humiliated them.

Clerics humiliated holy figures by moving those figures' remains (relics) or related corporeal extensions (crucifixes and holy texts) from their traditional places of exaltation to the ground. There, clerics covered them with brush or thorns. Similarly, clamoring clerics sometimes humiliated themselves – God's servants – by lying prostrate on the floor.

Clerics' logic was that humiliating holy figures (or themselves) would, in the eyes of their plunderers, provoke those figures, who expected to be venerated rather than denigrated. So provoked, supernatural overseers would turn their displeasure on the plunderers prompting clerics' rude call.[9]

---

[8] Technically, clamoring clerics clamored only God directly. Other holy figures, such as humiliated saints, clamored God on clerics' behalf together with clerics. However, it could be God's wrath or saints' (or both) that offending persons, who prompted the clamor, were supposed to fear because of the ritual.

[9] Persons who prompted clerical clamors weren't only supposed to fear divine wrath for their offenses. They were supposed to face pressure from neighbors, family members, and economic partners to change their ways and make restitution for their offense. This role is common to all forms of malediction this chapter discusses and constitutes an additional, supportive element of curses' power to improve property protection. There's no way to empirically distinguish or weigh the separate contributions of maledictions' supernatural

The third kind of malediction medieval clerical communities used to improve their property protection is the most familiar: excommunication and anathema.[10] Excommunication and anathema were predominantly the province of popes and bishops. But sometimes these higher-ranking ecclesiastics "licensed" lower-level clerics to excommunicate and anathematize the violators of Church property too.

Excommunication came in varying degrees that ranged from cutting one off from the sacraments to cutting him off from all members of the Holy Mother Church. Anathema was a kind of excommunication with gusto. It was a more dramatic excommunication reserved for contumacious excommunicates that often involved a ceremony of snuffing out candles or stomping them on the floor to symbolize the anathema's effect on the target's soul.

Clerics weren't averse to throwing in some curses against major excommunicates/anathematized persons when excommunicating or anathematizing them either, although this was not properly an excommunication – especially when their property was threatened. In these cases the lines between excommunication and malediction became blurred. Excommunication and anathema became a kind of malediction. Consider the following excommunication Pope Benedict VIII launched against some persons violating the property rights of the Abbey of Saint-Gilles in 1014 (Little 1993: 43):

May they be cursed in the East, disinherited in the West, interdicted in the North, and excommunicated in the South. May they be cursed in the day and excommunicated at night. May they be cursed at home and excommunicated while away, cursed in standing and excommunicated in sitting.... May they be cursed in the spring and excommunicated in the summer, cursed in the autumn and excommunicated in the winter.

The final form of malediction clerics used to improve their property protection isn't so much a different kind of malediction as it is a different use for it: contract cursing.[11] Besides imprecating strongmen who sought to violently seize their land and possessions, clerics threatened to imprecate persons who violated their land contracts.

---

versus shaming elements. But it's clear that their supernatural element was expected to do some of the work. For example, contract curses, discussed later, could be private. Clerics and their contractual counterparties witnessed and thus knew about these. Thus, if a counterparty violated his agreement, he would know he was cursed. But others may not know, precluding public shaming. In such cases the curse's expected effect operated solely through its supernatural element.

[10] On excommunication in the Middle Ages, see Vodola (1986).
[11] Besides Little (1993), see also Tabuteau (1988).

A common way that clerical communities came to possess property was for lay benefactors to gift it to them. A not infrequent occurrence was that some person might give land to, say, a monastic community, only to have his lord, his lord's heirs, or his own heirs challenge the community's property right to that land in the future. In an attempt to prevent this, a gifting layperson's lord, heirs, or both were often asked to make their consent to the gift explicit. Their consent was then recorded in a charter remembering the gift and held by the receiving clerics.[12]

To strengthen the enforcement of these persons' promises, clerics commonly included "curse clauses" in their charters.[13] These clauses, witnessed and consented to by the charter counterparties, threatened to imprecate them if in the future they tried to violate the Church's charter-identified property rights. Consider the following "curse clause" from a twelfth-century charter recording a land grant from a layperson to the Church (Little 1993: 56):

> And if any wish to destroy this charter . . . [m]ay they have the curses of the three patriarchs, Abraham, Isaac, and Jacob; and of the four evangelists, Mark and Matthew, Luke and John; and of the twelve apostles and of the sixteen prophets and of the twenty- four elders and of the 318 holy fathers who deliberated on the canons at Nicea; and may they have the curse of the 144,000 martyrs who died for the Lord; and may they have the curse of the cherubim and the seraphim, who hold the throne of God, and of all the saints of God.

Excluding the entire army of saints, which was undoubtedly large, this charter invokes the curses of no fewer than 144,380 people to be brought down upon the head of anyone who might try to violate it. That's a lot of curses.

Quantitative data that could shed light on the extent to which maledictions permitted clerics to improve their communities' property protection don't exist. However, narrative sources suggest that maledictions were often effective in this purpose. The fact that clerical communities used maledictions to defend their property for three centuries suggests that they must have been at least somewhat effective too. Commenting on the invocation of saintly interventions in particular, one historian of the Middle Ages notes that, "[i]n general, they seemed to have worked quite well, or at least better

---

[12] On the problems that consent rules created in Norman England and the peculiar legal system to which they gave rise, see Leeson (2011).

[13] Some charters involving Church property seem to have involved laypersons praying for curses to fall on contract violators. Presumably such persons only did so with churchman permission/approval or under churchman authority, given that only churchmen were seen as wielding the power to divinely curse.

than anything else available" for the protection of clerical communities' property (Geary 1991: 20).

Crucially, malediction as a mechanism of self-governance worked *because of*, not in spite of, medieval superstition: the objectively false belief according to which clerics could call on God to supernaturally punish persons who attacked the Church. That superstition had its foundation in a centrally important book that reflected medieval Christian belief – the Bible.[14]

Like medieval clerics themselves, the Bible is a curious mix of brotherly love and frightful wrath. It contains numerous curses. Consider this small sampling from Deuteronomy 28:

[I]f you do not obey the Lord your God and do not carefully follow all his commands and decrees I am giving you today, all these curses will come on you and overtake you:

You will be cursed in the city and cursed in the country. . . .

You will be cursed when you come in and cursed when you go out. . . .

The Lord will plague you with diseases until he has destroyed you from the land you are entering to possess. The Lord will strike you with wasting disease, with fever and inflammation, with scorching heat and drought, with blight and mildew, which will plague you until you perish. The sky over your head will be bronze, the ground beneath you iron. . . .

You will be pledged to be married to a woman, but another will take her and rape her. You will build a house, but you will not live in it. You will plant a vineyard, but you will not even begin to enjoy its fruit. Your ox will be slaughtered before your eyes, but you will eat none of it. . . . The Lord will afflict your knees and legs with painful boils that cannot be cured, spreading from the soles of your feet to the top of your head. . . .

All these curses will come on you.[15]

These curses should sound familiar. They're the same ones that graced liturgical maledictions, clamors, excommunications, and charters. Compare the

---

[14] A strongman who believes in the Bible, and thus biblical prohibitions on theft, may still be willing to appropriate Church property. For example, he may see himself as reclaiming property that's legitimately his rather than stealing, or for some other reason view his seizure as justified in God's eyes. A strongman who sees his appropriation as theft may be willing to steal because the discounted cost of the punishment he expects God to mete out to him when he dies is lower than the present benefit he expects to enjoy from the stolen property. In both cases malediction adds to the expected cost of appropriation and shifts much of that cost to the present, reducing the likelihood the strongman will take from the Church.

[15] The Book of Psalms is another hotbed of biblical cursing. See, for instance, Psalms 35:6; 35:8; 55:15; 69:22; 69:23; 69:25; 69:28; 83:17; 109:8; 109:9; 109:10; 199:11; 109:12; 109:13; and 140:10. On Psalm maledictions, see Curraoin (1963).

curses elaborated in Deuteronomy 28 with the following liturgical malediction from the Abbey of Saint-Martial of Limoges circa the late tenth century
(Little 1993: 60–61):

> We hereby inform you, brothers, that certain evil men are devastating the land of
> our lord Martial. . . . May the curse of all the saints of God come upon them. . . . May
> they be cursed in town. May they be cursed in the fields. May they be cursed inside
> their houses and outside their houses. . . . May their wives and their children and all
> who associate with them be cursed. . . . May their vineyards and their crops and their
> forests be cursed. . . . May the Lord send over them hunger and thirst, pestilence and
> death, until they are wiped off the earth. . . . May the sky above them be brass and
> the earth they walk on iron. . . . May the Lord strike them from the bottoms of their
> feet to the tops of their heads.

To render malediction an effective weapons against plunderers, clerics
needed to ground their curses firmly in plunderers' existing beliefs. Because
targets were Christians, grounding maledictions in "biblical curse tradi-
tions" achieved precisely that (Geary 1995: 96).[16]

   Notably, the superstition-based mechanism of self-governance reflected
in clerical cursing served to overcome a problem faced by persons in anarchy
that, as the essays in Part II discussed, the discipline of continuous dealings
has difficulty overcoming: the problem of violent theft. While in many
cases magical thinking won't be an effective safeguard against plunder,
in contexts in which the "belief framework" required to support magical
thinking's effectiveness in this regard exists, as it did in the context medieval
monks and canons confronted, superstition can be effective. It constitutes
another arrow in the self-governance quiver that individuals can and do use
to promote social order under anarchy.

SASSYWOOD

Leveraging objectively false beliefs to secure private law and order goes far
beyond cursing monks. There are many superstition-based mechanisms of
self-governance that individuals use when they can't, or prefer not to, rely

---

[16] Because maledictions' effectiveness depended on persons' belief in them, predators may
have had an incentive to develop disbelief in clerical curses in particular and the Bible/
Christianity more generally. I have found no evidence that they tried to do so. This isn't to
say that self-delusion isn't possible or never occurred. However, it may reflect the fact that
deliberately changing one's religious beliefs is difficult. A Christian who desires to drop his
religious beliefs confronts a time-inconsistency problem. At the time he considers doing
so, he believes that in the future, when his belief is gone, he will be damned as a consequence.
To be willing to deliberately jettison one's belief in Christianity today, one must already
significantly disbelieve in Christianity, and thus the consequences of rejecting it.

on government for this purpose. The judicial ordeals known as sassywood, used in contemporary Liberia, are a case in point.

Judicial ordeals have a long and rich history the world over. Most famously, trial by boiling water and burning iron was used by medieval European legal systems to determine persons' guilt or innocence in difficult criminal cases for hundreds of years leading up to the emergence of jury trial in England and the inquisitorial procedure on the continent in the thirteenth century.[17]

Judicial ordeals remain popular in contemporary Liberia because that country's government-supplied legal institutions are dysfunctional, where they exist at all. The state-provided judicial system is inaccessible to many Liberians, rife with corruption, and typically administrated by persons ignorant of the law, legal procedure, and without the resources required to perform basic judicial services adequately. In the face of this government failure, rural Liberians in particular, who constitute more than half of the country's population and face de facto "judicial anarchy," use private mechanisms – among them sassywood – to administer criminal justice instead.

Today people use the term "sassywood" to describe a variety of judicial ordeals that play a prominent role in the customary criminal justice systems of Liberians, the inhabitants of Sierra Leone, and smaller numbers of people elsewhere in Africa.[18] However, *the* sassywood ordeal, which I focus on, takes its name from the poison concoction these systems ask criminal defendants to drink to determine their guilt or innocence. The poisonous part of that concoction is made from the toxic bark of the *Erythrophleum suaveolens,* or sassywood tree.[19]

Sassywood is a "method of invoking the aid of supernatural powers to settle disputes or to test the truth of accusation" to adjudge the accused's guilt or innocence (Kirk-Greene 1955: 44).[20] Sassywood's particulars vary across time and place.[21] But its basics are similar. A criminal defendant imbibes a poisonous concoction, sometimes called "red water" (Wilson 1856: 225):

---

[17] On the law and economics of medieval judicial ordeals, see Leeson (2012c).

[18] For example, defendants are sometimes asked to place their hand in a pot of boiling oil in a manner similar to the medieval hot water ordeal. Alternatively, defendants may have a heated machete applied to their skin, similar to the medieval hot iron ordeal.

[19] The sasswood tree is also called *Erythrophleum guineense.*

[20] Kirk-Green's characterization here is made specifically in the context of Nigerian sassywood. But his characterization applies equally to Liberian sassywood.

[21] For example, in Eastern and Western Africa, citizens sometimes used animals as proxies for defendants in imbibing the poisonous mixture (Davies 1973: 33). However, in Liberia, the defendants themselves imbibe the poisonous concoction.

[T]he people who assembled to see [the sassywood] administered form themselves into a circle, and the pots containing the liquid are placed in the center of the enclosed place. The accused comes forward... his accusation is announced, he makes a formal acknowledgement of all of the evil deeds of his past life, then invokes the name of God three times, and imprecates his wrath in case he is guilty of the particular crime.... He then steps forward and drinks freely of the red water.[22]

The defendants' physiological reaction to his consumption of the sassywood concoction decides his guilt or innocence (Afzerlius 1967: 25):[23]

If the drinker by vomiting throws up all the [poison]... before the sunrise the following morning or much more if he does it during the very trial then he is innocent and publicly declared not guilty of the crime for which he was accused. But if he should die on the spot [or display signs of intoxication]... then he is believed and proclaimed Guilty.[24]

Historically, like its medieval predecessor, sassywood has typically been reserved for important crimes, such as theft or murder (Davies 1973: 44).[25] Also like its medieval predecessor, sassywood is reserved for difficult cases – cases in which "ordinary" evidence is inconclusive or lacking and thus traditional means of fact finding have failed. Accused criminals are charged publicly with a crime before their entire community. They can respond to the charge against them by confessing their guilt or proclaiming their innocence. In the latter case they're asked to undergo sassywood.

The logic behind sassywood's ostensible power to determine accused criminals' guilt or innocence lies in a widely held Liberian superstition according to which a spirit, or witch, "accompanies the draught, and searches the heart of the suspected individual for his guilt. If he be innocent, the spirit returns with the fluid in the act of ejection, but if guilty, it remains to do more surely the work of destruction" (Hening 1850: 45; see also Tonkin 2000: 368).

The fact-finding spirit inhabits the draught via the bark of the sasswood tree. Consider how one man tasked with collecting sasswood bark to make the sassywood concoction addressed the tree from which he harvested the

---

[22] Sassywood may also be used to determine the veracity or falsity of a witness's testimony.

[23] This description refers to sassywood in Sierra Leone but also characterizes the basics of sassywood in Liberia.

[24] According to Wilson (1856: 225), for example, if imbibing the concoction "causes vertigo and [the accused] loses self-control, it is [also] regarded as evidence of guilt."

[25] Accusations of witchcraft – of the use of supernatural means to perpetrate these or similar crimes – are also often adjudicated via sassywood. Such accusations are typically leveled when some crime or socially undesirable event has occurred but the culprit remains mysterious. This is consistent with the idea that sassywood is used to find fact about a criminal's identity when "ordinary" evidence to that effect is unavailable.

poisonous exterior: "You are a tree that never lies, a tree full of power. You give justice to all alike. If you agree that if it is true that the accused . . . is guilty of causing the death of deceased . . . show it to us when the cutlass touches your body" (Harley 1970: 156).

A "sassywood specialist" administers the ordeal *en toto* and acts as the trial's judge. He mixes the sassywood concoction and oversees the ordeal or chooses someone else to do so. The specialist's identity varies. But he's always a spiritual "leader" – an individual the community members seeking his assistance see as wielding special spiritual power that gives him authority to perform socioreligious rituals. Such individuals may include "witch doctors" – specialists in "medicines," poisons, and witchcraft – "zoes," or secret society leaders, elders with special standing in their communities, and chiefs. Regardless of sassywood specialists' particular identities, "only the men who know medicine, especially sasswood medicine, well and themselves possess strong medicine can conduct the ordeals" (Davies 1973: 43).

What seems like a senseless judicial procedure is in reality an ingenious, private judicial procedure for finding fact. The key to understanding how this is so is to recall the superstition that underlies sassywood – the superstition according to which a magical spirit that inhabits the sassywood concoction can infallibly detect a person's guilt or innocence, and acts on him accordingly to what it has found. Given this belief, persons confronted with the specter of imbibing deadly poison who are guilty of the crime of which they stand accused expect sassywood to reveal their guilt and kill them, or at least to inflict serious pain on them, in the process. In contrast, innocent persons expect to expel the sassywood potion, evidencing their innocence and leaving them unharmed.

Because confessing to his crime and suffering the resulting community-stipulated punishment for his misdeed is less costly for a guilty defendant than death (or at least severe pain) and suffering the community-stipulated punishment when sassywood reveals his guilt, the guilty criminal defendant prefers to confess to his crime rather than to undergo sassywood. Because being unharmed and exonerated by sassywood is less costly for an innocent defendant than confessing to a crime he hasn't committed and thus suffering the community-stipulated punishment for that crime, the innocent criminal defendant prefers to undergo sassywood rather than to confess. Indeed, because innocent defendants expect to be unharmed and exonerated by undergoing sassywood, they may *request* to be subjected to the ordeal to evidence their innocence. This explains why, rather than universally expressing fear at the specter of undergoing trial by ordeal, some Liberians volunteer to do so (Isser, Lubkemann, and N'Tow 2009: 58).

Because of the sassywood superstition, the ordeal imposes different expected costs on innocent and guilty defendants. This leads innocent and guilty defendants to choose differently when confronted with the specter of undergoing the ordeal. Innocent persons' expected cost of undergoing sassywood is lower than guilty persons' expected cost of doing so. Thus innocent persons are more likely to opt to undergo it.[26] Because of this, sassywood specialists – informal Liberian judicial administrators – learn important information about criminal defendants' guilt or innocence by observing how defendants choose when confronted with the specter of undergoing sassywood. Having learned the defendant's likely criminal status, the sassywood specialist rigs the ordeal to find the correct result, securing genuine criminal justice. Because innocent defendants are the ones who are most likely to choose to undergo sassywood, this means manipulating the potion such that it exonerates the accused.

"[F]ar from being the infallible and just 'judge' that the people as a whole th[ink] it to be, the sasswood ordeal offer[s] several opportunities for trickery and manipulation" (Harley 1970: 158). Specialists can manipulate the sassywood concoction to ensure that the "poison" criminal defendants drink isn't poisonous at all or at least that its presence in the concoction is low enough to prevent deleterious effects. Alternatively, specialists can include ingredients in the sassywood potion that induce vomiting, leading the defendant to expel the sasswood toxin (Harley 1970: 159). In these and doubtless other ways, sassywood specialists "can so arrange these tests as to make them produce any result they wish. By weakening or strengthening the decoction of sassy-wood, they can make it innocent or fatal, as interest or inclination may lead" (Hale 1853: 234).[27]

---

[26] As noted earlier, sassywood is far from the only judicial ordeal on which Liberians have historically relied. A common, nonlethal variant called cowfur is a kind of glorified oath taking. A criminal defendant or other person whose judicial testimony is in question may be asked to "swallow his oath" by consuming a clod of dirt or some other harmless substance. The logic here is that if the person is guilty (or lying), spiritual forces inhabiting or resulting from the oath will punish him. In some cases when even a suspect is lacking for some crime, an entire community may be asked to swallow their oaths. The economic mechanism underlying these variants of the judicial ordeal is the same basic one described in this essay. Believers who are innocent have nothing to fear by swallowing their oaths and therefore are happy to do so. Believers who are guilty fear the consequences of swallowing their oaths and therefore decline to do so, revealing their guilt.

[27] My theory of sassywood is consistent with cynical specialists and genuinely believing ones. A genuinely believing specialist may manipulate the poisonous concoction in a manner similar to the way that a believer in the occult manipulates the marker on a Ouija board. He may believe that "spirits" are guiding his actions or have some other internal justification that reconciles his intervention with the ordeal's supernatural mechanics (see, for instance,

Sassywood specialists' "trade secrets" of ordeal manipulation are kept secret by virtue of their monopoly on making and administering the sassywood mix. Recall that these specialists are spiritual leaders who allegedly have access to supernatural forces only they can wield. The importance of sustaining Liberians' superstition – their belief that trial by poison ingestion is supernaturally capable of revealing criminal defendants' guilt or innocence – helps explain why only certain, sanctified persons are permitted to administer sassywood as judicial administrators and helps ensure that only persons knowledgeable about and skilled in the manipulation of sassywood conduct ordeal trials.

The result of the sassywood procedure is a self-confirming equilibrium. The guilty defendant declines the ordeal, so his belief is never undermined. The innocent defendant undergoes the ordeal, but because the sassywood administrator rigs the ordeal to reflect his innocence, the ordeal exonerates him. Thus the innocent defendant's belief is confirmed. Sassywood reinforces the very belief that makes it effective. Moreover, it finds fact correctly and, similar to the case of the cursing monks, it does so *because of*, not in spite of, Liberians' superstition.

In practice sassywood fact-finding is more complicated that what I have described in this section. In large part this is because, in practice, potential criminal defendants may be skeptical in varying degrees of the superstition that underlies the ordeal. Still, the logic I sketched provides a basic sense of how this self-governing mechanism works: by leveraging the objectively false belief that underlies it, sassywood accurately "sorts" guilty and innocent defendants, revealing their criminal status where it would otherwise remain hidden. Most important, sassywood supplies evidence that even self-governing mechanisms that have objectively false beliefs as their basis are capable of outperforming their relevant governmental alternative – not, in the case of sassywood, because those mechanisms are free from problems, but rather because those mechanisms, which seem absurd on the surface, often work much better than their absurd façade would suggest, and most critically of all, because their relevant governmental alternative – corrupt and dysfunctional state courts – are riddled with still more severe problems.

Evans-Pritchard 1937). Whether this is the case or instead sassywood specialists are cynics is a question requiring empirical investigation. However, for mechanism described to "work," all that's needed is for the sassywood specialist to observe the defendant's decision to undergo the ordeal and, on the basis of that decision, to manipulate the ordeal's outcome to exonerate him – wittingly or unwittingly.

GOING FORWARD

The dual themes identified at the beginning of this chapter and highlighted by the superstition-based self-governing mechanisms discussed in the preceding sections point to a path forward for future considerations of anarchy. They suggest two "principles" or "rules of thumb" it would be wise to bear in mind for future thinking about self-governance.

First, persons in anarchy who must find private solutions to the obstacles that stand in the way of their ability to realize the gains from social cooperation are better at finding such solutions than you are. Thus the fact that you (or other researchers) haven't thought of a self-governing mechanism that can overcome some problem that anarchy presents doesn't imply that self-governance is unable to do so. The odds that you have failed are higher than the odds that anarchy has.

This book has focused on self-governance where the state is absent or dysfunctional. But anarchy, and thus self-governance, is ubiquitous. You can find it nearly everywhere if you know how to look. Hopefully, this book has improved your ability to find successful self-governance across time and space.

For example, even where highly functioning government is present, the state's eye can't be everywhere all the time and, even when it is, the state may be too slow to respond or be too expensive to use. The result is "pockets" of effective anarchy amid even "good" government. Thus we find "rent-a-cops," private arbitration, and reliance on superstition to produce contractual compliance even among law-abiding citizens in countries such as the United States (see, for instance, Benson 1998; Richman 2006).[28] Here citizens have a choice among governance alternatives. And they sometimes choose to use self-governing mechanisms to facilitate social cooperation instead of government.

This observation leads to the second "principle" for future thinking about anarchy that this book's dual themes point to. Upon observing a mechanism of self-governance that "obviously" underperforms its actual governmental alternative, ask yourself why, if this is so, the persons who rely on it do so. You may find that on closer inspection, a poorly performing anarchic arrangement is in fact underperformed still further by an even more poorly performing government.

Anarchy, in other words, may work better than you think.

---

[28] On extralegal contractual relations among Jewish diamond traders, see also Bernstein (1992).

References

Africa Watch Committee. 1990. *Somalia: A Government at War with Its Own People.* New York: Africa Watch Committee.

Afzerlius, Adam. 1967. *Sierra Leone Journal 1795–1796.* Uppsala, Sweden: Studia Ethnographica Upsaliensa.

Ahmed, Ismail. 2000. "Remittances and Their Economic Impact in Post-War Somaliland." *Disasters* 24: 380–389.

Akerlof, George. 1997. "Social Distance and Social Decisions." *Econometrica* 65: 1005–1028.

Akerlof, George, and Rachel Kranton. 2000. "Economics and Identity." *Quarterly Journal of Economics* 115: 715–753.

Alesina, Alberto, Reza Baqir, and William Easterly. 1999. "Public Goods and Ethnic Divisions." *Quarterly Journal of Economics* 114: 1234–1284.

Alesina, Alberto, Arnaud Devleeschauwer, William Easterly, Sergio Kurlat, and Romain Wacziarg. 2003. "Fractionalization." *Journal of Economic Growth* 8: 155–194.

Alesina, Alberto, and Eliana La Ferrara. 2002. "Who Trusts Others?" *Journal of Public Economics* 85: 207–234.

Alesina, Alberto, and Enrico Spolaore. 2003. *The Size of Nations.* Cambridge, MA: MIT Press.

Anderson, Annelise. 1979. *The Business of Organized Crime: A Cosa Nostra Family.* Palo Alto: The Hoover Institution.

Anderson, David A. 1999. "The Aggregate Burden of Crime." *Journal of Law and Economics* 42: 611–642.

Anderson, Gary M., and Adam Gifford, Jr. 1991. "Privateering and the Private Production of Naval Power." *Cato Journal* 11: 99–122.

Anderson, Gary M., and Adam Gifford, Jr. 1995. "Order Out of Anarchy: The International Law of War." *Cato Journal* 15: 25–38.

Anderson, Terry L., Bruce L. Benson, and Thomas E. Flanagan. 2006. *Self-Determination: The Other Path for Native Americans.* Stanford: Stanford University Press.

Anderson, Terry L., and Peter J. Hill. 2004. *The Not So Wild, Wild West: Property Rights on the Frontier.* Stanford: Stanford University Press.

Anderson, Terry L., and Fred S. McChesney. 2002. *Property Rights: Cooperation, Conflict and Law.* Princeton: Princeton University Press.

Arlacchi, Pino. 1988. *Mafia Business: The Mafia Ethic and the Spirit of Capitalism.* Oxford: Oxford University Press.

Armstrong, Robert. 1883. *The History of Liddesdale, Eskdale, Ewesdale, Wauchopdale, and the Debateable Land.* Edinburgh: Edinburgh University Press.

Arnot, Frederick S. 1889. *Garenganze; or, Seven Years' Pioneer Mission Work in Central Africa.* London: James E. Hawkins.

Arnot, Frederick S. 1893. *Bihe and Garenganze; or Four Years Further Work and Travel in Central Africa.* London: James E. Hawkins.

Ashworth, Tony. 1980. *Trench Warfare, 1914–1918: The Live and Let Live System.* New York: Holmes and Meier.

Auty, Richard M. 2001. "The Political Economy of Resource-Driven Growth." *European Economic Review* 46: 839–846.

Axelrod, Robert. 1984. *The Evolution of Cooperation.* New York: Basic Books.

Baland, Jean-Marie, and Patrick Francois. 2000. "Rent-Seeking and Resource Booms." *Journal of Development Economics* 61: 527–542.

Balfour, James. 1754. *Practicks: Or a System of the More Ancient Law of Scotland.* Edinburgh: Printed by Thomas and Walter Ruddimans, for A. Kincaid and A. Donaldson.

Baptista, P.J. 1873. "Journey of the 'Pombeiros.'" In: *The Lands of Cazembe: Lacerda's Journey to Cazembe, and Journey of Pombeiros, etc.*, edited by Richard F. Burton, pp. 167–244. London: John Murray.

Barclay, Harold. 1990. *People without Government: An Anthropology of Anarchy.* London: Kahn and Averill.

Barton, R.F. 1967. "Procedure among the Ifugao." In: *Law and Warfare*, edited by Paul Bohannan, pp. 161–182. Garden City: The Natural History Press.

Bates, Robert H. 1983. *Essays on the Political Economy of Central Africa.* Cambridge: Cambridge University Press.

Bates, Robert H., Avner Greif, and Smita Singh. 2002. "Organizing Violence." *Journal of Conflict Resolution* 46: 599–628.

Bauer, Peter T. 1954. *West African Trade.* Cambridge: Cambridge University Press.

Becker, Gary S. 1968. "Crime and Punishment: An Economic Approach." *Journal of Political Economy* 76: 169–217.

Becker, Gary S., and George J. Stigler. 1974. "Law Enforcement, Malfeasance, and Compensation of Enforcers." *Journal of Legal Studies* 3: 1–18.

Beito, David, Peter Gordon, and Alexander Tabbarok, editors. 2002. *The Voluntary City: Choice, Community and Civil Society.* Ann Arbor: University of Michigan Press.

Bell, Richard. 1605. *Bell Manuscript.*

Benson, Bruce L. 1989a. "Enforcement of Private Property Rights in Primitive Societies: Law without Government." *Journal of Libertarian Studies* 9: 1–26.

Benson, Bruce L. 1989b. "The Spontaneous Evolution of Commercial Law." *Southern Economic Journal* 55: 644–661.

Benson, Bruce L. 1990. *The Enterprise of Law: Justice without the State.* San Francisco: Pacific Research Institute for Public Policy.

Benson, Bruce L. 1998. *To Serve and Protect: Privatization and Community in Criminal Justice.* New York: NYU Press.

Benson, Bruce L. 1999. "An Economic Theory of the Evolution of Governance and the Emergence of the State." *Review of Austrian Economics* 12: 131–160.

Berman, Harold. 1983. *Law and Revolution.* Cambridge, MA: Harvard University Press.

Bernstein, Lisa. 1992. "Opting Out of the Legal System: Extralegal Contractual Relations in the Diamond Industry." *Journal of Legal Studies* 21: 115–157.

Betagh, William. 1728. *A Voyage Round the World*... London: Printed for T. Combes.

Bishop, Matthew. 1744. *The Life and Adventures of Matthew Bishop*... London: Printed for J. Bridley.

Bisson, T.N. 1994. "Feudal Revolution." *Past and Present* 142: 6–42.

Bliege Bird, Rebecca. 1999. "Cooperation and Conflict: The Behavioral Ecology of the Sexual Division of Labor." *Evolutionary Anthropology* 8: 65–75.

Böckstiegal, K.-H. 1984. *Arbitration and State Enterprises: A Survey of the National and International State of Law and Practice.* Deventer, Netherlands: Kluwer Law and Taxation Publishers.

Boettke, Peter J. 1990. *The Political Economy of Soviet Socialism: The Formative Years, 1918–1928.* Boston: Kluwer.

Boettke, Peter J. 2012a. "Anarchism and Austrian Economics." *New Perspectives on Political Economy* 7: 125–140.

Boettke, Peter J. 2012b. "An Anarchist's Reflection on the Political Economy of Everyday Life." *Review of Austrian Economics* 25: 1–7.

Bohannan, Paul. 1968. "Stateless Societies." In: *Problems in African History*, edited by Robert Collins, pp. 170–172. Englewood Cliffs: Prentice-Hall.

Botelho de Vasconcellos, Alexandre Jose. 1844 [1873]. "Annaes Maritimos e Coloniais." In: *Lacerda's Journey to Cazembe, and Journey of Pombeiros, etc.*, edited by Richard F. Burton, pp. 24–25. London: John Murray.

Bowes, Robert. 1551. *Manuscript of Sir Robert Bowes.*

Bromley, J.S. 1987. *Corsairs and Navies 1660–1760.* London: The Hambledon Press.

Buchanan, James M. 1975. *The Limits of Liberty: Between Anarchy and Leviathan.* Chicago: University of Chicago Press.

Buchanan, James M., and Gordon Tullock. 1962. *The Calculus of Consent: Logical Foundations of Constitutional Democracy.* Ann Arbor: University of Michigan Press.

Buchner, Max. 1883. "Das Reich des Mwata Yamvo und seine Nachbarlander." *Deutsche Geographische Blatter* 1: 56–67.

Bucquoy, Jacobus de. 1744. *Zestien Jaarige Reis nass de Inidien gedan door Jacob de Bucquoy.* Harlem: Bosch.

Burnett, John S. 2002. *Dangerous Waters: Modern Piracy and Terror on the High Seas.* New York: Plume.

Bush, Winston C., and Lawrence S. Mayer. 1974. "Some Implications of Anarchy for the Distribution of Property Rights." *Journal of Economic Theory* 8: 401–412.

California Department of Justice. 2003. *Organized Crime in California: Annual Report to the California Legislature 2003.* Available at: http://ag.ca.gov/publications/org_crime.pdf.

Cameron, Verney Lovett. 1877. *Across Africa.* New York: Harper and Brothers Publishers.

Capello, Hermengildo, and Roberto Ivens. 1969. *From Benguella to the Territory of Yacca*, translated by Alfred Elwes. New York: Negro Universities Press.

Casella, Alessandra. 1996. "On Market Integration and the Development of Institutions: The Case of International Commercial Arbitration." *European Economic Review* 40: 155–186.

Chang, Juin-Jen, Huei-Chung Lu, and Mingshen Chen. 2005. "Organized Crime or Individual Crime: Endogenous Size of a Criminal Organization and the Optimal Law Enforcement." *Economic Inquiry* 43: 661–675.

CIA World Factbook. 2006. *Somalia.* Available at: http://www.umsl.edu/services/govdocs/wofact2006/geos/so.html.

CIA World Factbook. 2007. *Somalia.* Available at: http://www.umsl.edu/services/govdocs/wofact2007/geos/so.html.

Clay, Karen. 1997. "Trade without Law: Private-Order Institutions in Mexican California." *Journal of Law, Economics, and Organization* 13: 202–231.

Coase, Ronald H. 1960. "The Problem of Social Cost." *Journal of Law and Economics* 3: 1–44.

Coggeshall, George. 1856. *A History of American Privateers and Letters of Marque.* New York: By and for the author.

Coggins, Jack. 2002. *Ships and Seamen of the American Revolution.* New York: Dover.

Cohen, Abner. 1969. *Custom and Politics in Urban Africa: A Study of Hausa Migrants in Yoruba Towns.* Berkeley: University of California Press.

Coillard, Francois. 1897. *On the Threshold of Central Africa,* translated by Catherine Mackintosh. London: Hodder and Stoughton.

Colson, Elizabeth. 1969. "African Society at the Time of the Scramble." In: *Colonialism in Africa 1870–1960: The History and Politics of Colonialism 1870–1914, Vol. 1,* edited by L.H. Gann and Peter Duignan, pp. 27–65. Cambridge: Cambridge University Press.

Cordingly, David, editor. 1996. *Pirates: Terror on the High Seas – From the Caribbean to the South China Sea.* Atlanta: Turner Publishing.

Cordingly, David. 2006. *Under the Black Flag.* New York: Random House.

Cotrugli, Benedetto. 1573. *Della mercatura et del mercante perfetto.* Venice.

Coyne, Christopher J. 2006. "Reconstructing Weak and Failed States: Foreign Intervention and the Nirvana Fallacy." *Foreign Policy Analysis* 2: 343–361.

Craig, W. Laurence, William Park, and Ian Paulsson. 2000. *International Chamber of Commerce Arbitration.* New York: Oceana Publications.

Crawford, David. 1914. *Thinking Black: 22 Years without a Break in the Long Grass of Central Africa.* London: Morgan and Scott.

Crowhurst, Patrick. 1977. *The Defence of British Trade 1689–1815.* Chatham: Dawson.

Crowhurst, Patrick. 1989. *The French War on Trade: Privateering 1793–1815.* Aldershot: Scolar Press.

Crowhurst, Patrick. 1997. "Experience, Skill and Luck: French Privateering Expeditions, 1792–1815." In: *Pirates and Privateers: New Perspectives on the War on Trade in the Eighteenth and Nineteenth Centuries,* edited by David J. Starkey, E.S. van Eyck van Heslinga, and J.A. de Moor, pp. 155–170. Exeter: University of Exeter Press.

Curraoin, Tomás Ó. 1963. "The Maledictions in the Psalms." *Furrow* 14: 421–429.

Curtin, Philp, Steven Feierman, Leonard Thompson, and Jan Vansina. 1995. *African History: From Earliest Times to Independence.* New York: Longman.

Dampier, William. 1697–1707 [2005]. *Buccaneer Explorer: William Dampier's Voyages,* edited by Gerald Norris. Woodbridge: Boydell Press.

David, Rene. 1985. *Arbitration in International Trade*. Deventer, The Netherlands: Kluwer Law and Taxation Publishers.

Davies, Louise Sarah. 1973. *The Sasswood Ordeal of the West Atlantic Tribes of Sierra Leone and Liberia: An Ethnohistoriographic Survey*. MA Thesis, Portland State University.

Davis, Ralph. 1962. *The Rise of the English Shipping Industry in the Seventeenth and Eighteenth Centuries*. London: Macmillan.

De Long, Bradford, and Andrei Shleifer. 1993. "Princes and Merchants: European City Growth before the Industrial Revolution. *Journal of Law and Economics* 36: 671–702.

Demsetz, Harold. 1969. "Information and Efficiency: Another Viewpoint." *Journal of Law and Economics* 10: 1–21.

Dias de Carvalho, Henrique Augusto. 1890. *Ethnographia e historia tradicional dos povos da Lunda (Expedicao portugueza ao Muatianvua, vol. 5)*. Lisboa: Imprensa Nacional.

Dick, Andrew R. 1995. "When Does Organized Crime Pay? A Transaction Cost Analysis." *International Review of Law and Economics* 15: 25–45.

DiIulio, Jr., John J. 1996. "Help Wanted: Economists, Crime and Public Policy." *Journal of Economic Perspectives* 10: 3–24.

Dixit, Avinash K. 2004. *Lawlessness and Economics: Alternative Modes of Governance*. Princeton: Princeton University Press.

Dixit, Avinash K. 2003. "Trade Expansion and Contract Enforcement." *Journal of Political Economy* 111: 1293–1317.

Dole, Gertrude. 1966. "Anarchy without Chaos: Alternatives to Political Authority among the Kuikuru." In: *Political Anthropology*, edited by Marc Swartz, Victor Turner, and Arthur Tuden, pp. 73–87. Chicago: Aldine.

Downing, Clement. 1737 [1924]. *A History of the Indian Wars*, edited by William Foster. London: Oxford University Press.

Duby, Georges. 1977. *The Chivalrous Society*. Berkeley: University of California Press.

Dunbabin, Jean. 1985. *France in the Making, 843–1180*. Oxford: Oxford University Press.

Easterly, William. 2001. "Can Institutions Resolve Ethnic Conflict?" *Economic Development and Cultural Change* 49: 687–706.

Easterly, William, and Ross Levine. 1997. "Africa's Growth Tragedy: Policies and Ethnic Divisions." *Quarterly Journal of Economics* 112: 1203–1250.

Evans-Pritchard, E.E. 1937. *Witchcraft, Oracles and Magic among the Azande*. Oxford: Oxford University Press.

Evans-Pritchard, E.E. 1940 [1980]. *The Nuer: A Description of the Modes of Livelihood and Political Institutions of a Nilotic People*. Oxford: Oxford University Press.

Exquemelin, Alexander O. 1678 [2000]. *The Buccaneers of America*, translated by Alexis Brown. Mineola: Dover.

Fanning, Nathaniel. 1912. *Fanning's Narrative, Being the Memoirs of Nathaniel Fanning, an Officer of the Revolutionary Navy, 1778–1783*, edited by John S. Barnes. New York: Naval History Society.

Fearon, James, and David Laitin. 1996. "Explaining Interethnic Cooperation." *American Political Science Review* 90: 715–735.

Federal Bureau of Investigation. 2008. *Freedom of Information and Privacy Acts Subject File: La Nuestra Familia*. Available at: http://foia.fbi.gov/filelink.html?file=/lanuestrafamily/lanuestrafamily_part01.pdf.

Foreign Policy/Fund for Peace. 2007. *Failed States Index 2007.* Available at: http://www.fundforpeace.org/web/index.php?option=com_content&task=view&id=229&Itemid=366.

Fraser, George MacDonald. 1995. *The Steel Bonnets: The Story of the Anglo-Scottish Border Reivers.* London: Harper Collins.

Friedman, David. 1973. *The Machinery of Freedom: Guide to a Radical Capitalism.* Chicago: Open Court Publishing.

Friedman, David. 1979. "Private Creation and Enforcement of Law: A Historical Case." *Journal of Legal Studies* 8: 399–415.

Fuentes, Nina. 2006. *The Rise and Fall of the Nuestra Familia.* Jefferson, WI: Know Gangs Publishing.

Furbank, Philip N., and W.R. Owens. 1988. *The Canonisation of Daniel Defoe.* New Haven: Yale University Press.

Gambetta, Diego. 1993. *The Sicilian Mafia: The Business of Private Protection.* Cambridge, MA: Harvard University Press.

Gambetta, Diego. 1994. "Inscrutable Markets." *Rationality and Society* 6: 353–368.

Gambetta, Deigo. 2009. *Codes of the Underworld: How Criminals Communicate.* Princeton: Princeton University Press.

Garitee, Jerome R. 1977. *The Republic's Private Navy.* Middletown: Mystic Seaport/Wesleyan University Press.

Garoupa, Nuno. 2000. "The Economics of Organized Crime and Optimal Law Enforcement." *Economic Inquiry* 38: 278–288.

Geary, Patrick J. 1991. *Furta Sacra: Thefts of Relics in the Central Middle Ages.* Princeton: Princeton University Press.

Geary, Patrick J. 1995. *Living with the Dead in the Middle Ages.* Ithaca: Cornell University Press.

Gettleman, Jeffery, and Mark Mazzetti. 2006. "Somalia's Islamists and Ethiopia Gird for War." *New York Times,* December 14.

Gibbons, Alfred St. Hill. 1904. *Africa from South to North through Marotseland.* 2 vols. London: John Lane.

Gifford, Adam Jr. 1993. "The Economic Organization of 17th- through Mid-19th Century Whaling and Shipping." *Journal of Economic Behavior and Organization* 20: 137–150.

Glaeser, Edward L., Bruce Sacerdote, and Jose A. Scheinkman. 1996. "Crime and Social Interactions." *Quarterly Journal of Economics* 111: 507–548.

Goeje, M.J. de. 1909. "International Handelsverkeer in de Middeleeuwen." *Verslagen en Mededeelingen der Koninklijke Akademie van Wetenschappan, Afdeeling Letter-kunde* 9: 245–269.

Gosse, Philip. 1946. *The History of Piracy.* New York: Tudor Publishing Company.

Graca, Joaquim. 1890. "Expedicao ao Muatayanvua. Diario de Joaquim Rodrigues Graca." *Boletim da Sociedade de Geographia de Lisboa* 9a ser: 365–468.

Greif, Avner, Paul Milgrom, and Barry R. Weingast. 1994. "Coordination, Commitment, and Enforcement: The Case of the Merchant Guild." *Journal of Political Economy* 102: 745–776.

Grossman, Herschel. 1998. "Producers and Predators." *Pacific Economic Review* 3: 169–187.

Grossman, Herschel, and Minseong Kim. 2002. "Predation, Efficiency and Inequality." *Journal of Institutional and Theoretical Economics* 127: 393–407.

Haddock, David. 2002. "Force, Threat, Negotiation: The Private Enforcement of Rights." In: *Property Rights: Cooperation, Conflict, and Law*, edited by Terry L. Anderson and Fred S. McChesney, pp. 168–194. Princeton: Princeton University Press.

Hale, Sarah J. 1853. *Liberia; or, Mr. Peyton's Experiments.* New York: Harper & Brothers Publishers.

Harding, Colin. 1905. *In Remotest Barotseland.* London: Hurst and Blackett, Ltd.

Harley, George Way. 1970. *Native African Medicine: With Special Reference to Its Practice in the Mano Tribe of Liberia.* London: Frank Cass.

Hart, Oliver, and John Moore. 1988. "Incomplete Contracts and Renegotiation." *Econometrica* 56: 755–785.

Hashim, Alice. 1997. *The Fallen State: Dissonance, Dictatorship and Death in Somalia.* Lanham: University Press of America.

Hassan, Mohamed Olad. 2007. "UNICEF: Somali Kids Urgently Need Food." *Associated Press*, September 12.

Hausken, Kjell. 2004. "Mutual Raiding of Production and the Emergence of Exchange." *Economic Inquiry* 42: 572–586.

Hayek, Friedrich A. 1944. *The Road to Serfdom.* Chicago: University of Chicago Press.

Hayward, Aurthur L., editor. 1735 [1874]. *Lives of the Most Remarkable Criminals... Collected from Original Papers and Authentic Memoirs.* 2 vols. London: Reeves and Turner.

Hening, E.F. 1850. *History of the African Mission of the Protestant Episcopal Church in the United States with Memoirs of Deceased Missionaries, and Notices of Native Customs.* New York: Stanford and Swords.

Hirshleifer, Jack. 1988. "The Analytics of Continuing Conflict." *Synthese* 76: 201–233.

Hirshleifer, Jack. 1994. "The Dark Side of the Force." *Economic Inquiry* 32: 1–10.

Hirshleifer, Jack. 1995. "Anarchy and its Breakdown." *Journal of Political Economy* 103: 26–52.

Hirshleifer, Jack. 2001. *The Dark Side of the Force: Economic Foundations of Conflict Theory.* Cambridge: Cambridge University Press.

Hobbes, Thomas. 1651 [1955]. *Leviathan.* Oxford: Blackwell.

Hoebel, E. Adamson. 1954. *The Law of Primitive Man.* Cambridge, MA: Harvard University Press.

Holcombe, Randall G. 2004. "Government: Unnecessary but Inevitable." *Independent Review* 8: 325–342.

Howell, Paul. 1968. "Nuer Society." In: *Problems in African History*, edited by Robert Collins, pp. 190–210. Englewood Cliffs: Prentice-Hall.

Hughes, Jonathan, and Louis P. Cain. 1994. *American Economic History*, 4th edition. New York: Harper Collins.

Iannaccone, Laurence. 1992. "Sacrifice and Stigma: Reducing Free-Riding in Cults, Communes, and Other Collectives." *Journal of Political Economy* 100: 271–291.

ICC. 2002. *International Court of Arbitration Bulletin*, Spring 13(1).

ICC. 2001. *International Court of Arbitration Bulletin*, Spring 12(1).

ICDR. 2002. *Press Release.*

IMF. 2006. *International Financial Statistics Online.* Available at: http://www.imfstatistics.org.

Isser, Deborah H., Stephen C. Lubkemann, and Saah N'Tow. 2009. *Looking for Justice: Liberian Experiences With and Perceptions of Local Justice Options.* Washington, DC: United States Institute of Peace.

Jameson, J. Franklin, editor. 1923. *Privateering and Piracy in the Colonial Period.* New York: Augustus M. Kelley.

Jankowski, Martin Sanchez. 1991. *Islands in the Streets: Gangs and American Urban Society.* Berkeley: University of California Press.

Jennings, William. 1984. "A Note on the Economics of Organized Crime." *Eastern Economic Journal* 10: 315–321.

Johnson, Charles. 1726–1728 [1999]. *A General History of the Pyrates: From Their First Rise and Settlement in the Islands... to which is Added a Short Abstract of Statue and Civil Law, in Relation to Pyracy,* edited by Manuel Schonhorn. New York: Dover.

Johnston, James. 1893. *Reality versus Romance in South Central Africa.* London: Hodder and Stoughton.

Kaminski, Marek. 2004. *Games Prisoners Play: The Tragicomic Worlds of Polish Prison.* Princeton: Princeton University Press.

Kinkor, Kenneth J. 2001. "Black Men under the Black Flag." In: *Bandits at Sea: A Pirates Reader,* edited by C.R. Pennell, pp. 195–210. New York: New York University Press.

Kirk-Greene, A.H.M. 1955. "On Swearing: An Account of Some Judicial Oaths in Northern Nigeria." *Africa: Journal of the International African Institute* 25: 43–53.

Klein, Benjamin, Robert Crawford, and Armen Alchian. 1978. "Vertical Integration, Appropriable Rents, and the Competitive Contracting Process." *Journal of Law and Economics* 21: 297–326.

Knox, George W. 2004. "The Melanics: A Gang Profile Analysis." In: *Gang Profiles: An Anthology,* edited by George W. Knox and Curtis Robinson, pp. 205–280. Peotone: New Chicago School Press.

Knox, George W. 2006. *An Introduction to Gangs.* Peotone: New Chicago School Press.

Konrad, Kai A., and Stergios Skaperdas. 1997. "Credible Threats in Extortion." *Journal of Economic Behavior and Organization* 33: 23–39.

Konrad, Kai A., and Stergios Skaperdas. 1998. "Extortion." *Economica* 65: 461–477.

Konstam, Angus. 2002. *The History of Pirates.* Guilford: The Lyons Press.

Konstam, Angus. 2007. *Scourge of the Seas: Buccaneers, Pirates and Privateers.* New York: Osprey.

Landa, Janet T. 1981. "A Theory of the Ethnically Homogeneous Middleman Group: An Institutional Alternative to Contract Law." *Journal of Legal Studies* 10: 349–362.

Landa, Janet T. 1994. *Trust, Ethnicity, and Identity: Beyond the New Institutional Economics of Ethnic Trading Networks, Contract law, and Gift-Exchange.* Ann Arbor: University of Michigan Press.

Landes, William M., and Richard A. Posner. 1975. "The Private Enforcement of Law." *Journal of Legal Studies* 4: 1–46.

Lansdowne Manuscript. Appox. 1450–1500.

Lapsley, Gaillard Thomas. 1900. "A Study in English Border History." *American Historical Review* 5: 440–466.

Lazear, Edward P. 1999. "Culture and Language." *Journal of Political Economy* 107: S95–S126.

Leeson, Peter T. 2005. "Endogenizing Fractionalization." *Journal of Institutional Economics* 1: 75–98.

Leeson, Peter T. 2008. "How Important is State Enforcement for Trade?" *American Law and Economics Review* 10(1): 61–89.

Leeson, Peter T. 2010a. "Rational Choice, Round Robin, and Rebellion: An Institutional Solution to the Problems of Revolution." *Journal of Economic Behavior and Organization* 73: 297–307.

Leeson, Peter T. 2010b. "Pirational Choice: The Economics of Infamous Pirate Practices." *Journal of Economic Behavior and Organization* 76: 497–510.

Leeson, Peter T. 2010c. "Rationality, Pirates, and the Law: A Retrospective." *American University Law Review* 59: 1219–1230.

Leeson, Peter T. 2011. "Trial by Battle." *Journal of Legal Analysis* 3: 341–375.

Leeson, Peter T. 2012a. "Poking Hobbes in the Eye: A Plea for Mechanism in Anarchist History." *Common Knowledge* 8: 541–546.

Leeson, Peter T. 2012b. "Oracles." Mimeo. Available at: http://www.peterleeson.com/Oracles.pdf.

Leeson, Peter T. 2012c. "Ordeals." *Journal of Law and Economics* 55: 691–714.

Leeson, Peter T. 2013. "Gypsy Law." *Public Choice* 155: 273–292.

Leeson, Peter T., and Douglas B. Rogers. 2012. "Organizing Crime." *Supreme Court Economic Review* 20: 89–123.

Leslie, John, Bishop of Ross. 1888–1895. *The Historie of Scotland Wrytten First in Latin by the Most Reverend and Worthy Jhone Leslie Bishop of Rosse and Translated by Father James Dalrymple*, edited by E.G. Cody. 2 vols. Edinburgh: Blackwood and Sons.

Levitt, Steven D. 1998. "Juvenile Crime and Punishment." *Journal of Political Economy* 106: 1156–1185.

Levitt, Steven D. 2004. "Understanding Why Crime Fell in the 1990s: Four Factors that Explain the Decline and Six That Do Not." *Journal of Economic Perspectives* 18: 163–190.

Lewis, George. 1980. "Social Groupings in Organized Crime: The Case of La Nuestra Familia." *Deviant Behavior* 1: 129–143.

Libecap, Gary D. 2002. "Contracting for Property Rights." In: *Property Rights: Cooperation, Conflict, and Law*, edited by Terry L. Anderson and Fred S. McChesney, pp. 142–167. Princeton: Princeton University Press.

Lipsey, R.G., and Kevin Lancaster. 1956–1957. "The General Theory of Second Best." *Review of Economic Studies* 24: 11–32.

Little, Lester K. 1993. *Benedictine Maledictions: Liturgical Cursing in Romanesque France.* Ithaca: Cornell University Press.

Little, Peter D. 2001. "The Global Dimension of Cross-Border Trade in the Somalia Borderlands." In: *Globalization, Democracy and Development in Africa: Challenges and Prospects*, edited by Taye Assefa, Severine M. Rugumamu, and Abdel Ghaffar M. Ahmed, pp. 179–200. Addis Ababa, Ethiopia: OSSREA.

Little, Peter D. 2003. *Somalia: Economy without State.* Bloomington: Indiana University Press.

Livingstone, David. 1857. *Missionary Travels and Researches in South Africa.* London: John Murray.

Livingstone, David. 1874. *The Last Journals of David Livingstone in Central Africa*, edited by Horace Waller. 2 vols. London: John Murray.

Livingstone, David. 1960. *Livingstone's Private Journals 1851–1853*, edited by Isaac Schapera. London: Chatto & Windus.

Livingstone, David. 1963. *Livingstone's African Journal 1853–1856,* edited by Isaac Schapera. 2 vols. London: Chatto & Windus.

Lopez, Robert S. 1976. *The Commercial Revolution of the Middle Ages, 950–1350.* Cambridge: Cambridge University Press.

Lopez, Robert S., and Irving W. Raymond. 1990. *Medieval Trade in the Mediterranean World.* Cambridge: Cambridge University Press.

Lubrano, Alfred. 2007. "Unconventional Wisdom: Get Real Rules for American Mobsters." *The Philadelphia Inquirer,* November 17, E1.

Lydon, James G. 1970. *Pirates, Privateers, and Profits.* Upper Saddle River: Gregg Press.

Maclay, Edgar Stanton. 1900. *A History of American Privateers.* London: Sampson Low, Marsten & Co.

Marsden, R.G., editor. 1915–1916 [1999]. *Law and Custom of the Sea.* 2 vols. Union: Lawbook Exchange.

Martens, Georg Friedrich von, and Thomas Hartwell Horne. 1801. *An Essay on Privateers, Captures, and Particularly on Recaptures, According to the Laws, Treaties, and Usages of the Maritime Powers of Europe.* London: Printed for E. and R. Brooke.

Marx, Jenifer G. 1996a. "The Brethren of the Coast." In: *Pirates: Terror on the High Seas – From the Caribbean to the South China Sea,* edited by David Cordingly, pp. 37–57. Atlanta: Turner Publishing, Inc.

Marx, Jenifer G. 1996b. "The Golden Age of Piracy." In: *Pirates: Terror on the High Seas – From the Caribbean to the South China Sea,* edited by David Cordingly, pp. 101–123. Atlanta: Turner Publishing, Inc.

Marx, Jenifer G. 1996c. "The Pirate Round." In: *Pirates: Terror on the High Seas – From the Caribbean to the South China Sea,* edited by David Cordingly, pp. 141–163. Atlanta: Turner Publishing, Inc.

Mattli, Walter. 2001. "Private Justice in a Global Economy: From Litigation to Arbitration." *International Organization* 55: 919–947.

McGuire, Martin, and Mancur Olson. 1996. "The Economics of Autocracy and Majority Rule: The Invisible Hand and the Use of Force." *Journal of Economic Literature* 34: 72–96.

Mehlum, Halvor, Karl Moene, and Ragnar Torvik. 2006. "Institutions and the Resource Curse." *Economic Journal* 116: 1–20.

Menkhaus, Ken. 1998. "Somalia: Political Order in a Stateless Society." *Current History* 97: 220–224.

Menkhaus, Ken. 2004. *Somalia: State Collapse and the Threat of Global Terrorism.* New York: Oxford University Press.

Menkhaus, Ken, and Kathryn Craven. 1996. "Land Alienation and the Imposition of State Farms in the Lower Jubba Valley." In: *The Struggle for Land in Southern Somalia: The War Behind the War,* edited by Catherine Besteman and Lee V. Cassanelli, pp. 155–178. Boulder: Westview Press.

Middleton, John. 1971. "Some Effects of Colonial Rule among the Lugbara of Uganda." In: *Colonialism in Africa 1870–1960, Profiles of Change: African Society and Colonial Rule, Vol. 3,* edited by Victor Turner, pp. 6–48. Cambridge: Cambridge University Press.

Milgrom, Paul, Douglas C. North, and Barry R. Weingast. 1990. "The Role of Institutions in the Revival of Trade: The Medieval Law Merchant, Private Judges, and the Champagne Fairs." *Economics and Politics* 1: 1–23.

Mill, John Stuart. 1848. *Principles of Political Economy.* London: John W. Parker.

Miller, Joseph. 1970. "Cokwe Trade and Conquest in the Nineteenth Century." In: *Pre-Colonial African Trade*, edited by Richard Gray and David Birmingham, pp. 175–201. London: Oxford University Press.

Miller, Joseph. 1988. *Way of Death*. Madison: University of Wisconsin Press.

Miron, Jeffrey A., and Jeffrey Zweibel. 1995. "The Economic Case against Drug Prohibition." *Journal of Economic Perspectives* 9: 175–192.

Mises, Ludwig von. 1949. *Human Action: A Treatise on Economics*. New Haven: Yale University Press.

Morales, Gabriel C. 2008. *La Familia – The Family: Prison Gangs in America*. San Antonio: Mungia Printers.

Morgan, Kenneth. 1989. "Shipping Patterns and the Atlantic Trade of Bristol, 1749–1770." *William and Mary Quarterly* 46: 506–538.

Morris, Richard B. 1965. *Government and Labor in Early America*. New York: Harper and Row.

Moselle, Boaz, and Benjamin Polak. 2001. "A Model of a Predatory State." *Journal of Law, Economics, and Organization* 17: 1–33.

Mubarak, Jamil. 1996. *From Bad Policy to Chaos: How an Economy Fell Apart*. Westport: Praeger.

Mubarak, Jamil. 1997. "The 'Hidden Hand' Behind the Resilience of the Stateless Economy in Somalia." *World Development* 25: 2027–2041.

Neary, Hugh. 1997. "Equilibrium Structure in an Economic Model of Conflict." *Economic Inquiry* 35: 480–494.

Nenova, Tatiana. 2004. *Private Sector Response to the Absence of Government Institutions in Somalia*. Washington, DC: The World Bank.

Nenova, Tatiana, and Tim Harford. 2004. "Anarchy and Invention: How Does Somalia Cope without Government?" *Public Policy for the Private Sector* 280: 1–4.

Neville, Cynthia. 1998. *Violence, Custom and Law: The Anglo-Scottish Border Lands in the Later Middle Ages*. Edinburgh: Edinburgh University Press.

Nicolson, Joseph, and Richard Burn. 1777. *The History and Antiquities of the Counties of Westmorland and Cumberland*. 2 vols. London: Printed for W. Strahan.

Nicolson, William, Lord Bishop of Carlisle. 1747. *Leges Marchiarum*. London: Printed for Mess. Hamilton and Balfour, Booksellers in Edinburgh.

North, Douglass C. 1981. *Structure and Change in Economic History*. New York: W.W. Norton & Co.

North, Douglass C. 1990. *Institutions, Institutional Change and Economic Performance*. Cambridge: Cambridge University Press.

Notten, Michael van. 2005. *The Law of the Somalis: A Stable Foundation for Economic Development in the Horn of Africa*. Trenton: Red Sea Press.

Olson, Mancur. 1993. "Dictatorship, Democracy, and Development." *American Political Science Review* 87: 567–576.

Oppen, Achim von. 1994. *Terms of Trade and Terms of Trust*. Hamburg: Lit Verlag.

Petrie, Donald A. 1999. *The Prize Game: Lawful Looting on the High Seas in the Days of Fighting Sail*. New York: Berkley Books.

Pinkerton v. United States. 1946. 328 U.S. 640.

Pogge, Paul. 1880. *Im Reich des Muata-Jamvo*. Berlin: Reimer.

Posner, Eric A. 1996. "Law, Economics, and Inefficient Norms." *University of Pennsylvania Law Review* 144: 1697–1744.

Pospisil, Leopold. 1963. *The Kapauku Papuans of West New Guinea.* New York: Holt, Rinehart, and Winston.

Powell, Benjamin, Ryan Ford, and Alex Nowrasteh. 2008. "Somalia after State Collapse: Chaos or Improvement?" *Journal of Economic Behavior and Organization* 67: 657–670.

Prendergast, John. 1997. *Crisis Response: Humanitarian Band-Aids in Sudan and Somalia.* London: Pluto Press.

Pringle, Patrick. 1953. *Jolly Roger: The Story of the Great Age of Piracy.* New York: W.W. Norton.

Rafaeli, Anat, and Michael Pratt. 1993. "Tailored Meanings: On the Meaning and Impact of Organizational Dress." *Academy of Management Review* 18: 32–55.

Rajan, Raghuram G., and Luigi Zingales. 1998. "Power in a Theory of the Firm." *Quarterly Journal of Economics* 113: 387–432.

Ranger, Terence. 1985. "The Invention of Tradition in Colonial Africa." In: *The Invention of Tradition,* edited by Eric Hobsbawm and Terence Ranger, pp. 211–262. Cambridge: Cambridge University Press.

Rankin, Hugh F. 1969. *The Golden Age of Piracy.* Williamsburg: Colonial Williamsburg.

Rediker, Marcus. 1981. "Under the Banner of King Death: The Social World of Anglo-America Pirates, 1716–1726." *William and Mary Quarterly* 38: 203–227.

Rediker, Marcus. 2004. *Villains of All Nations: Atlantic Pirates in the Golden Age.* Boston: Beacon Press.

Rediker, Marcus. 2006. *Between the Devil and the Deep Blue Sea: Merchant Seamen, Pirates and the Anglo-American Maritime World, 1700–1750.* Cambridge: Cambridge University Press.

Reporters Sans Frontieres. 2003. *Freedom of the Press throughout the World: 2003 Africa Annual Report.* Available at: http://www.rsf.org/article.php3?id_article=6451.

Reuter, Peter. 1985. *Disorganized Crime: The Economics of the Visible Hand.* Cambridge, MA: MIT Press.

Reynolds, Julia. 2008. "Gang Leader Took Unusual Route to the Top." *Monterey County Herald,* February 10.

Richman, Barak D. 2006. "How Communities Create Economic Advantage: Jewish Diamond Merchants in New York." *Law and Social Inquiry* 31: 383–420.

Ritchie, Robert C. 1986. *Captain Kidd and the War against the Pirates.* Cambridge, MA: Harvard University Press.

Robinson, James A., Ragner Torvik, and Thierry Verdier. 2006. "Political Foundations of the Resource Curse." *Journal of Development Economics* 79: 447–468.

Rogozinski, Jan. 2000. *Honor among Thieves: Captain Kiss, Henry Every, and the Pirate Democracy in the Indian Ocean.* Mechanicsburg, PA: Stackpole Books.

Roscoe, E.S., editor. 1905. *Reports of Prize Cases Determined in the High Court of Admiralty.* London: Stevens and Sons.

Rosenwein, Barbara H., Thomas Head, and Sharon Farmer. 1991. "Monks and Their Enemies." *Speculum* 66: 764–796.

Rothbard, Murray N. 1977. *Power and Market: Government and the Economy.* New York: Columbia University Press.

Rymer, Thomas. 1739–1745. *Foedera . . . fideliter exscripta.* 10 vols. Hagae Comitis, Apud Joannem Nuelme.

Sadler, Ralph. 1809. *The State Papers of Sir Ralph Sadler,* edited by Arthur Clifford. Edinburgh: Printed for A. Constable and Co.

Samatar, Abdi. 1987. "Merchant Capital, International Livestock Trade and Pastoral Development in Somalia." *Canadian Journal of African Studies* 21: 355–374.

Schelling, Thomas. 1960. *The Strategy of Conflict*. Cambridge, MA: Harvard University Press.

Schwartz, Warren F., Keith Baxter, and David Ryan. 1984. "The Duel: Can These Gentlemen be Acting Efficiently?" *Journal of Legal Studies* 13: 321–355.

Scott, Walter. 1802–1803 [1873]. *The Minstrelsy of the Scottish Border*. Edinburgh: A & C Black.

Scott, Walter. 1814–1817. *The Border Antiquities of England and Scotland*. 2 vols. London: Longman.

Sechrest, Larry J. 2004. "Public Goods and Private Solutions in Maritime History." *Quarterly Journal of Austrian Economics* 7: 3–27.

Senior, W. 1918. "Ransom Bills." *Law Quarterly Review* 34: 49–62.

Serpa Pinto, Alexandre de. 1881. *How I Crossed Africa*, translated by Alfred Alwes. 2 vols. Philadelphia: J.B. Lippencott & Co.

Shleifer, Andrei, and Daniel Treisman. 2004. "A Normal Country: Russia after Communism." *Journal of Economic Perspectives* 19: 151–174.

Silva Porto, Antonio Francisco Ferreira da. 1885. "Novas jornadas de Silva Porto nos sertoes africanos." *Boletim da Sociedade de Geographia e da Historia de Lisboa* 5a serie, nos. 1, 3, 9, and 10: 3–36, 145–172, 569–586, 603–642.

Skaperdas, Stergios. 1992. "Cooperation, Conflict, and Power in the Absence of Property Rights." *American Economic Review* 82: 720–739.

Skaperdas, Stergios. 2001. "The Political Economy of Organized Crime: Providing Protection when the State Does Not." *Economics of Governance* 2: 173–202.

Skaperdas, Stergios. 2003. "Restraining the Genuine Homo Economicus: Why the Economy Cannot be Divorced from its Governance." *Economics and Politics* 15: 135–162.

Skaperdas, Stergios, and Constantinos Syropoulos. 1997. "The Distribution of Income in the Presence of Appropriative Activities." *Economica* 64: 101–117.

Slush, Barnaby. 1709. *The Navy Royal: or a Sea-Cook Turn'd Projector*. London.

Smith, Adam. 1776 [1965]. An *Inquiry into the Nature and Causes of the Wealth of Nations*, edited by Edwin Cannan. New York: The Modern Library.

Smith, Alastair, and Federico Varese. 2001. "Payment, Protection, and Punishment: The Role of Information and Reputation in the Mafia." *Rationality and Society* 13: 349–393.

Smith, Eric, and Rebecca Bliege Bird. 2000. "Turtle Hunting and Tombstone Opening: Public Generosity as Costly Signaling." *Evolution and Human Behavior* 21: 245–261.

Smith, Eric, Samuel Bowles, and Herbert Gintis. 2001. "Costly Signaling and Cooperation." *Journal of Theoretical Biology* 213: 103–119.

Snelgrave, William. 1734 [1971]. *A New Account of some Parts of Guinea, and the Slave Trade*. London: F. Cass.

Soremekun, Fola. 1977. "Trade and Dependency in Central Angola: The Ovimbundu in the Nineteenth Century." In: *The Roots of Rural Poverty in Central and Southern Africa*, edited by Robin Palmer and Neil Parsons, pp. 82–95. London: Heinemann.

Spotswood, Alexander. 1882. *The Official Letters of Alexander Spotswood*. 2 vols. Richmond: Virginia Historical Society.

Starkey, David J. 1990. *British Privateering Enterprise in the Eighteenth Century*. Exeter: University of Exeter Press.

Starkey, David J. 1997. "A Restless Spirit: British Privateering Enterprise, 1739–1815." In: *Pirates and Privateers: New Perspectives on the War on Trade in the Eighteenth and Nineteenth Centuries*, edited by David J. Starkey, E.S. van Eyck van Heslinga, and J.A. de Moor, pp. 126–140. Exeter: University of Exeter Press.

Starkey, David J. 2001. "The Origins and Regulation of Eighteenth-Century British Privateering." In: *Bandits at Sea: A Pirates Reader*, edited by C.R. Pennell, pp. 69–81. New York: New York University Press.

Stopford, J.G.B. 1901. "Glimpses of Native Law in West Africa." *Journal of the Royal African Society* 1: 80–97.

Swanson, Carl E. 1991. *Predators and Prizes: American Privateering and Imperial Warfare, 1739–1748.* Columbia: University of South Carolina Press.

Tabarrok, Alexander. 2007. "The Rise, Fall, and Rise Again of Privateers." *Independent Review* 11: 565–577.

Tabuteau, Emily Zack. 1988. *Transfers of Property in Eleventh-Century Norman Law.* Chapel Hill: University of North Carolina Press.

Tek, Nathan. 2006. "The Profits of Islam." *Yale Globalist* 2: 31.

The Border Papers: Calendar of Letters and Papers Relating to the Affairs of the Borders of England and Scotland Preserved in Her Majesty's Public Record Office, London, edited by Joseph Bain. 1560–1603 [1894–1896]. 2 vols. Edinburgh: Her Majesty's General Register House.

The Economist. 2005. "Somalia Calling: An Unlikely Success Story." December 20.

Tonkin, Elizabeth. 2000. "Autonomous Judges: African Ordeals as Dramas of Power." *Ethnos* 65: 366–386.

Torvik, Ragnar. 2002. "Natural Resources, Rent Seeking, and Welfare." *Journal of Development Economics* 67: 455–470.

Tough, Douglas. 1928. *Last Years of a Frontier: A History of the Borders During the Reign of Elizabeth I.* Oxford: Clarendon Press.

Trakman, Leon E. 1983. *The Law Merchant: The Evolution of Commercial Law.* Littleton: Fred B. Rothman & Co.

Tullock, Gordon. 1967. "The Welfare Costs of Monopolies, Tariffs, and Theft." *Western Economic Journal* 5: 224–232.

Turnbull, Colin. 1961. *The Forest People.* New York: Simon & Schuster.

Umbeck, John. 1981. "Might Makes Rights: A Theory of the Formation and Initial Distribution of Property Rights." *Economic Inquiry* 19: 38–59.

United Nations. 1992. Resolution 751 1992. Available at: http://daccessdds.un.org/doc/RESOLUTION/GEN/NR0/010/92/IMG/NR001092.pdf?OpenElement.

United Nation. 2006. Somali *Reconstruction and Development Framework.* 4 vols. Available at: http://www.somali-jna.org/index.cfm?Module=ActiveWeb&Page=WebPage&s=clusters.

United Nations Children's Fund. 2005a. "Education." Available at: http://www.unicef.org/somalia/SOM_EducationFNL.pdf.

United Nations Children's Fund. 2005b. "Communities Unite Around Education in Somalia." Available at: http://www.unicef.org/girlseducation/somalia_25906.html.

United Nations Development Programme. 1999. *Human Development Report 1999.* New York: Oxford University Press.

United Nations Development Programme. 2001. *Human Development Report 2001 – Somalia.* New York: UNDP.

United Nations Development Programme. 2004. *Human Development Report 2004*. New York: Oxford University Press.

United Nations Development Programme. 2005. *Human Development Report 2005*. New York: UNDP.

United Nations Development Programme. 2006. *Human Development Report 2006*. New York: UNDP.

United Nations Security Council. 2013. "Report of the Monitoring Group on Somalia and Eritrea Pursuant to Security Council Resolution 2060 (2012): Somalia." Available at: http://www.un.org/ga/search/view_doc.asp?symbol=S/2013/413.

Upton, Francis H. 1863. *The Law of Nations Affecting Commerce during War: With a Review of the Jurisdiction, Practice and Proceedings of Prize Courts*. New York: John S. Voorhies.

Uring, Nathaniel. 1726 [1928]. *The Voyages and Travels of Captain Nathaniel Uring*. London: Cassell and Company Ltd.

U.S. Library of Congress. 2006. "Country Studies: Somalia." Available at: http://countrystudies.us/somalia/.

Varese, Federico. 2006a. "How Mafias Migrate: The Case of the 'Ndrangheta in Northern Italy." *Law and Society Review* 40: 411–444.

Varese, Federico. 2006b. "The Secret History of Japanese Cinema: The Yakuza Movies." *Global Crime* 7: 105–124.

Vellut, Jean-Luc. 1979. "Diversification de l'economie de cueillette miel et cire dans les societes de la foret Claire d'Afrique centrale (c. 1750–1950)." *African Economic History* 7: 93–112.

Vodola, Elizabeth. 1986. *Excommunication in the Middle Ages*. Berkeley: University of California Press.

Weber, Max. 1919 [1958]. "Politics as a Vocation." In: *From Max Weber: Essays in Sociology*, edited and translated by H.H. Gerth and C. Wright Mills, pp. 77–128. New York: Oxford University Press.

Wheaton, Henry. 1815. *A Digest of the Law of Maritime Captures and Prizes*. New York: Forbes & Co.

Wick, Katharina, and Erwin Bulte. 2006. "Contesting Resources – Rent-Seeking, Conflict and the Natural Resource Curse." *Public Choice* 128: 457–476.

Williamson, Oliver E. 1975. *Markets and Hierarchies: Analysis and Antitrust Implications*. New York: The Free Press.

Williamson, Oliver E. 1983. "Credible Commitments: Using Hostages to Support Exchange." *American Economic Review* 73: 519–540.

Williamson, Oliver E. 1985. *The Economic Institutions of Capitalism*. New York: The Free Press.

Wilson, John Leighton. 1856. *Western Africa: Its History, Condition and Prospects*. New York: Harper & Brothers.

Wolfe, Adam. 2005. "Intelligence Brief: Somalia." *World Security Network*, July 18. Available at: http://www.worldsecuritynetwork.com/showArticle3.cfm?article_id=11680.

Woodard, Colin. 2007. *The Republic of Pirates*. New York: Harcourt.

World Bank. 2005. *World Development Indicators*. Washington, DC: World Bank.

World Bank and United Nations Development Programme. 2003. *Socio-Economic Survey 2002 – Somalia*. Washington, DC and New York: UNDP and World Bank.

World Health Organization. 2004. *WHO Somalia Annual Report 2003*. Somalia: WHO.

World Health Organization. 2006. *WHO Mortality Database*. Available at: http://www3.who.int/whosis/menu.cfm?path=whosis,mort.

World Trade Organization. 2004. *Recent Trends in International Trade Policy Developments*. Geneva: World Trade Organization.

Wright, Charles, and C. Ernest Fayle. 1928. *A History of Lloyd's*. London: Macmillan.

Index

Printed in the United States
By Bookmasters